Escalate English

English

Houghton Mifflin Harcourt

6

Printed in the U.S.A.

ISBN   978-0-544-57882-1

5 6 7 8 9 10   0868   25 24 23 22 21 20 19 18 17

4500656139   B C D E F G H

Cover, Title Page Photo Credits: Escalator ©Rodrigo Apolaya/APU Imagenes/Getty Images. All Other Photos ©HMH

Escalate  English

6

Dear Student,

Welcome to *Escalate English*! This program is designed to help you take the final steps to becoming fully proficient in English. You will practice and master the skills you need to listen, speak, read, and write English at home, in your community, and at school. This is your opportunity to fine tune your skills so that your English is great in both social and academic situations. You will be ready to conquer the next phase of your education.

Escalate English and your teachers will help you, but you also have a job to do. As you work through this program, ask questions, share what you are learning, and discuss your ideas. The more you practice, the faster your skills will improve. Being an active partner in your learning will ensure that you reach your goals—one step at a time!

What is

Escalate English is a program designed to help you quickly increase your English skills so that you can fully participate in all of your classes. You will master the academic language you need to excel—now and in the future.

escalate *verb*

1. to increase rapidly
2. to rise quickly

synonyms: soar, climb, accelerate

Escalate English?

You are ready.

Ready to increase
your English skills.

Ready to achieve more in
school, in life, in a career.

Ready to tackle the language
you need to succeed.

You are ready to Escalate!

UNIT 1 Facing Fear

Animal Intelligence

UNIT 3

Dealing with Disaster

Making Your Voice Heard

UNIT 5 Decisions That Matter

What Tales Tell

Student Resources

Connecting to Your World

Every time you read something, view something, write to someone, or react to what you've read or seen, you're participating in a world of ideas. You do this every day, inside the classroom and out. These skills will serve you not only at home and at school, but eventually (if you can think that far ahead!), in your career.

The digital tools in this program will tap into the skills you already use and help you sharpen those skills for the future.

Start your exploration at my.hrw.com.

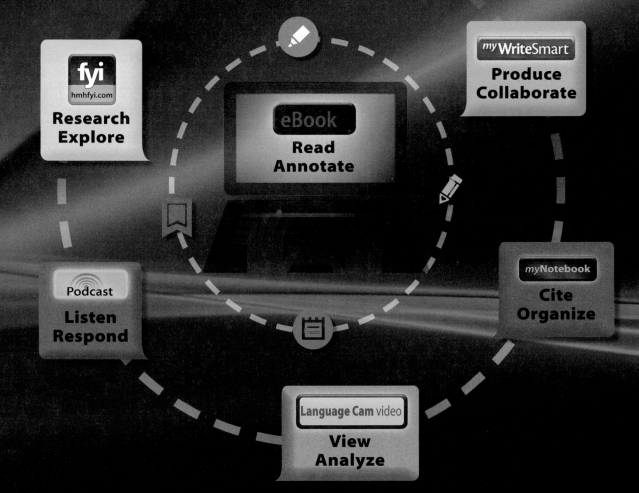

fyi hmhfyi.com
Research Explore

eBook
Read Annotate

*my*WriteSmart
Produce Collaborate

Podcast
Listen Respond

*my*Notebook
Cite Organize

Language Cam video
View Analyze

Interacting in Meaningful Ways

Every day you interact with people in many different situations. You text with friends, make plans with family, give directions to your siblings, talk with people in your community, and participate in discussions at school. You have probably noticed that the language you use in one situation might not work in another. In *Escalate English*, you will see and hear examples of English used in meaningful ways. You will have opportunities to practice using words, phrases, and structures so that you are able to successfully interact in every situation.

Collaborating

You have a lot of knowledge to share with others and there is a lot you can learn from others. Whether at home, at school, or in the workplace, it is important to learn the language you need to participate in collaborative discussions. You will be successful if you are prepared for discussions, listen carefully to what others say, and can ask questions and provide feedback.

It is also important to pay attention to the rules of conversation, such as knowing when to take your turn.

Sometimes your interactions are spoken and sometimes they are written. Either way, it is important to understand your purpose and your audience. Exchanging social texts and emails with friends is different than exchanging information for school or work. In *Escalate English*, you will practice writing and responding to blogs as well as collaborating with your classmates on a variety of academic topics. The more you practice, the more you will be able to express what you know.

In *Escalate English,* you will learn about many topics and you will have an opinion about what you hear, view, and read. You may need to support your opinion and persuade others. It is important to provide facts and examples to support your opinion. In *Escalate English*, you will learn the language you need to clearly make claims and to persuade others. You will know what language to use in every situation.

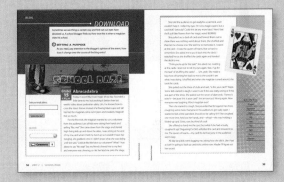

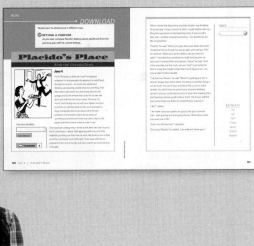

Interacting in Meaningful Ways

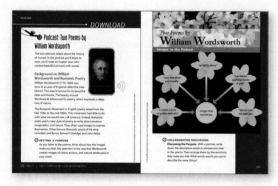

To effectively communicate, you need to listen and read as carefully as you speak and write. Sometimes it is easy to understand what we hear and read and other times the language and the topic may be less familiar and more challenging. In *Escalate English*, you will learn many strategies for listening, viewing, and reading.

Interpreting

It is important to know how to ask questions when you do not understand or when you want more information. In *Escalate English*, you will learn when and how to ask questions effectively.

Even when what you are viewing or reading seems difficult, don't give up. In *Escalate English*, you will learn to view and read closely. The skills you learn will help you figure out what unfamiliar words and phrases mean and explain what you understand.

You will see that some words and phrases have different meanings in different contexts. As you learn more about language choices, you will be able to impress people with your ability to use language accurately.

Language Cam video
Watch the video to find out more about ways people can reach out and help others.

We Can Help!

Language Cam video
Watch the video to find out more about kids making discoveries.

Seeing Old Things with New Eyes

Language Cam video
Want to learn more about revolution? Watch the video.

Sybil Ludington

Language Cam video
Watch this video to learn about nature at work.

Hawks and Beavers

Producing the Right Language

One of the most important skills you will develop in school is the ability to talk to a group of people in a formal situation. You will be asked to do this frequently in *Escalate English*. At first, it can be frightening to prepare and present to a group of people, but, with practice, you will find it gets easier. Learning to present formal oral presentations on a variety of topics is a skill you will need throughout your life.

Producing

Sometimes, instead of expressing your ideas orally, you will be asked to write them. You will learn a variety of formats and will practice using different technology tools to organize your thoughts and to write. Being able to explain your ideas and opinions, to present your argument, and to clearly share information with others will prepare you for college and for your future career.

at the Right Time

In *Escalate English,* you will learn that "one size does not fit all." The way you write will change if you are communicating with friends via social media, completing homework or a test, or doing a writing assignment for class. You will learn to select the most appropriate vocabulary and language structures to effectively convey ideas depending on the situation.

Understanding How English Works

Have you ever noticed that texts look different depending upon where you see them? Some texts might be easier for you to read and some might be more difficult. Is it easier for you to read a magazine, a story, or something from your science or social studies text? That is because texts are put together differently for different purposes. In *Escalate English*, you will practice reading varied texts. As you do, you will also learn how these texts are put together and why. You will practice writing using these texts as models. Soon, you will be able to write accurately for multiple purposes.

Some texts are harder to follow than others. Sometimes readers get lost in a story or article and have to use strategies to find their way. In *Escalate English*, you will learn how to identify words and phrases that help you, as a reader, understand how the text is glued together. This will help you read more fluently and, with practice, reading and understanding will become much easier.

You will also learn to watch for language that tells you the important details in a text. You will begin to notice language that indicates when something happened. You will begin to tune into the language that describes what is going on in the text. You may be surprised by how exciting it can be when you understand all the details.

xxi

Understanding How English Works

The more you read and listen to English for different purposes, the more you will be able to express yourself in many ways. As you prepare for your future college and career experiences, you will want to be sure you are able to write and speak fluently and efficiently.

In *Escalate English*, you will learn the language you need to connect your thoughts. You will practice this orally and, with enough practice, you will be able to use the language in writing. The people who listen to what you say and read what you write will be able to understand exactly what you mean.

You will also learn words and phrases that will help you become more efficient with your language. Learning how to condense your ideas will enable you to say what you mean and mean what you say!

This is your opportunity to become
academically proficient in English.
Work hard, practice, and prepare
for your successful future!

Stream to Start

fyi
hmhfyi.com

Facing Fear

I'm not afraid of storms, for I'm

learning how to sail my ship.

— Louisa May Alcott, author

Essential Question

How do fears affect actions?

The Language of Fear

There are many different kinds of fears. Fear can help us survive by making us act more carefully in unsafe or dangerous situations. For example, while climbing a tall ladder, the fear of falling and hurting yourself will make you more cautious. Caution is not bad!

There is the fear of the unfamiliar. Moving to another neighborhood and trying to make new friends can be frightening. So can trying to do something different, like learning to play a new instrument.

Sometimes a fear is rational. If you're hiking in an area where there are poisonous snakes, it is wise to tread carefully. The fear of getting bitten is sensible.

But sometimes a fear can become irrational or excessive. Then the fear becomes a phobia. If looking at a picture of bats makes you break into a sweat and feel nauseous, you might have chiroptophobia. Although bats may look odd to you, they are rarely dangerous to humans. They rarely bite people. In fact, bats are quite amazing. A single brown bat can catch around 1,000 mosquito-size insects in an hour. So the next time you're scratching those bites, you may wish more bats lived in your neighborhood.

In this unit, you will learn about another common phobia — the fear of being trapped in an enclosed space. You will also explore situations where fear is not irrational, but well-founded. Finally, you will look at fears that are made up.

> **Why do we put ourselves in situations that we know will scare us?**

Big Words Go a Long Way: Etymology

The word *phobia* comes from the Greek root *phobos* which means "fear."
If a word ends with -*phobia*, it is a specific type of irrational or excessive fear.

	Latin or Greek Root	Phobia	Meaning
	chiropter = hand and wing	**chiroptophobia** *chiropto + phobia*	fear of bats
	arachne = spider	**arachnophobia** *arachno + phobia*	
	ophis = snake	**ophidiophobia** *ophidio + phobia*	
	acro = at the top	**acrophobia** *acro + phobia*	
	claustrum = enclosed space	**claustrophobia** *claustro + phobia*	

↻ Performance Task

Choose a phobia. You don't have to suffer from it. It can be one listed above, one in **Browse** magazine, or you can research to find others. Begin preparing a short speech about your chosen phobia. Use the supports in your **Activity Book**. What makes it interesting to you?

➡ *Browse magazine*

DOWNLOAD

If bats don't scare you, maybe what happens to the narrator of this story will.

⏻ SETTING A PURPOSE

As you read, pay attention to the order of events that the blogger describes in her frightening adventure.

» Bloggergirl

Enter your email address:

[ ]

Subscribe me!

SEARCH

[🔍]

💬 **Comments** [0]

September 22, 4:10 p.m.

As I write this, I am trapped in the school elevator, waiting to be rescued. Most kids don't know about the school elevator. That's because the school principal and the other teachers don't want you to know. To ride it, you need a doctor's note, a letter from the school nurse, and a special elevator pass. I have none of these things. So no one knows I'm here, with the possible exception of Mr. Koch, the school custodian, or whoever it was that heard the siren that went off when I pushed the red EMERGENCY button.

September 22, 4:30 p.m.

GR8. Where is everyone? Someone must have heard the siren. I'm sure they did. I bet they have a whole wall of CCTVs in the basement somewhere, monitoring the situation. I bet the repair people had to go back to the factory for parts.

September 22, 4:45 p.m.

Clanking noises! Yes! They are obviously on it! Just in time, too. I'm beyond starving. Whoever invented food was brilliant.

September 22, 5:00 p.m.

The clanking noises stopped. Now I'm worried. But it's more like pre-worry. I'll wait another ten minutes before I get really worried. I've been here only an hour anyway. If you look at the big picture, an hour is nothing.

September 22, 5:12 p.m.

I remember my mom saying that she was roasting a chicken, so I'd better be hungry. If she only knew!

September 22, 5:14 p.m.

I rummage around in my backpack and find the paper bag that once contained my lunch. There's an apple core, a rubbery lettuce leaf, and — what's this? — the tiniest dollop of tuna salad. This is a judgment call. I decide it isn't worth it. Food poisoning is one thing you don't want when you're stuck in an elevator.

September 22, 5:15 p.m.

I'm trying not to imagine that the walls are closing in on me. I feel sick, I'm sweating, I can recognize the beginnings of a WORLD CLASS PANIC ATTACK. Yoo Hoo! Where is everyone?

Oh, no! My battery is dying! Soon I won't even be able to write . . . Way to go, laptop! I might just punch the walls. YES!

September 22, 7:45 p.m.

I'm home now. The chicken was delicious. You want to know what happened? It's a little embarrassing . . .

Well, the battery did die. I did punch the walls. I punched, and punched, and punched — and I must have punched in the exact right place, because all of a sudden the elevator gave a jerk and started moving, all the way down to the lobby, where the doors parted for me and I walked out of the building and into the sunlight.

So, long story short, if you're ever stuck in an elevator, try pushing "L" for Lobby. If you don't push anything, the elevator will not move. Trust me on that, people! Trust me! LOL

More next time from Bloggergirl. TTYL

ARCHIVES

September

August

July

June

May

April

March

February

January

7

UPLOAD

⏻ COLLABORATIVE DISCUSSION

Discussing the Purpose With a partner, discuss how the tension builds as the blogger describes what happens to her. How does her experience change from the beginning to the end of her story? Cite evidence from the text to support your analysis.

Exploring the Setting Could this event take place in a different setting? Defend your opinion.

Staying Safe What are the possible risks of communication online? How can bloggers stay safe? Work in a group. Make a list of rules that bloggers should follow to help limit risks.

Write On!

Like many blogs, "Bloggergirl" gives readers the opportunity to post a comment about the blog. Write a short comment on Bloggergirl's post. State your opinion about what happened to the blogger and how she responded. Then exchange your comment with a classmate and write something in reaction to his or her comment. ⏺ Comments 0

↻ Performance Task

Writing Activity: Start a Blog There are blogs about everything. Some blogs are about a favorite hobby, while others are just about the blogger's day-to-day experiences. Do you blog?

1 Start and maintain a blog as you complete this unit. The first and most important thing to decide is what you're going to write about. Pick a topic you care about.

2 Next, decide what website you'll use to host your blog. There are many free blogging websites out there. Using one of these sites would be your cheapest option because you don't have to pay anything to get started.

3 Then, decide what your blog will look like. There are many free themes on the Internet to choose from. Free blogging websites also come with many themes built-in. Pick a catchy, unique title for your blog and maybe even add an image at the top or in the background. Be safe! Use a nickname when blogging.

4 Finally, start writing and spread the word! Share your blog posts with people you know. If you use a free blogging website you can often follow other users of that website if you like their posts, and they can follow you back. You can also keep a "blogroll" that lists all of the other blogs you enjoy reading. It's common for bloggers you add to your blogroll to add you back, which lets you reach even more readers.

Language Cam video

Do you want to learn more about facing a fear?
Watch the video.

Trapped!

This Is Your Brain on Fear

Think about Bloggergirl's physical reaction while she was in the elevator. What might have been happening in her brain? Read ahead to find out.

READING TOOLBOX

Reading Hard Words

This selection contains scientific terms that name parts of the body. You can't break most of them down into recognizable root words, prefixes, and suffixes. These terms are just large, unfamiliar words.

▶ **Give the text a first read** to see what it's mainly about. Decide how much you need to know about the technical terms. Don't let them slow you down.

▶ **Use the resources provided** to understand the terms. Is there a diagram that gives information about them? Does context help? Do you need to use a dictionary or look them up online?

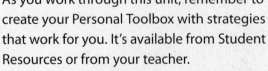

As you work through this unit, remember to create your Personal Toolbox with strategies that work for you. It's available from Student Resources or from your teacher.

⏻ SETTING A PURPOSE

As you read, pay attention to specific facts and details that explain what happens in your brain when you are scared.

This Is Your Brain on Fear

by Valerie Field

Think back to the last time you were afraid of something. It could have been something in your real life, such as having to perform onstage, or it could have been something such as a scary movie or TV show you were watching alone. It could even have been a strange noise in the middle of the night that turned out to be nothing. What did you feel like at the time? Did your mouth get dry? Did your heartbeat speed up and even seem to get louder? Did you draw in your breath or start breathing hard? Did you get a prickly feeling at the back of your neck, or **goose bumps** on your arms? Did you break out into
10 a sweat or feel a chill? Did you cry out before you even realized it? Did you freeze into position for a moment? Or did you almost start running away? You may not have experienced all of these, but you probably felt at least a few. These reactions show that fear can affect you physically.

> Many languages refer to the little bumps that you get on your arms as some sort bird skin such as **goose bumps**. Share what you know.

It's All in Your Brain — Sort Of

What's interesting is that physical reactions caused by fear all originate in your brain without your doing anything to set them off. They are **reflex actions** caused by your brain's response to an outside event. The fight-or-flight response is a reflex action in response to a potentially harmful situation. Do you stay and fight? Or do you run
20 away? What happens in the rest of your body is a result of signals sent by different parts of your brain. It all happens very quickly, too—in a matter of split seconds.

> Reread the previous sentence to understand the meaning of **reflex actions**.

You probably think of your brain as a one-piece organ that stores your thoughts and knowledge and helps you do such things as think and move. But the brain is far more complex than that. It's actually made up of many different sections and structures.

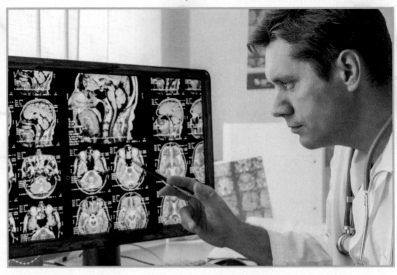

A doctor reviews MRIs of the brain. ▶

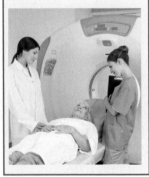

MRI: This is an acronym that stands for **m**agnetic **r**esonance **i**maging. A special machine takes a photo of what's inside your body.

Today, thanks to various medical procedures such as **MRI** scans, scientists have learned a lot about which parts and structures of the brain control certain processes and activities. Amazingly, many parts

30 of the brain can all be working at once. This complexity makes the human brain one of the greatest supercomputers in existence.

When it comes to fear, different areas of the brain exchange signals and also send signals to other parts of the body to be ready for action. That way, if there is a real threat, you can act on it at once. You can fight off the threat, or you can get away quickly. This reaction is called the fight-or-flight response, and it's been part of human nature probably for as long as there have been humans. In fact, this is why you're here now. Your human **ancestors** were able to react to danger very quickly in order to survive. If they hadn't, maybe the Earth of

ancestors: people in your family from a past time

40 today would be populated mainly by wolves, birds, and bison!

What Was That?

You're in the middle of a town or city, walking along a busy street. Suddenly, you hear a cracking sound and then glass breaking very close by. Your sense of hearing takes in these sound signals, and right away they are transmitted from your ears to your brain. The sensory

Use the information before and after **zips over** to help you understand its meaning.

information **zips over** to a part of your brain called the thalamus. This structure relays the information to the amygdala. That's when the action begins.

The amygdala sends signals to several other locations in your brain. One is your brain stem, which can cause you to stiffen or freeze
50 in place. This reaction keeps you from moving toward the threat. Another signal goes to a part of the brain called the hypothalamus. This structure sends messages throughout your body. Many things happen at once. Your heart rate speeds up, and your blood pressure rises. The pupils of your eyes widen so you can take in as much light as possible. Your lungs get ready to take in more oxygen, which is why you might start breathing more quickly without even realizing it. Blood supply is **diverted** from your skin to major muscles so that they can be as strong as possible. All these reactions are preparing your body to act if needed—either to fight, or to flee from the source of
60 danger. Your reflexes go into overdrive, and you might automatically yelp, duck, or even break into a run on the busy street when something dangerous has happened!

diverted: changed the direction of

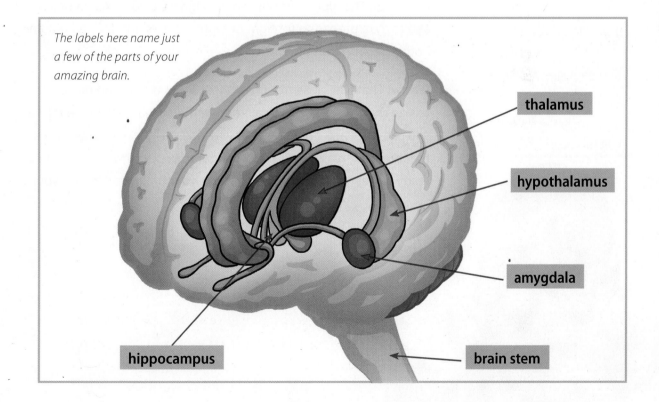

The labels here name just a few of the parts of your amazing brain.

thalamus

hypothalamus

amygdala

hippocampus

brain stem

13

Wait Just a Minute!

However, that's not the only thing your brain is doing. At the same time, another set of signals is zipping along to a structure called the hippocampus. This structure is not as fast-acting as the hypothalamus. Instead, it evaluates the sense clues more carefully, using memory of your earlier experiences and knowledge.

Maybe the sound of breaking glass is really dangerous. In that case, you can keep on reacting and getting ready to deal with the threat.
70 Suppose, however, that the sound is not coming from right next to you. Maybe it's coming from a short distance away, where the broken glass won't cause any harm to you. Sure enough, after a moment's thought, you notice that construction workers are breaking some old glass as they're tearing down a building. Nothing's spilling out onto the street. The hippocampus sends a signal for you to calm down and to stop preparing for fight or flight. There's nothing to fight and nothing to run from.

Whew! That was close. Your heartbeat slows down, and maybe you realize that you're sweating a bit more than usual. But you're safe, and
80 you can just keep going on your way. Still, it's good to know that if that breaking glass really was a danger to you, you would have been ready to get out of the way fast. That's your brain working for you!

Whew! sounds like and means that you are relieved. It is an example of onomatopoeia, or use of words that sound like their meanings. Another example of onomatopoeia is *Boom*! Do you know any others?

⏻ COLLABORATIVE DISCUSSION

Discussing the Purpose With a partner, take turns explaining what happens in your brain when you are frightened. Cite evidence from the text to support your explanation.

Vocabulary Strategy: Scientific Terminology

There were many long and complex words in this selection. Was it important to know the exact definition of each word? What was important to know about these words?

LISTENING TOOLBOX

Active Listening

Always be respectful of others when they are talking.

▶ **Wait for your turn.** As excited as you may be to add to the conversation, don't interrupt.

▶ **Ask if you don't understand** what has been said.

▶ **Let the speaker know that you understood** the point, even if you disagree.

Useful Phrases

▷ Would you please repeat that? I'm not sure what you mean.

▷ I agree with most of what you say, but ____.

▷ I heard Maria say ____, and Julio just pointed out ____.

Speak Out! Should people try to overcome the fight-or-flight response? Work in a small group to share your opinion. What factors might persuade your group to agree with your position?

A Leap of Faith

Will the brain's automatic reaction to fear help or hurt the narrator of this story?

ONE CHOICE CAN TRANSFORM YOU

DIVERGENT
#1 NEW YORK TIMES BESTSELLING AUTHOR
VERONICA ROTH

Know Before You Go

The novel *Divergent* is set in a future Chicago where the population is divided into five **factions**. All sixteen-year-olds must choose the faction that they will be a part of for the rest of their lives. If the chosen faction is different from the one they were raised in, they become initiates. Initiates must prove that they belong in their faction. Each faction is built around one human trait.

> **factions** (n): Factions are groups within a larger group that have different opinions and ideas from the rest of the group.

Faction	Amity	Erudite	Candor	Abnegation	Dauntless
Trait	friendship	knowledge	truth	selflessness	bravery

The narrator of this story was born into the Abnegation faction, but has chosen to become part of the Dauntless faction.

READING TOOLBOX

Making Inferences

Look for clues about characters.

Authors don't always tell you everything you need to know about a character. They assume you'll use what you already know about people. Ask yourself, "If my friend did what that character just did, what would I know about my friend?"

⏻ SETTING A PURPOSE

As you read, pay attention to the narrator's **point of view.** When a story has a **first-person point of view,** the narrator is a character in the story. The pronouns *I, me,* and *we* are used.

A Leap of Faith

from *Divergent*

by Veronica Roth

"Listen up! My name is Max! I am one of the leaders of your new faction!" shouts a man at the other end of the roof. He is older than the others, with deep **creases** in his dark skin and gray hair at his temples, and he stands on the **ledge** like it's a sidewalk. Like someone didn't just fall to her death from it. "Several stories below us is the members' entrance to our compound. If you can't muster the will to jump off, you don't belong here. Our initiates have the privilege of going first."

"You want us to jump off a *ledge*?" asks an Erudite girl. She is a
10 few inches taller than I am, with mousy brown hair and big lips. Her mouth hangs open.

I don't know why it shocks her.

"Yes," Max says. He looks amused.

"Is there water at the bottom or something?"

"Who knows?" He raises his eyebrows.

The crowd in front of the initiates splits in half, making a wide path for us. I look around. No one looks eager to leap off the building — their eyes are everywhere but on Max. Some of them nurse minor wounds or brush gravel from their clothes. I glance at Peter. He is
20 picking at one of his cuticles. Trying to act casual.

I am proud. It will get me into trouble someday, but today it makes me brave. I walk toward the ledge and hear **snickers** behind me.

Max steps aside, leaving my way clear. I walk up to the edge and look down. Wind whips through my clothes, making the fabric snap.

What words and phrases around **creases** help you understand the meaning of the word?

ledge: a narrow, flat surface that sticks out

Make Inferences What do you learn about the Erudite girl's character?

Watch the pronunciation! *Sneakers* are a type of shoe. **Snickers** are disrespectful laughs or noises.

The building I'm on forms one side of a square with three other buildings. In the center of the square is a huge hole in the concrete. I can't see what's at the bottom of it.

This is a scare tactic. I will land safely at the bottom. That
30 knowledge is the only thing that helps me step onto the ledge. My teeth chatter. I can't back down now. Not with all the people betting I'll fail behind me. My hands fumble along the collar of my shirt and find the button that secures it shut. After a few tries, I undo the hooks from collar to hem, and pull it off my shoulders.

Beneath it, I wear a gray T-shirt. It is tighter than any other clothes I own, and no one has ever seen me in it before. I ball up my outer shirt and look over my shoulder, at Peter. I throw the ball of fabric at him as hard as I can, my jaw clenched. It hits him in the chest. He stares at me. I hear **catcalls** and shouts behind me.

40 I look at the hole again. Goose bumps rise on my pale arms, and my stomach lurches. If I don't do it now, I won't be able to do it at all. I swallow hard.

I don't think. I just bend my knees and jump.

The air howls in my ears as the ground surges toward me, growing and expanding, or I surge toward the ground, my heart pounding so fast it hurts, every muscle in my body tensing as the falling sensation drags at my stomach. The hole surrounds me and I drop into darkness.

I hit something hard. It gives way beneath me and cradles my
50 body. The impact knocks the wind out of me and I wheeze, struggling to breathe again. My arms and legs sting.

A net. There is a net at the bottom of the hole. I look up at the building and laugh, half relieved and half hysterical. My body shakes and I cover my face with my hands. I just jumped off a roof.

⏻ COLLABORATIVE DISCUSSION

Discussing the Purpose With a partner, identify the narrator's point of view. How can you tell which point of view is being used? Support your explanation with examples from the text.

READING TOOLBOX

Making Inferences

When you're asked to make inferences from a text, look for what the text actually says and think about logical assumptions you can make based on the evidence. Sometimes, you need to use what you know about how people react in certain situations.

Useful Phrases

▷ ___ is based on ___

▷ ___ shows that ___

▷ ___ suggests that ___

▷ ___ leads to ___

▷ ___ indicates that ___

▷ ___ influences ___

Analyzing the Text   Cite Text Evidence

1. **Make Inferences** In lines 12–20, what could explain the way the initiates are acting?

2. **Make Inferences** In line 29, how does the narrator know that she will land safely at the bottom?

Vocabulary Strategy: Using Context Clues

This is a scare tactic. (line 29)

What does *tactic* mean in the sentence above? You can look for clues in the sentence or paragraph, but how do you know what the clues are? You don't. You need to make a good guess at the meaning of the word. If your definition does not make sense, look up the word. "Land safely" is a clue. A tactic is a way to get someone to do what you want.

Practice and Apply Use context clues to determine the meaning of these words from the story:

compound (line 6)   **stories** (line 5)   **cradles** (line 49)

DOWNLOAD

Podcast: Oh Captain, My Captain!

There are many novels about facing fear. People face fear in real life, as well.

Background on the Vietnam War

Vietnam is a country located in Southeast Asia. After winning its independence from France, Vietnam was divided into two rival states—the Democratic Republic of Vietnam in the North and the State of Vietnam in the South. South Vietnam was supported by the United States and other anti-communist countries. North Vietnam was supported by communist allies including the Soviet Union and China.

The two states were at war until 1975, when North Vietnam gained control of Saigon, the capital of South Vietnam. Vietnam was unified, but the war had left the country devastated.

 SETTING A PURPOSE

As you listen, pay attention to the story as it unfolds. This podcast is over ten minutes long. Use the timeline to follow along with the main events of the narrative.

Oh Captain, My Captain!

The Podcast Timeline

Pha Le's father achieves the rank of Lieutenant Commander in the navy of South Vietnam.

↓

Pha Le is born.

↓

Pha Le's father survives the concentration camp and returns home.

↓

Pha Le and his family move to Saigon, where the police come to the house and interrogate his father.

↓

Pha Le's parents tell him that they are leaving Vietnam with him, but they will have to leave his two brothers with his grandmother.

→

Pha Le and his family take a bus to Bình Long. They then take a riverboat taxi and a transport boat to the escape boat that brings them to a refugee camp in Indonesia.

↓

Pha Le and his family live at the refugee camp before coming to America as political asylum refugees.

↓

Pha Le and his family are reunited with his brothers.

↓

Pha Le goes to medical school and becomes an emergency medicine physician, while his other brothers work in accounting and sales.

⏻ COLLABORATIVE DISCUSSION

Discussing the Purpose In a small group, discuss the different types of fear Pha Le and his family faced when they experienced events during the Vietnam War.

DOWNLOAD

When you read the informational text, evaluate the sources of information. Can you rely on them? Why or why not?

⏻ SETTING A PURPOSE

As you read, think about how the two opinions presented in this text are similar and different.

Can Animals Sense People's Fear?

by Susan Buckley

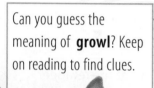

Can you guess the meaning of **growl**? Keep on reading to find clues.

A girl encounters a large dog on a leash. The girl is nervous, though she tries to hide it. The dog gives a short **growl** and turns aside. Nearby, a boy approaches a horse to take his first horseback ride. He is a bit fearful of this new experience. As he reaches to grasp the reins, the horse moves away.

"The dog smells fear on you. I'll just move him away so he calms down," says the dog's owner to the girl.

"The horse smells your fear, so he's acting up a bit," says the riding trainer to the boy. "He doesn't know

10 whether you'll treat him right or pull too hard on the reins."

What would fear smell like, and can a dog or a horse really smell it? People often say that animals detect fear in human beings by scent. However, scientists have differing opinions about whether animals sense a person's fear through smell or in other ways.

One Scientist's Opinion

Alexandra Horowitz studies cognitive science, the science of how the mind works. Her special focus is the minds of dogs. In her book *Inside of a Dog*, she writes, "It is likely that dogs do smell fear, as well as anxiety and sadness." Horowitz points out that a dog's sense of smell is much more powerful than that of a human being. A human nose has about 6 million receptors for smell. The average beagle's nose contains more than 300 million receptors! Also, the **olfactory bulb** of a dog's brain is about one-eighth the mass of the entire brain. In fact, even though a dog's brain is smaller than a human brain, a dog's olfactory bulb is actually larger than that of a human being. This means that a huge part of a dog's brain is given over to processing scents. Clearly, a dog gets a lot of information about its environment from its sense of smell.

20

The **olfactory bulb** is the part of the brain in mammals, birds, and some other animals that processes scents.

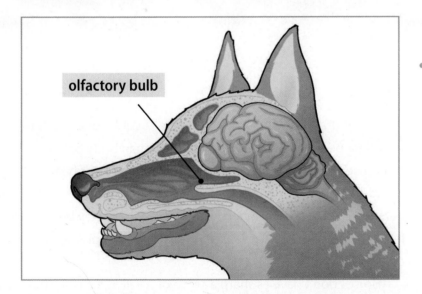

olfactory bulb

Canine olfactory bulbs are **4 times larger** than those of humans, even though their brains are **10 times smaller.**

30   People have always known that dogs have an acute sense of smell by observing their skills. Many dogs can track a person across miles of countryside. Dogs can detect injured or dead people buried under the rubble of buildings after an earthquake. Many dogs are trained for these tasks even today, because we haven't yet invented machinery that's better than an ordinary bloodhound's sense of smell. But can a dog's super-sense of smell tell what people around it are feeling?

▲ *A mare and her foal*

Alexandra Horowitz explains that it's possible for animals to smell fear because of ways in which the human body behaves. Fear can cause several automatic reactions in people. Their heart rate

40 speeds up, for example. They also tend to perspire. The smell of that perspiration is a clue to an animal that the person may be anxious or fearful. So it may be true that scent is how animals pick up a person's emotions.

Horses don't have as sharp a sense of smell as dogs do, but they have a much better one than human beings do. Like dogs, horses take in a lot of information by scent. A mare can identify the individual aroma of her newborn **foal**. Even when all the foals in a herd are crowded together, the mare can distinguish her own baby from the other ones. Horses also seem to use their sense of smell to locate

50 water and to identify whether feed is fresh or stale.

You can get clues about the word **foal** by looking at the picture and caption above.

A Second Opinion

However, scent might not be the way that dogs or horses know when we humans are afraid. Nancy Diehl is an **equine** scientist at Pennsylvania State University. Diehl believes it is misleading to say that animals smell fear. Diehl notes that animals such as horses and dogs do have a complex set of scent receptors. These receptors can pick up and interpret chemical signals from the environment. One kind of signal is carried through chemicals called **pheromones**. All living things emit pheromones. These substances give information about feelings such as aggressiveness. However, Diehl points out that

60 currently, most scientists believe that **pheromone** communication happens only among animals of the same species. For example, a dog might pick up on another dog's aggressive mood through its pheromones. This view suggests that the dog wouldn't be able to identify a horse's mood—or a person's.

Diehl suggests that "an animal's fear may depend more on behavioral clues than on olfactory signals." Both horses and dogs might react to a person's way of moving. (A fearful person might move stiffly.) There might also be sound clues. A frightened or nervous person often breathes rapidly or has a different tone of

70 voice from a calm person.

> The word **equine** refers to horses, as *canine* refers to dogs and *feline* to cats.

> **pheromone:** chemical produced by animals that attracts other animals

UPLOAD

⏻ COLLABORATIVE DISCUSSION

Discussing the Purpose With a partner, compare and contrast the two opinions presented. Be specific when citing evidence from the text.

Judging the Sources

A **source** is a person, a book, or an organization that gives information about a topic. The information a source provides may or may not be reliable. That is why it is important to check your facts and make sure that your sources really know what they are talking or writing about.

You just read an informational article titled "Can Animals Sense People's Fear?" Writers of informational articles or informational books must be very careful about their facts. They need to check their sources. Writers call that process **fact checking**.

The writer of this article, Susan Buckley, has written many informational articles for students. In this article, Ms. Buckley cites two sources for the conclusions she makes about whether animals can sense people's fear. Here is what Ms. Buckley found out about those sources:

Dr. Alexandra Horowitz is the author of a book titled *Inside of a Dog*. She does research to determine what animals know and understand. Dr. Horowitz is a professor of psychology at Barnard College, and runs the Dog Cognition Lab at Columbia University.

Dr. Horowitz is the source of information in this article about dogs and what they know and understand. Given her job and her experience, the reader should be able to rely on the accuracy of the information about dogs.

Dr. Nancy Diehl was an equine (horse) scientist at Penn State University. Dr. Diehl is a veterinarian who works with the Pennsylvania Department of Agriculture. She received her veterinary degree from the University of Pennsylvania, which is considered one of the top veterinary schools in the United States, particularly for horses.

Dr. Diehl is cited in the article for the information given about horses. Dr. Diehl has an impressive background on this topic.

↻ Performance Task

Writing Activity: Judge Sources Answer the following questions.

- Is it evident that Ms. Buckley's sources are trustworthy? How do you know?

- Give examples of sources that would not be reliable for information about animals sensing fear.

- Find at least one more source that supports what Dr. Horowitz says about dogs. How did you know this source was trustworthy?

- Find at least one more source that supports what Dr. Diehl says about horses. How did you know this source was trustworthy?

RESEARCH TOOLBOX

Gathering Information

When you have to talk or write about a topic you don't know much about, you probably do research at the library or online to learn more. But ... be careful where you get your information from!

▶ **Check your sources.**

Whether you are getting information from a book or from the Internet, it is important to verify that the authors of the information are reliable. Are they experts in that topic? Have they studied in that field? Have they worked in that field for many years? Or are they just interested in the topic as a hobby?

▶ **Check your facts.**

Confirm your research against more than one source. For instance, if you are writing about an event in history, check two or more sources to verify that the date of the event is the same in all of them.

▶ **Double check your work.**

Once you have information you can trust, organize it in a clear way. Then, go over it again to make sure you have included the information correctly. The clearer it is, the better your audience will understand it.

The Epic of Gilgamesh

When the animal you are facing is a monster, does it really matter whether or not it senses your fear?

Historical Background

The Epic of Gilgamesh may be the world's oldest epic. It was probably first created more than 4,500 years ago, in an area of the world that is now part of Iraq and other nearby countries. Historians often call this area Mesopotamia. The hero, King Gilgamesh of the city of Uruk, may really have existed, though of course his real-life deeds were not as fantastic as his adventures in the epic. The story was transmitted orally for centuries before it was finally written down in various versions from about 2000 BCE to about 600 BCE. No single written version of the epic is complete, and the details of each version vary.

A cuneiform tablet from the library of the Assyrian King Ashurbanipal that tells part of The Epic of Gilgamesh

THE CHARACTERS As in most ancient epics, some of the characters are human beings and others are gods. The gods often take direct action in the lives of people. In this epic, the characters' names may be a little difficult to remember. Here is the "who's who" to help you.

Gilgamesh, the king of Uruk

Enkidu, Gilgamesh's friend

Shamash and Enlil, gods worshipped in many Mesopotamian cultures

Humbaba, a monsterlike creature who lives in a forest

Ninsun, a goddess who is the mother of Gilgamesh

⏻ SETTING A PURPOSE

As you read, compare and contrast Gilgamesh and Enkidu's personalities.

The Epic of Gilgamesh

Retold by Judy Rosenbaum

The city of Uruk was ruled by its mighty king, Gilgamesh. Gilgamesh was descended from gods as well as men. He was strong and bold; no one could defeat him in battle. But Gilgamesh could be a cruel king who abused his power. He forced the people of Uruk to work hard constructing buildings and walls for the city.

The gods decided to take a hand in the matter. They created a man named Enkidu to be an equal to Gilgamesh. Their intention was to give Gilgamesh a friend, but one who would stand up to him. The gods threw a lump of clay down far away in the wilderness. From this clay, Enkidu was born. He grew up in the care of the wild animals.

In time, Enkidu left the wilderness and came to live with people in a small settlement far from the city. He used his great strength for the benefit of his neighbors. He helped shepherds by chasing away lions and wolves that tried to attack the flocks of sheep. After a while, word of this powerful wild man reached Gilgamesh in Uruk, and Gilgamesh traveled to the distant village to see whether this stranger was a threat to him or to his kingdom.

An alabaster statue of Gilgamesh, king of Uruk

At first the two men fought, but soon these strong warriors became friends. Gilgamesh's behavior toward his people changed. His friendship with Enkidu made him less cruel.

Among the many adventures the two friends had was the battle with the monster Humbaba. A great distance from Uruk, Humbaba lived in a dense forest of cedar trees. Gilgamesh, who could never resist a challenge, said to Enkidu, "You know the way to the cedar forest. Let's go together and fight Humbaba. Defeating him will bring undying glory to us both."

Enkidu was troubled by Gilgamesh's wish to fight Humbaba. From his years of living in the wild, Enkidu knew how dreadful the monster was. Enkidu said, "Even you will be no match for Humbaba. The sound of his roars is like the storm floods, and his breath is fire. He is death to all who come near him. When an animal stirs in the forest, even many miles away, he hears it. What man would willingly walk into his territory? The god Enlil put him in the cedar forest to terrorize people and keep them away."

Gilgamesh answered, "Humbaba sounds fearsome, but I'm not afraid. It will be a worthwhile battle whether I win or lose. Even if I am killed in this battle, I will be remembered for being the one who fought with the fierce forest monster, and my fame will live on long past my life."

Enkidu realized that he would never **dissuade** Gilgamesh from seeking out and fighting Humbaba. Moreover, Enkidu
50 knew that he would have to go along, no matter what he thought of the idea, because he alone was familiar with the route to the monster's territory. Gilgamesh would get lost wandering across the mountains and into the deep forest on his own. Out of loyalty to Gilgamesh, Enkidu knew that he must accompany the king.

To prepare for the journey, Gilgamesh went to the craftsmen of Uruk and said, "We are going to fight a battle like none other that we have ever fought. We need all the strength your weapons can give us."

60 Right away, the craftsmen began to make armor, swords, and axes. While they worked, Gilgamesh went to the **Elders** of the city and asked for their blessing. The Elders, worried about the danger of the fight, reminded Gilgamesh not to trust his strength alone, but to keep on the alert and fight cleverly. They urged Enkidu to do everything possible to protect his friend the king. Gilgamesh also visited his mother, the goddess Ninsun, to ask for advice, and then went to the temple of the god Shamash to ask for the god's protection.

When the armor and weapons were ready, Gilgamesh and
70 Enkidu set out on their journey. The route was long and took Gilgamesh and Enkidu across steep mountains. When the two men reached the edge of the forest, Enkidu once more tried to persuade Gilgamesh not to continue. But Gilgamesh said, "Don't be afraid, Enkidu. Forget your fear of death and follow me. We are each strong, but together we will be unbeatable. When two people go into something frightening together, they can protect each other."

dissuade: to persuade someone not to do something, or to discourage. The prefix *dis-* means "not."

Elders: people respected for their wisdom, or those who serve as advisors to a king. The word *elder* is related to the word "older."

Enkidu sighed and remained with his friend.

Gilgamesh and Enkidu still had a great distance to
80   travel, and many days and nights passed. Each night, as
they slept, Gilgamesh had a disturbing dream. In one, a
mountain fell on the two friends; in another, Gilgamesh
encountered a wild bull; in a third, lightning struck and
caused a fire that almost consumed Gilgamesh and Enkidu.
Again and again Gilgamesh dreamed. After every dream,
Gilgamesh told Enkidu what he had seen, and each time,
Enkidu interpreted the dream in such a way that it foretold
victory for Gilgamesh. This gave Gilgamesh the confidence
to continue toward his goal.

90   At last, the companions reached the forest home of
Humbaba. Gilgamesh took his axe and cut down a tree,
because he knew that this noise would bring Humbaba, and
the two men stood and waited.

Sure enough, the giant monster came crashing through
the trees. His head was as large as that of a water buffalo,
and his legs were as thick as tree trunks. Gilgamesh raised
his axe; Enkidu gripped the axe he held.

The battle went on and on, shaking the ground with its
force. Although Gilgamesh and Enkidu were clever fighters,
100   Humbaba was far larger and stronger. To help Gilgamesh,
the god Shamash sent strong winds to hold Humbaba in
place. At last, Gilgamesh had Humbaba at his mercy, and he
killed the monster.

Gilgamesh and Enkidu returned to Uruk. Their victory
over Humbaba was celebrated by the people of Uruk.

⏻ COLLABORATIVE DISCUSSION

DIscussing the Purpose The Epic of Gilgamesh is probably the world's oldest story about two friends. Many superheroes have a best friend, or a sidekick, who shares their adventures. They often save each other's lives.

Do Gilgamesh and Enkidu share many similarities? Do they have differing qualities? Work in a small group to share your opinion. What factors might persuade others to agree with you? Cite concrete details from the text.

↻ Performance Task

Speaking Activity: Collaborative Discussion With a partner, read the first question and the two answers. Then respond to the two questions that follow.

QUESTION: Would it help to have a friend with you when you go through a frightening situation?

Yes: It might make you feel better and braver if you had someone with you.

No: It might make you feel embarrassed, because your friend could see how afraid you are.

How you answer the question would depend on the situation. With your partner, come up with at least three situations for each question below. Take turns expressing your ideas and the details that support them. When you share your opinions, be respectful of your partner's ideas.

- What kinds of scary situations would be easier to deal with if you had a friend with you?
- What kinds of scary situations would be easier to deal with if you were alone?
- Record your ideas.

Theseus and the Minotaur

There are stories about monsters from many different cultures.

Know Before You Go

THE SETTING This story takes place in Ancient Greece, between Athens, a city-state, and Crete.

THE CHARACTERS Many ancient Greek myths include a hero—someone who is usually stronger and more courageous than ordinary people. Heroes are typically courageous, strong, honorable, and intelligent. They are protectors of society who hold back the forces of evil and fight to make the world a better place. The hero of this story is Theseus.

The characters in this story are:

Theseus
son of King Aegeus

King Aegeus
ruler of Athens

King Minos
ruler of Crete

Ariadne
daughter of King Minos

⏻ SETTING A PURPOSE

As you read, think about how Theseus compares to heroes you know from other classic stories. Which of Theseus's qualities make him a hero?

THESEUS AND THE MINOTAUR

A GREEK MYTH retold by Candy Rodó

EVERY NINE YEARS, KING AEGEUS OF ATHENS HAS TO SEND SEVEN BOYS AND SEVEN GIRLS TO CRETE.

It is that sad time of the year again . . .

Why do we send our youth to Crete? They never come back!

THE MINOTAUR WAS A BEAST, HALF HUMAN, HALF BULL, THAT LIVED IN A LABYRINTH, A HUGE MAZE OF COMPLEX, INTERCONNECTED DARK PASSAGES.

It's the price we have to pay for peace with Crete. And they don't come back because King Minos feeds them to the Minotaur!

MANY YEARS AGO . . . Minos sent his only son Androgeus on a trip to Athens.

During his visit, King Aegeus sent Androgeus on an expedition to kill a very dangerous bull.

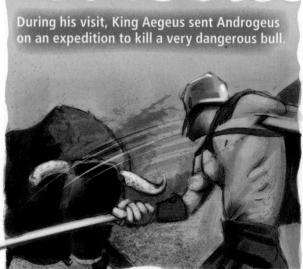

35

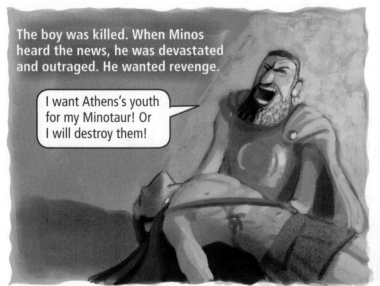

The boy was killed. When Minos heard the news, he was devastated and outraged. He wanted revenge.

I want Athens's youth for my Minotaur! Or I will destroy them!

THIS YEAR'S YOUTH HAVE ALREADY BEEN SELECTED, BUT . . .

Father, let me go as one of the sacrificial victims. I will kill the Minotaur.

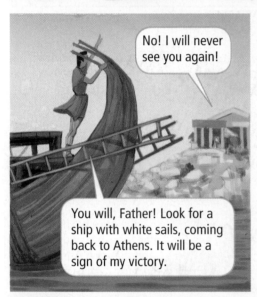

No! I will never see you again!

You will, Father! Look for a ship with white sails, coming back to Athens. It will be a sign of my victory.

THE YOUNG ATHENIANS ARE PARADED THROUGH THE STREETS OF CRETE. MINOS'S DAUGHTER ARIADNE SEES THESEUS AND FALLS IN LOVE WITH HIM.

I'm going to help this handsome youth!

ARIADNE HIDES NEAR THE LABYRINTH ENTRANCE, WAITING FOR THESEUS.

I will help you if you promise to take me away from Crete, away from my cruel father.

If I get out of this, I promise I will take you to Athens and marry you.

You are brave and strong. You can kill the Minotaur, but you'll never find your way out of the labyrinth.

Tie the end of this yarn to the entrance, and let off yarn as you go in. Then you'll be able to trace your steps back here.

THESEUS CAN'T SEE ANYTHING INSIDE THE DARK LABYRINTH, BUT FROM TIME TO TIME HE HEARS A BOY OR A GIRL SHRIEKING AND SCREAMING.

Ugh!!!

Argh!!!

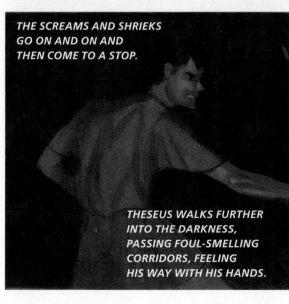

THE SCREAMS AND SHRIEKS GO ON AND ON AND THEN COME TO A STOP.

THESEUS WALKS FURTHER INTO THE DARKNESS, PASSING FOUL-SMELLING CORRIDORS, FEELING HIS WAY WITH HIS HANDS.

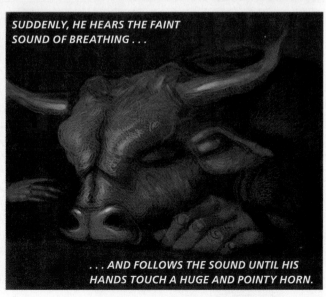

SUDDENLY, HE HEARS THE FAINT SOUND OF BREATHING . . .

. . . AND FOLLOWS THE SOUND UNTIL HIS HANDS TOUCH A HUGE AND POINTY HORN.

THESEUS HAS NO WEAPONS. BUT HE IS STRONG, THE SON OF A KING, A HERO. WITH HIS BARE HANDS HE GRABS THE MINOTAUR'S HORNS AND TWISTS ITS HEAD . . .

. . . UNTIL THE BEAST IS DEAD.

WHEN THESEUS COMES OUT OF THE LABYRINTH, ARIADNE IS WAITING FOR HIM.

Quickly! The ship is waiting for us in the harbor.

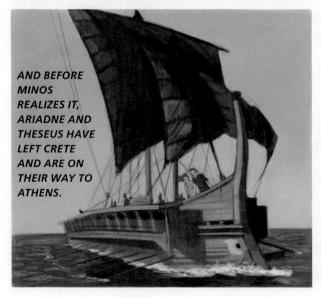

AND BEFORE MINOS REALIZES IT, ARIADNE AND THESEUS HAVE LEFT CRETE AND ARE ON THEIR WAY TO ATHENS.

BUT ARIADNE NEVER MADE IT TO ATHENS.

SOME SAY THAT THESEUS, GOING BACK ON HIS WORD OF MARRIAGE, ABANDONED HER ON A SMALL ISLAND AND OTHERS SAY THAT SHE GOT SICK AT SEA AND DIED.

WHICHEVER WAY IT WAS, THE GODS DIDN'T LIKE THE OUTCOME. THEY MADE THESEUS FORGET TO CHANGE THE SAILS TO WHITE BEFORE ARRIVING IN ATHENS. . . .

WHEN KING AEGEUS SAW THE BLACK SAILS OF HIS SON'S SHIP COMING BACK, HE THOUGHT THESEUS HAD DIED . . .

. . . AND HE JUMPED OFF A CLIFF INTO THE SEA.

THAT IS WHY THE SEA AROUND THE COAST OF GREECE IS CALLED THE AEGEAN SEA.

UPLOAD

⏻ COLLABORATIVE DISCUSSION

Discussing the Purpose With a partner, review the characteristics of a classic hero given in the Download section. Then talk about and respond to the following questions. Cite text evidence to support your ideas.

1. What actions make Theseus brave and heroic?

2. Which of Theseus's actions are more **ambiguous**?

3. Would you put Theseus in a list of famous heroes? Why?

> **ambiguous:** an adjective meaning "not clear"

↻ Performance Task

Writing Activity: Essay Explain which of Theseus's **character traits** indicate that he is a hero. Write an essay that supports your explanation. Cite examples from the story.

- First, introduce your topic by briefly describing Theseus.

- Then, tell how and what Theseus thinks, says, and does.

- Finally, end your essay with a concluding statement that tells which of Theseus's heroic qualities are evident.

> **character traits:** The qualities shown by a character. They can be physical or expressions of personality.

Here are some words you can use in your essay. Check their meaning in a dictionary if they are unfamiliar to you.

Useful Words

- ▷ contradict
- ▷ ambiguous
- ▷ protagonist
- ▷ capable
- ▷ controversial
- ▷ encounter
- ▷ motive
- ▷ react
- ▷ version
- ▷ relentless

Speak Out! You have now read two stories in which the main character had to face a frightful beast. Both stories are from the distant past. As a class, discuss the similarities and differences between the two stories.

SPEAKING TOOLBOX

Using Academic Language

Even when participating in a class discussion, you should be mindful of the differences between the expressions and interjections that you use every day among your friends, and the academic language appropriate for the classroom. Here are some examples of expressions that you can use when contributing your opinions or when asking for clarification of someone else's.

Everyday Language	▶	Academic Language
Huh?	▶	Will you please repeat that?
What?	▶	Will you please restate your idea?
What do you mean?	▶	Can you explain what you mean by ____?
I don't get it.	▶	I don't quite understand your (response/ suggestion/example).
That's not true!	▶	I don't agree.
Think about . . .	▶	Consider . . .
I think . . .	▶	I believe . . . / In my opinion . . . / From my perspective . . .

Performance Task

Writing Activity: Short Story

You have been reading stories and informational texts about facing fear. Now, it's your turn to write a short story about it!

Planning and Prewriting

Connect to the Theme

Your story could be based on a personal experience, or it could be completely fictional. Whatever you decide, the best place to start is with yourself! Read the list below. What things on this list do you find scary?

- Being embarrassed in front of others (public speaking, etc.)
- Facing danger
- Getting lost
- Heights
- Enclosed spaces
- Oceans, rivers, lakes, etc.
- The dark
- Animals (spiders, dogs, sharks, snakes, insects, etc.)
- Forces of nature (storms, earthquakes, tornadoes, etc.)
- Going to the doctor, principal, dentist, etc.
- Elevators
- Failure
- Exams
- Being alone
- Being left out
- Not fitting in

Can you think of any other situation or thing that would be scary to you?

Write Down Three Story Ideas

Using the list above or topics of your own, write three possible story ideas featuring a situation that you think is frightening.

Read your ideas. How excited are you about each one? Rate them, from 0 (not excited) to 5 (really excited). Which one has the highest rating? That's your story line!

Decide the Basics

Now that you have your story idea, it's time to plan the structure of your narrative. Make decisions about your main conflict or problem, your characters, your setting, and your point of view. Use the notes below to help guide your decision making.

Conflict or Problem

A **conflict** is a struggle between opposing forces that is the focus of the story.

Think about:

- What is the conflict or problem in your story?
- Who faces this conflict or problem?
- Is your conflict exciting enough? If not, go back and think of a problem that would be more interesting or exciting.

Characters

Characters are the people, animals, or imaginary creatures who take part in the action of a work of literature.

Think about:

- Who is the main character of your story?
- Are there other characters?
- How would you describe your characters?
- Do you feel strongly about your characters? Do you love them or dislike them? If you don't feel strongly about your characters, neither will your reader.

Setting

The **setting** is the time and place of the action.

Think about:

- **Time**: When is your story set?
- **Place**: Where is your story set?
- Is the setting going to play an important role in your story?

Point of View

The **point of view** refers to how a writer chooses to narrate (or tell) a story. When a story is told from **first-person** point of view, the narrator is a character in the story. In a story told from **third-person** point of view, the narrator is not a character in the story. A writer's choice of narrator affects the information the readers receive.

Performance Task

Finalize Your Plan

You know the basics of your story: the conflict, the characters, the setting, and the point of view. Now it's time to plan your plot structure. Follow the structure of the diagram in the Writing Toolbox.

WRITING TOOLBOX

Elements of a Story

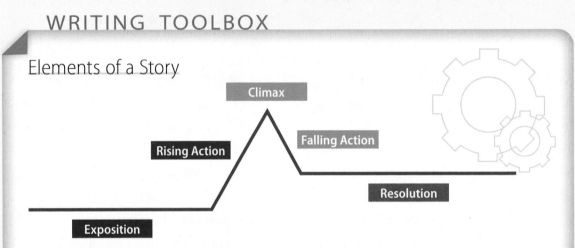

▶ **Exposition** — the part of the story where the main character, setting, and conflict are introduced. The **exposition** is the introduction to the story. Think about the beginning of "A Leap of Faith." The author introduces you to the characters and the setting.

▶ **Rising action** — where the obstacles that the character must overcome are introduced and suspense is built. The **rising action** is where the author lays out the story for the reader. In "A Leap of Faith," it begins when the narrator volunteers to jump first.

▶ **Climax** — the most important or exciting event. In "A Leap of Faith," the **climax** is when the narrator takes the plunge.

▶ **Falling action** — how the conflict is resolved, and the lesson the character learns. The **falling action** in "A Leap of Faith" is very short. The narrator explains what she finds after the jump.

▶ **Resolution** — the final part of the plot, where any outstanding questions are answered. The **resolution** in "A Leap of Faith" is also very short. We learn that the narrator feels both relieved and empowered after her jump.

> Don't forget to refine your Personal Toolboxes with strategies that work for you.

Draft Your Argument

You have the basics of your story. Start writing! As you write, think about:

- **Purpose and Audience** What effect do you want the story to have on readers? Who will read or listen to your story?
- **Main Character, Setting, and Conflict** Introduce the main character, setting, and conflict.
- **Point of View** Establish your point of view quickly.
- **Elements of a Story Diagram** Use your Elements of a Story diagram to create the sequence of events.
- **Transitions** Use transitional words and phrases to help your reader follow the sequence of events.
- **Descriptive Language** Use descriptive words and sensory language to create a vivid picture.
- **Climax** Make sure the story has an exciting climax.
- **Conflict Resolution** Tell how the conflict is resolved.

Revise

Self Evaluation

Use the checklist and rubric to guide your analysis.

Peer Review

Exchange your story with a classmate. Use the checklist to give feedback on your classmate's story.

Edit

Edit your short story to correct spelling, grammar, and punctuation errors.

Publish

Finalize your short story and choose the way to share it with your audience.

Stream to Start

fyi
hmhfyi.com

Animal Intelligence

Any glimpse into the life of an animal quickens our own and makes it so much more the larger and better [in] every way.

— **John Muir, naturalist**

Essential Question

What are the different ways that animals show intelligence?

The Language of Perspective

You will explore various perspectives about animal intelligence. Perspective, or point of view, is the lens through which an author, narrator, or another character looks at a topic or an issue. Perspective is important both when telling a story and when presenting information.

Animals can be the main characters of fictional stories. There are many fictional tales that feature an animal as the main character. You may know, or maybe even have read, *Black Beauty* or *White Fang*. When you read a story from the perspective of an animal narrator, you find out how that animal narrator thinks or responds as a human narrator might think or respond.

The subject of animal behavior and intelligence is explored in many informational texts. Some researchers and scientists believe that the environments where animals live influence their behavior. Others think that animals have taught themselves to be intelligent.

Authors have a specific purpose when writing about animals. When an author writes an informational text, he or she aims to inform or persuade you about that topic. When an author writes a fictional tale, he or she might write to entertain you. No matter what genre the text is, the author is expressing a thought or a feeling that he or she wants you to know.

In this unit, you will learn how different animals show intelligence. You will also learn about animals from different places and cultures—even different time periods. You will explore how animals show human emotions, such as kindness and pity. You will even find out how meaningful the relationship between humans and animals can be.

> ### How does perspective shape the way that we see animals?

Let's Hoof It: Figurative Language

Authors often use **figurative language**, or language that communicates meaning beyond the literal meaning of words. Figurative language helps writers express ideas in imaginative ways. For example, *Let's hoof it* means "Let's get going!" It refers to a horse's hoof, or foot. It is an example of figurative language that is related to an animal trait. Look at the chart below for more examples.

Figurative Language	Animal Traits	What Does It Mean?
cunning as a fox	Foxes are thought of as clever and tricky.	to be clever at getting what you want by tricking someone
horse around	Horses play by kicking up their hooves.	to play roughly
an eager beaver	Beavers are known to be excited to work hard.	a ready and willing worker
Your bark is worse than your bite.	A dog who acts threateningly may turn out to be harmless.	Your words are stronger than your actions.
to smell a rat	Rats are known to be smart and shrewd.	to be suspicious of someone or something
ahead of the pack	A pack is a group of wolves or dogs that live and travel together.	in the lead or at the front of a group

↻ Performance Task

Choose an example of figurative language that is related to an animal trait.
Choose one of the examples above, one in **Browse** magazine, or you can research others. Write a short speech about your chosen example. Why might writers use animal traits to describe human personalities in a figurative way? Use the supports in your **Activity Book**.

➔ **Browse**
magazine

DOWNLOAD

Read ahead to find out what the blogger thinks about riding a horse for the first time.

⏻ SETTING A PURPOSE

As you read, pay attention to the order of the events that allow this blogger doing something she always wanted to do.

Learning to Be Me

• September **7** •

Cowboy and Me

Enter your email address:

Subscribe me!

SEARCH

💬 Comments 0

I rode a horse! Well, almost. His name was Cowboy. I can't wait to tell you all about it!

Regular readers will know how much I've been begging my parents to let me ride a horse. This has been one of my top ten things I most want to do since . . . I don't know . . . maybe 3rd grade? The problem wasn't just that riding is expensive and takes lots of time. It was also the whole ADHD thing. I'm kind of over-excitable, especially around animals. I love them! But I don't always know when to stop loving them and give them some space. My parents were worried that I might get into some real trouble with a horse—it's a big animal, almost as big as a tank.

However, they found a riding program for special kids like me. I could bore you with all the tasks I had to complete and goals I had to meet first, but let's just say in the end my parents *finally* agreed and today was the BIG DAY!

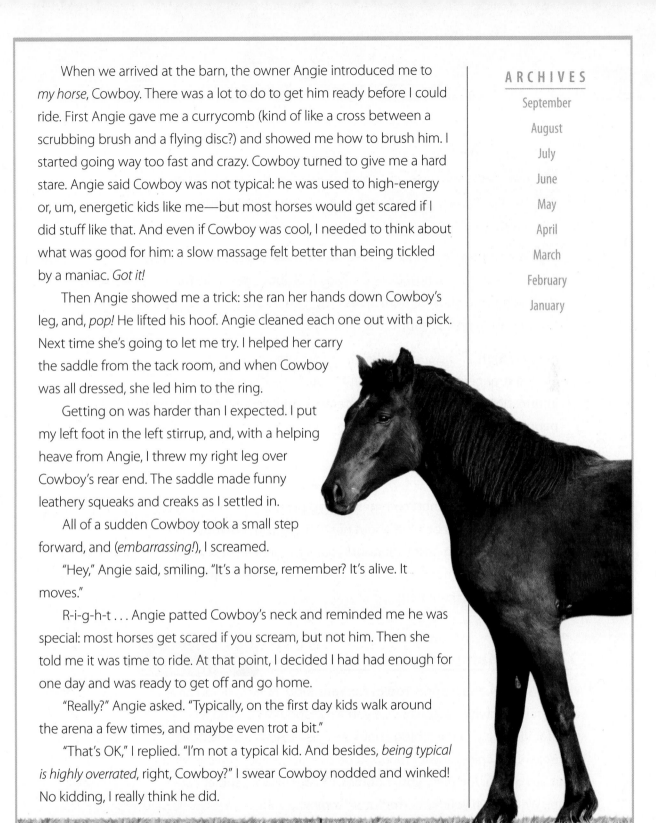

When we arrived at the barn, the owner Angie introduced me to *my horse*, Cowboy. There was a lot to do to get him ready before I could ride. First Angie gave me a currycomb (kind of like a cross between a scrubbing brush and a flying disc?) and showed me how to brush him. I started going way too fast and crazy. Cowboy turned to give me a hard stare. Angie said Cowboy was not typical: he was used to high-energy or, um, energetic kids like me—but most horses would get scared if I did stuff like that. And even if Cowboy was cool, I needed to think about what was good for him: a slow massage felt better than being tickled by a maniac. *Got it!*

Then Angie showed me a trick: she ran her hands down Cowboy's leg, and, *pop!* He lifted his hoof. Angie cleaned each one out with a pick. Next time she's going to let me try. I helped her carry the saddle from the tack room, and when Cowboy was all dressed, she led him to the ring.

Getting on was harder than I expected. I put my left foot in the left stirrup, and, with a helping heave from Angie, I threw my right leg over Cowboy's rear end. The saddle made funny leathery squeaks and creaks as I settled in.

All of a sudden Cowboy took a small step forward, and (*embarrassing!*), I screamed.

"Hey," Angie said, smiling. "It's a horse, remember? It's alive. It moves."

R-i-g-h-t . . . Angie patted Cowboy's neck and reminded me he was special: most horses get scared if you scream, but not him. Then she told me it was time to ride. At that point, I decided I had had enough for one day and was ready to get off and go home.

"Really?" Angie asked. "Typically, on the first day kids walk around the arena a few times, and maybe even trot a bit."

"That's OK," I replied. "I'm not a typical kid. And besides, *being typical is highly overrated*, right, Cowboy?" I swear Cowboy nodded and winked! No kidding, I really think he did.

ARCHIVES

September

August

July

June

May

April

March

February

January

👍 Like   👎 Dislike

⏻ COLLABORATIVE DISCUSSION

Discussing the Purpose In a small group, describe the order of events, or sequence, of the blogger visiting the riding program and becoming familiar with her horse.

Understanding Characters The blogger is excited to meet Cowboy for the first time, but how does Cowboy feel about her? Take turns sharing how Cowboy demonstrates intelligence. Use precise details from the blog post to support your answer.

Staying Safe Avoid specific details in your blog that would allow a stranger to be able to identify you. Do not share personal information with the people you interact with through your blog (like people who make comments). Staying anonymous is a good way to stay safe.

Write On! Write a short comment to this post on the "Learning to Be Me" blog. State your opinion about her first day with Cowboy. Give examples from the blog post to support your opinion. Then exchange your comment with a member of your small group. Write a comment in response to his or her comment. 💬 Comments 0

↻ Performance Task

Writing Activity: Brainstorm Topics for Your Blog Now that you have successfully started a blog, what do you write about when you are stuck for ideas? If you don't blog about your day-to-day experiences, brainstorming topics for your blog can be overwhelming. You can write about any of your interests, your hobbies, or your favorite subject at school. Write down your notes for future topics.

- If you are interested in animals and are knowledgeable about them, you can share new and exciting facts that your friends may not know.

- You can also write about a new place that you may have visited recently. If you have not taken a trip lately, you can write about a location that you want to visit someday. You can even create a blog travelogue or a diary that recounts your experiences during your travels. Using descriptive words and phrases makes your readers feel as if they are traveling with you on your journey!

- You may wish to discuss one of your favorite music bands. If so, you can upload audio files or links to music videos. Adding links to your posts can give your readers more information about a subject. Describing why you like a particular song or band shows your readers how much you care about the music.

- Other ideas for topics can include writing a review about a new book, movie, or food; giving step-by-step directions for a craft project; or sharing your opinion about a current event at school or in your town.

Language Cam video

Watch the video to learn more about animal intelligence.

Dolphins or Chimpanzees?

DOWNLOAD

The Divine Felines of Ancient Egypt

Think about the blogger and Cowboy's first meeting. How does the blogger benefit from Cowboy's ability to understand her feelings? Read ahead to find out more about the deep relationship between animals and humans.

READING TOOLBOX

Determine Central Idea and Details

A **central idea**, or **main idea**, is the most important idea about a topic. When you're asked to give the central idea of a story or an article, it is the most important idea that the author wants you to know about a topic.

The central idea can be an overall main idea for the entire article, as well as the most important point in a single section or paragraph.

Details are the examples, definitions, facts, quotations, and other elements that support the main idea.

As you work through this unit, remember to create your Personal Toolbox with strategies that work for you. It's available from Student Resources or from your teacher.

⏻ SETTING A PURPOSE

As you read, pay attention to facts and details that explain how and why ancient Egyptians nurtured, or cared for, cats.

The Divine Felines of Ancient Egypt

by Leila Ali

When **archaeologists** opened an Egyptian tomb in the year 1888, they did not know what they would find. Perhaps there would be the mummy, or preserved body, of a king or queen. They never expected to see what this tomb contained, however. Inside were the mummies of more than 80,000 cats! Each small body was carefully wrapped in linen. They had been placed there thousands of years earlier. Why?

The First People to Domesticate Cats

Egyptians in ancient times—thousands of years ago—respected all animals, but they loved cats. Scholars believe that Egyptians were the first to **domesticate** cats, about 4,000 years ago. Most Egyptians
10   were farmers and raised grains to survive. They came to depend on cats to kill the **vermin**, such as mice and rats, which ate their grain. Over a long period of time, African wild cats became used to humans, who fed them and took care of them. Some believe that wild cats lived with people in Mesopotamia years and years ago. But scholars think Egyptians were probably the first to truly domesticate cats.

In ancient Egypt, cats were more than pets. They were almost gods. Egyptian gods and goddesses were connected with certain qualities and parts of daily life. In fact, there were two important goddesses who were associated with cats. Bast had the body of a woman and
20   the head of a cat. A playful and affectionate **deity**, Bast was the goddess of the household. She protected women and children as well as cats. The second cat goddess, Sekhmet, represented very different qualities than Bast. Sekhmet was a goddess of war and destruction, with a lion's head, and considered the protector of the Pharaohs.

archaeologists: scholars who study human life in ancient times, especially by examining the physical remains of the past

domesticate: to train an animal to need and accept the care of humans

What other words in the sentence help you understand the meaning of **vermin**?

deity: (n.) a god or goddess

Break this sentence down into **clauses** to help you understand its meaning.

Sekhmet, an Egyptian goddess

What's in a Name?

- The English word *cat* comes from the same root as the Arabic *qitt*, Nubian *kadis*, and Berber *kadiska*.

- Ancient Egyptians called their cats *miu*, which meant "he or she who mews."

Important at Home and on the Battlefield

Cats were considered so important that the penalty for killing a cat was death! A special government agency made sure no one exported any cats to other countries. If a house caught fire, people were concerned with rescuing the house cats before anyone else. Cats lived with families as companions. They also accompanied family
30 members on trips outside their homes. When a family cat died, family members shaved their eyebrows. This was a sign of deep mourning in ancient Egypt.

Egyptians' love of cats was well-known even to their enemies. One story tells of how Persian soldiers used cats to defeat an Egyptian army at the Battle of Pelusium more than 2,500 years ago. Persian soldiers had painted pictures of cats on their shields. Some historians say the soldiers held live cats in their arms. Others add that the Persians released an army of cats onto the battlefield. According to the story, the Egyptian soldiers instantly stopped fighting. They would
40 rather lose the battle than take a chance on harming the cats!

The Valley of the Kings was a holy place in ancient Egypt. There, an inscription in stone records the Egyptians' attitude toward cats: "You are the Great Cat, the avenger of the gods, and the judge of words . . . you are indeed the Great Cat."

⏻ COLLABORATIVE DISCUSSION

Discussing the Purpose With a small group, discuss whether it would have been hard for the domesticated cats to survive in the wild. Would the Egyptians' nurturing have benefited the cats? Cite specific facts and details to support your answer.

Analyzing the Text Cite Text Evidence

1. **Summarize** What is the central idea of this text?

2. **Summarize** Explain how each paragraph supports this central idea.

Speak Out! During battle, the Egyptian soldiers stopped fighting because they didn't want to hurt the cats. Do you agree? Share your opinion with a partner.

Vocabulary Strategy: Word Families

This story contains some unfamiliar words that you may not recognize. One strategy for determining their meaning is to look for words that have roots you may know. Words with the same root make up a word family and have related meanings.

The following chart shows words from the story. Notice how the meanings of the related words are related to the meanings of their roots.

Story Words	Origin	Root	Related Words
preserved (line 3)	Latin	*serv*: to save, to protect	service, reserve
companions (line 29), **accompanied** (line 29)	Latin	*col, con, com*: together, with	company, collective
inscription (line 42)	Latin	*scrib, script*: to write	subscribe, prescribe

Practice and Apply Can you think of other related words that have one of the roots listed above?

Bast, an Egyptian goddess

DOWNLOAD

Podcast: What Bailey Taught

Animals cannot speak any sort of human language, but they can definitely make their perspective, or point of view, known to us.

Background on Monkeys and the Human Mind

To study the way human minds work, research can be conducted by testing monkeys. Monkeys have brains that are similar to our brains. The way that monkeys' brains are organized is very similar to the way our brains are organized. However, the size of a monkey's brain is smaller than a human's brain. When researchers want to gain more knowledge about the way our minds understand ideas, process information, and make decisions, they often conduct research studies examining monkeys' brains.

⏻ SETTING A PURPOSE

As you listen, pay attention to what Jackson states about Bailey. Use the evidence in the chart to help you determine how the monkey inspires Jackson to make an important decision.

What Bailey Taught

Conclusions Chart

Evidence	**Evidence**	**Evidence**
Jackson describes Bailey in very personal terms. He calls him "feisty," "opinionated," and "bright." Bailey's decisions are discussed in terms of what he wants and what he can do.	Jackson tries very hard to persuade Bailey to open the door. Jackson is puzzled that Bailey won't open the door. Jackson feels that Bailey should know exactly what to do.	Jackson explains that Bailey could open the door at any time, but that he needed to make the decision to do so. After realizing this, Jackson makes his final decision to accept the job offer in Germany. This shows that Jackson relates to Bailey's response.

Conclusion

Jackson's statements about Bailey show that he identifies with Bailey.

⏻ COLLABORATIVE DISCUSSION

Discussing the Purpose Summarize the relationship between Bailey's response and Jackson's decision. Why do you think that Jackson named this podcast "What Bailey Taught"? With a partner, share your ideas.

The Crow and the Pitcher

You've read and heard about how intelligent cats and monkeys are. Now you will read a retelling of "The Crow and the Pitcher" from *Aesop's Fables*. It is one of the first stories about animal intelligence.

Know Before You Go

A **fable** is a brief story that teaches a moral, or lesson. The moral of a fable is usually stated in a distinct and significant declaration at the end.

Aesop was an ancient Greek storyteller. It is not known exactly when he created his fables, but they have been handed down from generation to generation. His fables usually feature animal characters that talk as humans do.

READING TOOLBOX

Problem and Solution

When you are struggling to determine what the conflict, or problem, of the selection is, follow these steps:

1. Find the cause of the problem. This may appear in the first or second paragraph of a story or article.

2. Look for words such as *challenge* and *reason*. These words can signal an explanation of the problem.

3. To find a solution, ask: "What does the author offer to solve the problem?"

4. Look for words such as *answer, conclude,* and *propose*. These words can signal a solution.

⏻ SETTING A PURPOSE

As you read, think about how Crow's solution to his problem is related to the moral of the fable.

The Crow and the Pitcher

An Aesop's Fable retold by Nicole Gee

It was a **sweltering, stifling** day in the summer, when the heat of the sun burned and scorched those below. After flying all day over fields and plains, Crow was tired and hot, but most of all, he was thirsty.

As wide and open this land of fields and plains was for soaring and swooping, Crow desperately needed to find a river or a lake.

Crow could not find any body of water, but he did not want to give up the search. He flew on with determination
10 until he was **weary**.

He decided to fly low to the ground to find shade. He looked into the distance and spotted a farm with a large orchard.

"An orchard would provide nice shade for me," thought Crow, "And it would cool me off." He was terribly winded from his long flight.

> Read the paragraph to help you understand the meaning of **sweltering** and **stifling**.

> **weary:** (adj.) very tired; needing rest or sleep

What words in the sentence help you understand the meaning of **dismay**?

Aesop

When Crow touched the ground, he found a pitcher by one of the trees. "The pitcher must be full of water!" he thought, his eyes wide with anticipation.

Crow peered inside the pitcher eagerly, then cried out in shock, for there was so little water at the bottom of the pitcher. To add to his **dismay**, he couldn't even reach the water. His beak was too short to reach the bottom of the pitcher.

"I am so thirsty and tired that I cannot fly," moaned Crow. "I need to drink that water!"

He glanced around for help. There were no animals or people in sight. Above him, leaves from the trees drooped heavily. Around him, sticks and stones were scattered on the ground.

Crow's eyes landed on the stones, and widened as an idea popped into his mind. "Maybe if I drop a stone in the pitcher, the water would rise . . ."

Crow dropped a stone into the pitcher. The water level did rise slightly, but it was still not enough to reach the opening at the top.

He then dropped a second stone, and a third. Each time the water rose, but Crow still could not reach the water.

Crow gathered all of the stones he could find. He even searched deep into the orchard to collect large stones. When he collected all of these stones, he dropped them into the pitcher, one by one. Finally, the water had risen high enough to reach the opening at the top. He gulped the water gratefully.

Crow looked at the pitcher that was now partially full of stones and empty of water. The stones had saved him.

Necessity is the mother of invention.

⏻ COLLABORATIVE DISCUSSION

Discussing the Purpose In a small group, discuss the moral of the story. How does Crow use his intelligence to solve a problem?

Alliteration and Tone

It was a sweltering, stifling day in the summer, when the heat of the sun burned and scorched those below.

The first sentence of the fable uses **alliteration**, or the repetition of a consonant sound at the beginning of words. Writers use alliteration to direct attention to a certain feeling, rhythm, or meaning.

The repeated *s* sound immediately creates for the reader a sensation, or feeling, of being intensely overheated because of the sun's warmth. This feeling is called **tone**, or the author's attitude, or how he or she feels about a topic. The *s* alliteration in the sentence above shows us how thirsty Crow must be. Crow had been flying during an extremely hot summer day.

Practice and Apply Find another example of alliteration in the fable. What is the alliterative sound you hear most often? Which words are emphasized with this sound? How does alliteration affect the tone of the fable?

Write On! Do you know of other stories from *Aesop's Fables*? Do the animal characters examine and respond to a problem as Crow does? Write down your ideas.

DOWNLOAD

Researcher Explains How Crows Solved a Challenge from *Aesop's Fables*.

The following text references "The Crow and the Pitcher" fable that you read in the previous selection.

READING TOOLBOX

Analyze Structure: Text Features

Text features are the elements of a text that help organize and call attention to important information.

▶ The **title** of a piece of writing is the name that is attached to it. It often identifies the topic of the whole text and is sometimes referred to as a heading.

▶ A **photograph** is a visual record of real objects, animals, or people in real places. Photographs help readers understand exactly what something looks like.

▶ A **caption** is a brief description of what is in a photograph. Captions indicate how the photographs relate to the text.

⏻ SETTING A PURPOSE

As you read, think about how the information you are reading might change the way you think about crows' intelligence.

National Geographic News

Researcher Explains How Crows Solved a Challenge From *Aesop's Fables*.

New Caledonian crows were able to apply their natural understanding of cause and effect and the properties of objects.

by Virginia Morell for National Geographic

PUBLISHED APRIL 3, 2014

New Caledonian crows are known for using tools in the wild. A team is investigating the **cognitive** abilities of these crows, which live on the archipelago of New Caledonia in the southwest Pacific Ocean, 750 miles (1,200 kilometers) east of Australia.

> **cognitive:** relating to thinking, learning, and understanding

It was there, on the island of Grand Terre, that Sarah Jelbert, a doctoral student at Auckland University in New Zealand, and her colleagues tested the crows' understanding of cause and effect by presenting them with a test straight out of *Aesop's Fables*.

New Caledonian crows are known to make tools in the wild, something that very few animal species do.

Measure up is a phrasal verb that means "to meet the required standard."

In one fable, "The Crow and the Pitcher," a thirsty crow can't reach the
10 water at the bottom of a pitcher, but then begins to drop one pebble
after another into the vessel. Slowly, the water rises to the top, and the
bird gets its drink. How did Jelbert's New Caledonian crows **measure
up** when presented with a similar test?

The scientists recently published their results in *PLOS One*. National
Geographic caught up with Jelbert by phone to ask her more about
the study and these smart birds.

Why did you choose to work with New Caledonian crows?
They make tools in the wild, something that very few animal species
do. They make tools out of sticks and shape them with their beaks to
20 form a hook on the end. And then they use their sticks to lever **grubs**
out of holes in rotting logs.

Continue reading the next paragraph to get clues about the meaning of **grubs**.

The grubs are fat and gel-like, so if they just poked a stick into them,
they'd end up popping them and would have only a horrible mush
of grub. But by using the hook on the end of their stick, they can lift
them out.

We actually have a go at this ourselves at times. We have to collect the grubs for our work; we use them to catch the crows. Most of the grubs are inside the logs, and we have to hack them out with machetes. It's one of the more disgusting parts of the job.

30 The birds also make a tool from Pandanus leaves; it's a small bush that grows something like a palm. They use their beaks to snip into the side of a leaf, and then rip it up about 10 to 15 centimeters [4 to 6 inches], and snip it off at the top. The Pandanus leaves have natural barbs on their edges, so they make great tools. The birds use them to drag out insects that live beneath leaf litter.

What else can the crows do that surprises people?

We're still getting our heads around all they can do. One interesting thing: They don't use their tools just to get food, but [also] to investigate things they find that are scary, like a plastic snake in a
40 box. They'll poke it first with a stick to see if it is dangerous.

What's your **experimental setup** like? You're working with wild crows?

Yes. We have a large aviary on Grande Terre. We set up nets in the wild, and will catch 6 to 12 birds, and bring them back to the aviary where they're nicely fed and cared for. We keep them for three months, and then return them to the wild so they can carry on with their lives.

> **Experimental setup** is a term for a scientific process of arranging and organizing tools for testing something.

How did you come up with your idea to give the *Aesop's Fable* test to the crows?

50 Our study was based on the fantastic work of two other researchers, Christopher Bird and Nathan Emery. [They showed that rooks would use stones to raise the water level in a tube so that they could reach a worm.] Dropping stones into water isn't something

*A mosiac depicting
Aesop's fable*

Hollow is the opposite of **solid**. It means "empty inside."

New Caledonian crows do in the wild; no animal does. But it is also a completely natural thing, and so is a fair test of animals' cognition.

We trained six crows to drop small stones into tubes. And then we gave them different tests to see how much they understand or can learn about the cause and effect of water displacement. Would they understand that dropping stones into water in a tube [to get a piece of meat to float to the top] is different from dropping them into sand in a tube? Or that **hollow** objects have a different effect from **solid** ones?

They did very well at four of the six tests, where they were able to apply their natural understanding of cause and effect and the properties of objects. They understood that solid objects sink and hollow ones float, for instance, and that it doesn't make any sense

60

to drop stones into sand. But they were incredibly poor at the **counterintuitive** test, which involved a U-[shaped] tube; they had to infer that there was a connection between the two tubes, but none of them could do this.

Break down the compound word **counterintuitive** to help you understand its meaning.

70 **And what do their successes and failures at these tests tell us about the cognitive abilities of New Caledonian crows?**
We're trying to understand the cognitive mechanisms of animal minds, and to do that you need to look at tests that animals can pass and those that they fail. In human psychology, researchers have discovered that the way people make mistakes is often most informative about how they think. The errors give away how they are solving problems. Is this true for animals, too? Or do they have a completely different way of conceptualizing problems? By looking at the errors the crows make, we may get a better understanding of
80 how they successfully solve problems.

Are the New Caledonian crows that you've used in your experiments putting what they've learned in your aviary to use in the wild?
Well, I hope so [laughs]. But we normally don't see them again after we set them free. We go to new areas to catch new birds.

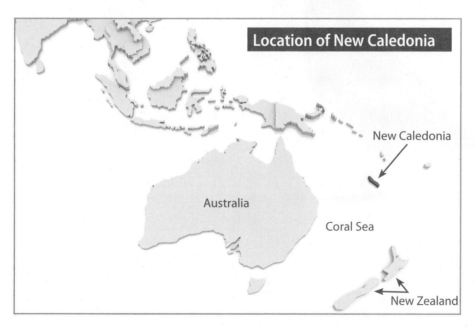

Location of New Caledonia

New Caledonia

Australia

Coral Sea

New Zealand

COLLABORATIVE DISCUSSION

Discussing the Purpose With a partner, discuss the series of tests mentioned in the article. How did this information change what you thought about crows before reading? When you share your opinion, cite examples from the text.

LISTENING TOOLBOX

Active Listening

Ask yourself the following questions:

▶ Did I know most of the words?

▶ Did I understand most or all of the sentences?

▶ Was the main point of the topic clear or confusing?

Analyzing the Text Cite Text Evidence

1. **Analyze** What text features did you recognize in this magazine article? What was the purpose of including them?

2. **Interpret** According to the first question in the interview, the crows are able to use tools successfully in the wild. What point does the researcher raise about the crows' cognition? Cite details from the text to support your answer.

3. **Evaluate** Are you convinced by the evidence about the crows' intelligence? Why, or why not?

4. **Integrate** Using information from the fable and the interview, explain how effectively each of the two selections presented a problem and solution. How do the two selections make each problem and solution interesting? What distinctive techniques does each selection use to help you understand the cognitive skills of a crow?

↻ Performance Task

Writing Activity: Notes for an Informative Essay Do research on a local issue that involves animals. Find information about this issue. Begin to compile and organize your information as if you were preparing to write an informative essay.

- You might want to make searches on the Internet to get started.

- Use books, magazines, online and digital resources such as encyclopedias, or other text resources to find facts and details.

- Write down your notes about the issue.

- Make a list of the sources you are using to get your facts.

How Did Wolves Become Dogs?

You've read about researchers who have studied crows' intelligence. Now you will read what some researchers believe about the intelligence of wolves.

Know Before You Go

READING TOOLBOX

Cause-and-Effect

A **cause-and-effect** pattern of organization shows the relationship between any event's **cause**—the action that makes another event happen, and its **effect**—the outcome of the event or action.

▶ To find the effect or effects, ask yourself, "What happened?"

▶ To find the cause or causes, ask yourself, "Why did it happen?"

▶ Look for words and phrases such as *because, since, therefore, due to,* and *as a result.* These words signify direct relationships between events.

⏻ SETTING A PURPOSE

As you read, pay attention to how ideas about wolf adoption and events leading to wolf domestication are related.

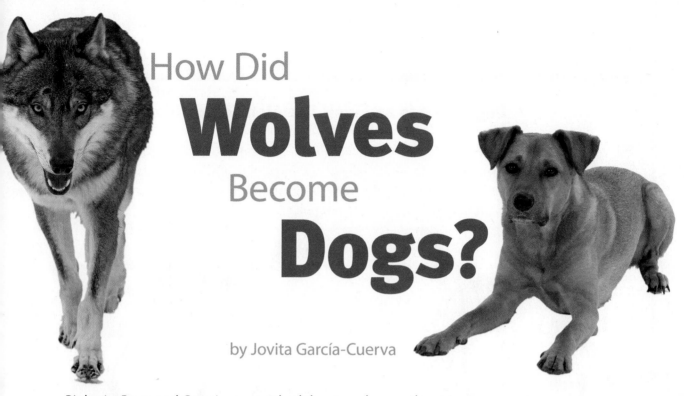

How Did
Wolves
Become
Dogs?

by Jovita García-Cuerva

Biologist Raymond Coppinger watched the stray dogs as they searched for food at a giant garbage dump. It may have been a smelly site, but Dr. Coppinger was doing scientific research. Through **DNA** studies, scientists have proven that modern dogs are descendants of gray wolves. But how did that happen, and when?

> **DNA:** This is an acronym for **d**eoxyribo**n**ucleic **a**cid, a genetic substance that carries information about human, animal, and plant cells.

At one time, most scientists believed ancient people first domesticated, or tamed, wolves by adopting wolf cubs. Over time, humans would have bred the dogs for characteristics that made them good companions for humans. In Russia, scientists have experimented
10 with taming silver foxes. Over a period of 40 years, they have bred silver foxes to become more and more friendly. As a result, the foxes have developed many dog-like qualities. They seek and respond to human affection. Some even bark!

One Theory

Dr. Coppinger does not think the adoption theory makes sense, however. Coppinger says wolf cubs have to be adopted before they are about two weeks old in order to be tamed. And even tame wolves can turn on humans when they are eating.

Dog Skeleton and Wolf Skeleton Comparison

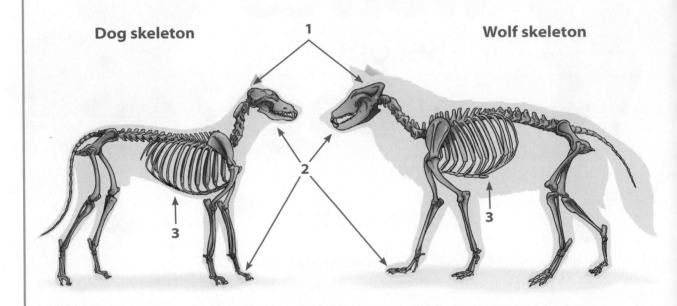

Dog skeleton   **Wolf skeleton**

1. Wolves have larger brains for their size than dogs, and thus have larger skulls.

2. Wolves have more pronounced teeth and claws, and their teeth curve more to help with biting live prey.

3. Wolves have thinner chests for their size than dogs do.

4. Wolves have longer legs and bigger paws than dogs; they are better distance runners.

More than behavior changed as dogs evolved. The bodies of these dogs were different from wolves, too. Wolves have to hunt and kill other animals in order to survive. But domesticated dogs did not need such large brains and bodies, or such sharp teeth. Over time, the bodies of dogs evolved to match their new lives.

Coppinger believes some wolves domesticated themselves. This happened about 15,000 years ago, he says. At the end of the last Ice Age, humans began to settle down and live in small communities. Their garbage would have attracted wild animals as an easy source of food. Many wild animals, Coppinger explains, do not ever eat when people are around. But some do. The "most social and least fearful" animals could eat in the presence of humans. Because these wolves stayed around the villages, they became used to humans. This interaction between wolves and humans was an early step in the domestication of dogs, Coppinger believes.

Other Theories

Dr. Brian Hare also believes ancient people did not adopt wolf cubs. Throughout history, human beings have tended to kill large animals. Hare says early humans would more likely have killed wolves than adopted them. We often talk about "survival of the **fittest**," Dr. Hare writes. But in the case of taming wolves, the "survival of the fittest" may have meant "survival of the friendliest." Imagine the wolves that hung out around the **prehistoric** village. Those who were the friendliest could come closest to the people. Therefore, they would get the most food and the most protection. "Dogs may have domesticated themselves by seeking out humans, to eat from their scrap-heaps," said Kerstin Lindblad-Toh, a Swedish scientist.

So far no one knows just when the first dogs were domesticated. Scientists call the earliest dogs "proto-dogs." Proto-dogs are a stage between wolves and dogs. Some scientists have studied DNA in fossils to see when the first proto-dogs existed. These scientists think there may have been proto-dogs as early as 32,000 years ago, and at least as early as 16,000 years ago. People often call dogs "man's best friend." As scientists find older and older evidence, they may find that dogs are also our oldest animal friends.

Suffix -est When comparing three or more people or things, look for the -est suffix. The -est suffix is the superlative form of an adjective.

Reread lines 19–20 to help you understand the meaning of **prehistoric**.

UPLOAD

⏻ COLLABORATIVE DISCUSSION

Discussing the Purpose With a small group, discuss why some scientists believed that wolf cub adoption caused wolf domestication. What was the effect of wolf cub domestication in their opinion? Cite evidence to support your analysis.

READING TOOLBOX

Cause-and-Effect

Cause-and-effect organization may directly state or indirectly imply the order in which information is presented.

Make sure to look closely at each cause-and-effect relationship. Sometimes, it may seem as if one event caused a second event because the first event is presented before the second event, but check again.

If you are having trouble identifying cause-and-effect relationships, use the following graphic organizer to help you record them as you read.

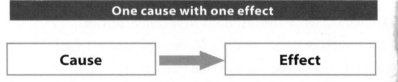

One cause with one effect	
Cause →	**Effect**

READING TOOLBOX

Analyze Structure: Text Features

Additional text features include the following:

▶ **Subheadings** appear at the beginnings of sections within a text and indicate the focus of that section.

▶ **Boldface type** is dark, heavy print that is used to draw attention to unfamiliar vocabulary or important text points.

▶ **Diagrams** are illustrations that show how something works or how different parts are related.

Analyzing the Text `Cite Text Evidence`

1. **Summarize** State the central ideas, or main ideas, about wolf domestication theories suggested by the three scientists identified in this article.

2. **Analyze** What cause-and-effect relationships can you identify in this text? Cite words and phrases that helped you identify the cause-and-effect relationships. Use a graphic organizer to help you record your information, if necessary.

3. **Integrate** What information do you learn from the diagram and text on page 74? How does this information help you understand the comparison between wolves and dogs?

The Call of the Wild

You've read about how some wild animals became domesticated. Find out what happens when a domesticated dog must survive in the wild.

Jack London's *The Call of the Wild,* published in 1903, is a classic wilderness adventure that explores the thin line that separates the tame from the wild—within animals and humans alike.

Know Before You Go

POINT OF VIEW *The Call of the Wild* is the unemotional account of one dog's life from the point of the view of the dog. Buck is the main character in this story. The events of the story are experienced through his eyes. London does not make any attempt to humanize, or soften, Buck. London also chooses not to tell Buck's story in the first person.

THE SETTING *The Call of the Wild* recreates the world of the Klondike Gold Rush during the late 1890s. The discovery of gold in northwestern Canada's Yukon Territory led thousands of men to head north. These fortune-seekers needed dogs to pull sleds across the harsh arctic trails.

⏻ SETTING A PURPOSE

As you read, consider how Buck's behavior changes throughout the story. Also, notice if Buck's actions are a response to intelligence or instinct. Instinct is the natural type of behavior in response to certain events or feelings.

The Call of the Wild

retold by Dina McClellan

BUCK WAS A GOOD DOG, INTELLIGENT AND STRONG, LOYAL AND TRUE. HE LIVED WITH JUDGE MILLER IN A BIG HOUSE IN THE SUN-KISSED SANTA CLARA VALLEY.

BUT BUCK'S CAREFREE DAYS WERE NUMBERED. HE WOULD SOON FALL VICTIM TO HUMAN GREED.

IT'S 1878. GOLD IS DISCOVERED IN THE FROZEN CANADIAN WILDERNESS. THOUSANDS OF ADVENTURERS GO NORTH, HOPING TO STRIKE IT RICH. THERE'S A GREAT DEMAND FOR SLED DOGS.

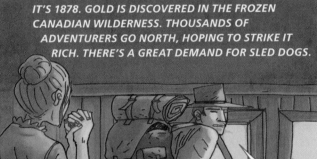

I'm taking off, Ma. Goin' up to Alaska. We're gonna be rich, you'll see!

A GARDENER KIDNAPS BUCK . . .

C'mere doggy! Nice doggy!

. . . AND SELLS HIM TO DOG TRADERS. THE TRADERS STUFF BUCK INTO A CRATE AND LOAD HIM ONTO A TRUCK HEADED FOR SEATTLE.

IN SEATTLE, THE TRADERS CARRY THE CRATE TO A SMALL BACKYARD. IT IS HERE THAT BUCK MEETS HIS NEXT TORMENTOR—A MAN WITH A RED SWEATER. THE MAN TRIES TO GET BUCK TO OBEY HIM BY BEATING HIM.

Come here, you red-eyed monster or I'll take a club to you!

BUCK LOSES HIS TEMPER AND LUNGES. THE MAN KICKS HIM AWAY AND BEATS HIM TWICE AS HARD. BUCK DOESN'T GIVE IN. HE KEEPS COMING BACK FOR MORE.

Take that, you lousy no-good mutt! And that! And that!

THE MAN SEES RED. HE LIFTS HIS ARM AND STRIKES THE CRUELEST BLOW. BUCK SHRIEKS IN AGONY. HE CRUMPLES AND GOES DOWN.

That'll teach you who's boss around here!

STRANGERS COME TO LOOK AT THE DOGS. MONEY CHANGES HANDS. SUDDENLY THERE'S A ROPE AROUND BUCK'S NECK, JERKING HIM THIS WAY AND THAT.

Just throw him in the truck with the others.

Sure thing, Boss.

FOR TWO DAYS AND TWO NIGHTS BUCK SUFFERS TERRIBLY. HE HAS NOTHING TO EAT OR DRINK.

ARRIVING IN THE CHILLY NORTH, BUCK IS AMAZED BY THE CRUELTY HE SEES AROUND HIM. THE MEN ARE SAVAGE, RUTHLESS CREATURES; THE DOGS, NO BETTER.

WHEN A GENTLE DOG NAMED CURLY TRIES TO BEFRIEND A MEAN HUSKY NAMED SPITZ, SPITZ BRUTALLY ATTACKS HER, RIPPING HER FACE FROM EYE TO JAW.

AS SHE LIES THERE DYING, THE OTHER HUSKIES CLOSE IN ON HER AND TEAR HER TO PIECES. ONCE DOWN, THAT'S THE END OF YOU.

SPITZ THROWS HIS HEAD BACK AND LAUGHS AND LAUGHS. FROM THAT MOMENT ON BUCK HATES HIM WITH A WHITE-HOT FURY HE'D NEVER KNOWN BEFORE.

BUCK AND SOME OF THE OTHERS ARE SOLD TO TWO MAIL CARRIERS FROM CANADA. THE MEN HITCH THE DOGS TO A SLED WITH CHAINS, STRAPS, AND BUCKLES. BUCK BEGINS HIS LIFE AS A SLED DOG.

THE MEN WORK THE DOGS HARD, AND FEED THEM BARELY ENOUGH TO KEEP THEM GOING.

FASTER! FASTER!

Go on! Mush! Mush!

THE MEN BEAT THE DOGS TO MAKE THEM GO FASTER.

AT NIGHT, WHEN THE MEN AND DOGS ARE ASLEEP, BUCK ROAMS WILD, IN THE MANNER OF HIS WOLFISH ANCESTORS. HE FEELS THE SHARP STIRRINGS OF OLD INSTINCTS.

BUCK LEARNS TO FIGHT AND SCAVENGE FOR FOOD. HE SLEEPS BENEATH THE SNOW.

HE THROWS HIS HEAD BACK AND HOWLS AT THE MOON. IT ALL FEELS FAMILIAR SOMEHOW.

AT THE SAME TIME, BUCK'S HATRED OF SPITZ GROWS DAILY. AS LEAD DOG ON THE TEAM, SPITZ DOESN'T TAKE KINDLY TO CHALLENGES TO HIS AUTHORITY.

EVENTUALLY, THE TWO DOGS GET INTO A BAD FIGHT. BUCK FEELS THE THRILL OF BATTLE. FIGHTING IS IN HIS BLOOD, IN HIS BONES.

AS THEY FIGHT, THE OTHERS FORM A CIRCLE AROUND THEM, SILENTLY LICKING THEIR CHOPS.

SUDDENLY, SPITZ GOES DOWN. THE OTHERS, SEEING THAT THEIR LEADER HAS FALLEN, FINISH HIM OFF. BUCK TAKES HIS PLACE AS LEAD DOG, AND THE JOURNEY CONTINUES.

AT THE END OF THE RUN THE DOGS ARE HALF-DEAD FROM EXHAUSTION. YET THEY'RE SOLD AGAIN, THIS TIME TO A GROUP OF AMERICAN GOLD-SEEKERS . . .

. . . INEXPERIENCED AND OUT OF PLACE IN THE WILDERNESS. THEY OVERLOAD THEIR SLED AND PLAN POORLY FOR THE JOURNEY. THE DOGS HAVE NO CONFIDENCE IN THESE PEOPLE.

BUCK AND THE TEAM STRUGGLE TO KEEP THE SLED UPRIGHT. BUT WHEN THEY MAKE A TURN, IT TIPS OVER. THE NEW MASTERS ARE FURIOUS.

Take that, you canine lowlife!

THE VILLAGERS ARE QUICK TO CONDEMN THE GOLD-SEEKERS.

What do you expect when you overload the sled like that?

You should haul the sled yourselves!

You need half the load and twice the dogs!

ONLY HALFWAY THROUGH THE JOURNEY, THEY'RE RUNNING OUT OF FOOD. THE HUMANS BICKER ABOUT WHO'S TO BLAME . . .

Idiot! Can't you do anything right?

. . . WHILE THE DOGS BEGIN TO STARVE.

ONE OF THE MEN COMES UP WITH A SOLUTION.

We'll cut their rations and make them go faster! We'll club them if they slow down!

OF THE ORIGINAL TEAM OF FOURTEEN, ONLY FIVE DOGS MAKE IT TO JOHN THORNTON'S CAMP. THE DOGS LIMP ALONG, JUST SKIN AND BONES, THEIR HAIR MATTED WITH DRIED BLOOD.

ZAS!

THORNTON WATCHES THEM. HE KNOWS SOMETHING ABOUT THE ICE IN THESE PARTS, AND TRIES TO WARN THE GOLD-SEEKERS OF THE DANGER THEY'RE IN.

That ice won't hold. Better lie low a couple of days.

Too bad! We're shoving off. Can't keep all that gold waiting!

THE GOLD-SEEKERS ORDER THE DOGS TO MOVE. ALL DO, EXCEPT BUCK. HE MAKES NO EFFORT. BUCK SENSES THAT CROSSING THE ICE WOULD BE DANGEROUS.

Get going, or you'll be sorry!

HAL FLIES INTO A RAGE. HE GOES AFTER BUCK WITH A KNIFE. THORNTON INTERVENES, KNOCKING THE KNIFE OUT OF HAL'S HAND AND USING IT TO CUT BUCK LOOSE.

Don't you worry about that, John Thornton! Team, start up the sled!

This dog stays with me! And I never want to see your faces again!

THE SLED TAKES OFF ACROSS THE ICE. ABOUT A QUARTER OF A MILE IN, THE ICE BREAKS OPEN, SWALLOWING UP THE HUMANS AND THE DOGS.

THORNTON BECOMES BUCK'S MASTER. BUCK IS DEVOTED TO HIM. BUCK WOULD DO ANYTHING FOR THORNTON.

Whew! Thanks, Buddy! You saved my life!

WITH THORNTON'S HELP, BUCK SLOWLY WINS BACK HIS STRENGTH. FOR THE FIRST TIME IN HIS LIFE, BUCK KNOWS GENUINE LOVE.

BUT BUCK'S LOVE FOR THORNTON IS MIXED WITH A GROWING ATTRACTION TO THE WILD. THE WILDERNESS CALLS OUT TO HIM. THE FEELING GROWS STRONGER EVERY DAY.

OFTENTIMES, BUCK RANGES FAR AFIELD, BEFRIENDING WOLVES. HIS CUNNING IS A WOLF'S CUNNING. HE MUST KILL TO STAY ALIVE.

ONE DAY, BUCK RETURNS TO CAMP AND FINDS HIS MASTER HAS BEEN MURDERED. HE FOLLOWS THE SCENT AND FINDS THE KILLERS BY THE RIVER. THROWING HIMSELF UPON THEM, HE DRAGS THEM DOWN LIKE DEER.

BUCK RETURNS TO THE WILD AND BECOMES THE LEADER OF A PACK OF WOLVES. BUT EVERY YEAR HE RETURNS TO THE PLACE WHERE THORNTON DIED, TO PAY HIM TRIBUTE.

THE LOCALS BELIEVE THEY CAN SEE HIM THERE, HOWLING AT THE MOON, MOURNING HIS BELOVED MASTER.

⏻ COLLABORATIVE DISCUSSION

Discussing the Purpose With a small group, discuss the events of the story. Respond to the following questions and cite evidence from the story.

1. How does Buck's behavior change from the time when he is in California to the time when he is living in the wild? What does the northern wilderness setting tell you about Buck's survival skills?

2. How is Thornton's treatment of Buck different from the treatment Buck receives from the three gold-seeking masters?

3. Do you consider Buck's survival skills to be a sign of intelligence or instinct?

↺ Performance Task

Writing Activity: Short Response You've now discussed how Buck's behavior changes throughout the story. Write a short response about the theme, or central idea, of "The Call of the Wild."

1. Explain the theme.

2. Give reasons for Buck's actions.

3. Cite evidence from the story to support your reasons.

Consider using the following Useful Words in your writing. Using these words can help you develop the theme in your response. These descriptive words can also help you convey Buck's experiences. Check their meanings in a dictionary if they are unfamiliar to you.

Useful Words

▷ dignity	▷ antagonistic	▷ formidable	▷ inevitable	▷ resilient
▷ overthrow	▷ ferocity	▷ impulsive	▷ impending	▷ advantage

SPEAKING TOOLBOX

Monitoring Speaking

Ask yourself the following questions:

▶ Can I retell the story by describing the beginning, middle, and end?

▶ Can I support my opinions, feelings, and ideas with details from the story?

▶ Can I explain my opinions and ideas about the story in a way that others understand?

Useful Phrases

▷ I'm not sure what you mean by ____.

▷ I understand what you mean, but ____.

▷ That sounds right, but I still think ____.

Speak Out! You have now read two stories that feature an animal as the main character: Crow from "The Crow and the Pitcher" and Buck from "The Call of the Wild." What ideas about Crow's and Buck's intelligence does each writer present? In a small group, take turns comparing and contrasting the two animal characters. Use the Useful Phrases as a guide for expressing your ideas respectfully.

Performance Task

Writing Activity: Informative Essay

In this unit, you have read about different aspects of animal intelligence. You have read about animals from their point of view. You have also read about how their relationship to humans has changed as a result of new knowledge. Your task is to write an informative essay on the theme of animal intelligence.

Planning and Prewriting

Connect to the Theme

The bond between humans and animals is as strong as ever. But do we respect animals as intelligent beings—or think that their purpose is to serve us? How has the relationship between humans and animals changed over time? What part do culture and geography play? To write your informative essay, you will need a main idea. What will it be?

Write Down Some Possible Main Ideas

Write down several possible main ideas using the information you learned in the selections you've read. Here are some examples of main ideas:

- Animals and humans can find ways to communicate with each other.

- Domesticated animals often retain aspects of their ancestors.

- Sometimes connecting with an animal can cause problems.

Choose the main idea that seems most promising. You can use an idea from the list above or one you've thought of yourself.

Decide the Basics

Now that you have a main idea that reflects the theme of the unit, you'll need to figure out how to support your idea with examples and details from the selections. Use the notes below to help guide your decision making.

Main Idea

The main idea is the "big idea" of your essay.

- Write your main idea in the form of a sentence.
- Think about the most important point you're making.
- Use an interesting, thought-provoking quote from one of the selections.
- Present a fact that will surprise readers or make them curious.
- Ask a question that readers can relate to.

Supporting Details

Supporting details are facts or examples that tell more about the main idea.

- Find details in the selections that support your main idea.
- Use enough details to support your main idea.
- Include evidence that is relevant to the topic.
- Include details from a variety of sources so that your main idea is wide-ranging.

Vocabulary

Think about vocabulary and word choice.

- Be mindful of writing style. Use a formal and objective tone.
- Explain any proper nouns that a reader may not be familiar with.
- Make sure you include transitional words and phrases (however; first/next; for example; specifically) to help readers connect one idea to the next and to clarify the relationships between ideas.

Text Features

Informative essays often contain one or more text features to help organize the information you want to present.

- **Title:** The title of your essay should identify the topic or refer to the topic in a way that catches the reader's interest.
- **Subheadings:** If some of your supporting details can be grouped together, you can use a subheading for each grouping.

Performance Task

Finalize Your Plan

You know the basics of your essay. You have a main idea based on the theme of animal intelligence. You know which facts, examples, and details from the selections you'll use to support your main idea. You may have even decided on the title of your essay.

Now you need to decide how to present the information. Follow the structure of the diagram in the Writing Toolbox as a guide.

WRITING TOOLBOX

Elements of an Informative Essay

Opening Paragraph	Present your main idea. "Hook" your audience with an interesting detail, question, or quotation that relates to your main idea. The first sentence in your essay should refer to the overall main idea.
Supporting Detail Paragraphs	Each of these paragraphs should include a supporting detail for your main idea, or a group of examples that have a common thread.
	If your main idea has several aspects or parts, you may want to use subheadings to introduce paragraphs that deal with each aspect. Each new paragraph can begin with a sentence that refers to the main idea of the paragraph.
Conclusion	The conclusion should follow and sum up how the details support your main idea. You may want to include an insight about the topic such as a provocative question that will make the reader think more deeply about the topic.

Don't forget to refine your Personal Toolboxes with strategies that work for you.

Draft Your Essay

You have the basics of your informational essay. Start writing! As you write, think about:

- **Purpose and Audience** What effect do you want your essay to have on readers? Try to present your information in such a way that your audience understands and learns from what you've written..

- **Point of View** Establish your main idea reasonably quickly, so that the reader can follow the key points you are making.

- **Structure** Use the diagram to help you organize the information you are presenting. Use subheadings where necessary. Be sure to link your ideas together in a way that makes sense.

- **Conclusion** Use a concluding paragraph to tie your ideas together. You may want to restate your main idea, which will have more weight now that you have supported it with examples. You may want to present your own conclusion based on evidence you found in the selections.

Revise

Self Evaluation

Use the checklist and rubric to guide your analysis.

Peer Review

Exchange your essay with a classmate. Use the checklist to comment on your classmate's essay.

Edit

Edit your essay to correct spelling, grammar, and punctuation errors.

Publish

Finalize your essay and choose a way to share it with your audience.

Stream to Start

fyi
hmhfyi.com

Dealing with Disaster

Bad things do happen in the world, like war, natural disasters, disease. But out of those situations always arise stories of ordinary people doing extraordinary things.

—Daryn Kagan, journalist

Essential Question

How do people deal with the impact of disasters?

The Language of Disaster

There are many different kinds of disasters. Disasters can be extensive or everyday: losing a beloved pet, missing an event when you're sick, or getting lost in a new city or in a new country. Whatever the disaster is, people may feel a range of emotions when faced with a crisis. One person might respond by being scared and feeling helpless—and another person might want to take immediate action.

Sometimes disasters are caused by nature. Natural disasters can have a wide range of magnitude, strength, and force. Earthquakes, fires, floods, tornados, hurricanes—these are all examples of natural disasters that cause destruction and devastation. People must be able to respond to these natural disasters quickly in order to save lives.

Sometimes people or animals cause disasters. Living things such as people and animals live together in a small world. When there is a conflict among them, both people and animals will respond to the conflict in various ways. They might attack. They might start war.

But disaster can inspire some people to help others, or to make a change. Reacting to a disaster is one action. Preventing future disasters so that they don't happen again takes that action one step further.

In this unit, you will learn about how different characters react and respond to disasters. You will also explore how people have coped with dangerous situations in different cultures and different time periods. You will find out why people disagree about what would be the best solution to a crisis. You will even read about how a reaction to a disaster can be significant and momentous.

What are the different ways of responding to a disaster?

Many Words for Disaster: Synonyms

Disaster can mean many things. Since there are so many different kinds of disaster, there are many words that express aspects of it.

↻ Performance Task

Choose a synonym for **disaster**. Use one of the words above, one that you find in **Browse** magazine, or another one you know. Begin preparing a short speech about how to prepare for a small everyday disaster, such as missing the bus or forgetting your lunch at home. Use the supports in your **Activity Book**.

DOWNLOAD

Read to find out how the narrator of the next story deals with having to relocate temporarily after his home has been severely flooded.

⏻ SETTING A PURPOSE

As you read, think about what the narrator reveals about being relocated temporarily.

Tales of a Sixth-Grade Skateboarder

Floating Man

Subscribe me!

Enter your email address:

SEARCH

After the Flood
Anybody Out There Know How I'm Feeling?

November 15

Hey. Thanks for listening as I think out loud about being "temporarily relocated" after the flood. That horrible night when the water just wouldn't stop rising was a month ago now. There are lots of things to be thankful for, I know. Here's my list:

- We're **all alive**! That is obviously the most important thing, more important than everything else put together.

- We got our **dog and both cats** out safely. That is HUGE.

- We have a **place to stay** for now, while we figure things out. OK, it's tiny, temporary, overcrowded, and I'm sharing a room with my sister (AWKWARD!). But still, I know we are lucky to not be in a shelter.

- I've started at a **new school**. My teachers at Elmhurst have gone out of their way to be super welcoming and friendly.

Staying busy at school helps me keep my mind off the bad stuff. I'm starting to make a few new friends, especially on the cross-country team. Go me!

But, despite all the good stuff, I've been having a pretty hard time. Here's why:

- I miss **my friends**. Staying in touch online is not the same. The fact that they are together and I'm not there makes me feel bad.

- I miss **my stuff, my room, my house, my street** . . . OK, I know it's shallow to miss THINGS, but it's more like I just miss stuff being familiar and comfortable and NORMAL. When we left, I took my school backpack, my baseball cap (of course), and my skateboard. Now I wish I could have taken a lot more—even impossible things like the giant tree on the corner, Mrs. Brown always waving from her front porch, and the Lindy Freeze (my favorite place to get ice cream after school).

- I hate the **uncertainty**. I hate not knowing when we'll be going back to our old place, or even IF we'll be going back. I don't know if my new school (and friends, etc.) is forever, or just for now.

- I hate the fact that **NO ONE GETS WHAT I'M FEELING**. It makes me feel so alone.

Anybody out there know what I mean?

👍 Like   👎 Dislike

ARCHIVES

November

October

September

August

July

June

May

April

March

💬 **Comments**   2

Posted at **7:38 PM** by **SurferDude**   Hang in there, Floating Man. We had to leave our home for a whole year, after a fire. But now, I'm back with my old buddies. Plus, I have new friends from the place we were for that year. It can be a good thing. Don't stress. You're not alone.

◯ **Reply**   ◯ **Share**

Posted at **9:17 PM** by **PizzaPartyGirl**   Dude! I'm a "floodster" relocated to Elmhurst, too. I thought I was the only one here. Man, I know EXACTLY what you're feeling.

I've been missing the Lindy Freeze like crazy. I used to go there after every game!

◯ **Reply**   ◯ **Share**

⏻ COLLABORATIVE DISCUSSION

Discussing the Purpose With a partner, share your thoughts about what Floating Man reveals about being relocated. What words or phrases reveal the most about what he feels and thinks?

Staying Safe Think carefully about uploading pictures of yourself. Once you've posted a picture of yourself online, anyone can see it. People also may be able to download it. Be cautious.

Write On! Write a short comment on Floating Man's post. State your opinion, but remember to be respectful of his feelings. Give examples from his blog post to support your comment. Then write a comment in response to Floating Man's readers' comments. 💬 Comments 0

🔄 Performance Task

Writing Activity: Design Your Blog Your personality immediately shines from your blog design. Your blog software should have a feature for designing its appearance, where you can choose among the different templates or themes. These range in color and style. They also allow you to design your layout. You can choose how many columns you need, as well as the size of the columns. You might have a sidebar column where you want to manage a list of website links that you often visit. If any photographs or art images have inspired your design, you can upload these photos and art images as part of your template.

NOTE: If you are using a photo or an image that is not yours, you must be sure to give proper credit. You must give the person or organization's name and the date of the photo or image.

1 Write a blog post describing why you chose this particular template and any art or images. You can use a bulleted or numbered list to organize your thoughts. This step would be a good place to insert a link to one of your design inspirations or upload an image. Adding links to your posts gives your readers more information about a subject.

2 Preview your draft. At this point, you may want to spell check or fix any grammatical errors. If you have added a link, check that it is correct and does not load to an incorrect site.

3 Publish your post.

Language Cam video
Do you want to learn more about dealing with disaster?
Watch the video.

Super Storm Sandy

DOWNLOAD

Floating Man finds a way to cope with a flooding disaster by blogging about his experience. Find out how a community decides to deal with a water crisis.

⏻ SETTING A PURPOSE

As you read, think about how well the facts and details are presented for both sides of the desalination plant issue.

Desalination:
Solution or Disaster?

San Diego Project Raises Big Questions

by Malik Mohammed

Poseidon: the Greek god of the sea. Think about why the company would choose this for its name.

Break down the term **desalination** into word parts if you are unfamiliar with its meaning. You can also get clues by reading ahead.

SAN DIEGO—the state of California has a big problem: too little water for too many people. **Poseidon** Resources, a private company, is building a $1 billion solution to the problem: a **desalination** plant. At least, this is what supporters of the plan say. Those in favor of the plan believe that plants—industrial buildings like this one—can solve the water crisis. Others disagree. The cost in dollars and in damage to the environment is too great, they claim.

The plant is being built in Carlsbad, California. And every day the plant will turn the seawater into 50 million gallons of fresh drinking water. The process is called desalination.

How does this process of getting 50 million gallons of fresh water work? First, the Carlsbad plant receives seawater that is used for cooling the Encina Power Station. One hundred million gallons of this seawater are piped into the plant. Filters rid the water of any

10

solids and bacteria. Next, machines **pump** the water through other filters. These remove more than 99% of the salt and other minerals. The end products will be 50 million gallons of purified water and 50 million gallons of double-salty water. This salty water is called brine. The brine will then be diluted and then returned to the ocean. The

20 remaining fresh water is treated with chlorine and minerals. This makes it taste like "regular" drinking water. It's now ready to be used by a city's water system.

The desalinated water from the Carlsbad plant will supply enough water for 112,000 households. In a region suffering from **drought**, this is important. This is especially true in San Diego County. The area receives only about ten inches of rain per year. (Nearby areas such as Los Angeles receive two-thirds more rain.) And San Diego does not have much **groundwater** to tap for drinking. Currently San Diego has to buy 70 percent of its water from other places.

pump: to raise and transfer fluids or gases by pressure or suction

Use context clues to determine the meaning of the term **drought**.

Guess the meaning of the compound word **groundwater**.

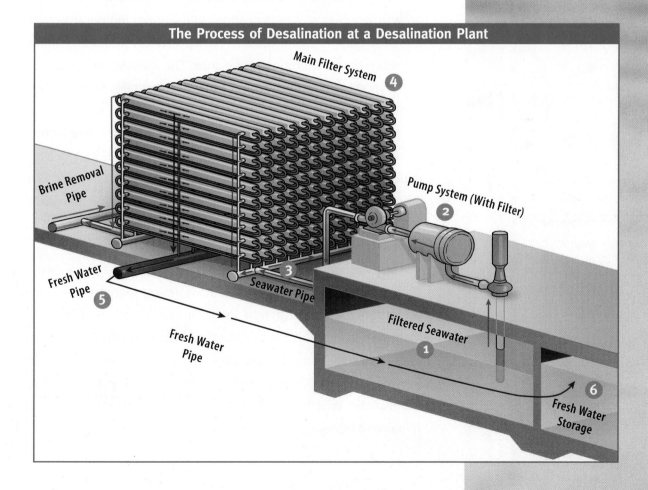

The Process of Desalination at a Desalination Plant

Main Filter System ④

Brine Removal Pipe

Pump System (With Filter) ②

Fresh Water Pipe ⑤

③

Seawater Pipe

Filtered Seawater ①

Fresh Water Pipe

Fresh Water Storage ⑥

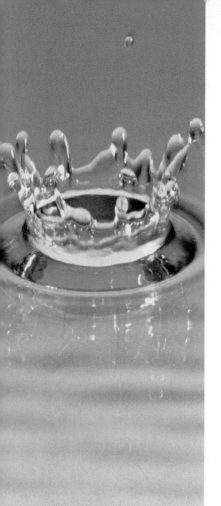

Reverse osmosis water purification plant

30   Several factors are adding to the water crisis. One is population growth. Another is climate change, with warmer temperatures and less snowpack in the mountains. Poseidon notes that desalination is a "drought proof" solution to the crisis. The water source does not depend on melting snow from California mountains or on rainfall. Specifically, the Pacific Ocean is right there.

Why do many people oppose desalination? Cost is one factor. Experts say buying water from the Carlsbad plant will be twice as expensive as buying water from sources such as the Colorado River. **Opponents** would prefer that the region develop less expensive ways
40 to save water. Environmentalists propose developing new ways to recycle "used" water, for example.

Environmentalists have other worries, too. They say the energy used in desalination will add to global warming. Moreover, pumping water from the ocean can trap and harm sea life such as marine mammals. In addition, the brine pumped back into the Pacific is saltier than regular sea water. This, too, could cause environmental problems.

The Carlsbad Desalination Plant will be the largest in the Western Hemisphere. Whether or not it is a solution to San Diego's water crisis remains to be seen.

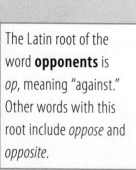

The Latin root of the word **opponents** is *op*, meaning "against." Other words with this root include *oppose* and *opposite*.

⏻ COLLABORATIVE DISCUSSION

Discussing the Purpose With a partner, discuss both sides of the issue. First, examine the circumstances that led to this issue. Which side of the issue made more of an impact on you? Do you and your partner agree? Cite facts and details to support your answer.

SPEAKING TOOLBOX

Reading with Expression

1. Read with energy.
2. Read with strong feeling.
3. Pause for punctuation marks such as commas and periods.

> As you work through this unit, remember to create your Personal Toolbox with strategies that work for you. It's available from Student Resources or from your teacher.

↻ Performance Task

Speaking Activity: Practicing for an Oral Presentation Work with your partner to practice delivering an oral presentation that expresses your opinion of the side that you found more persuasive.

1 Using your discussion as a guide, organize your notes in an outline. Review your facts and details to determine the most important ideas, or **talking points**, that support your opinion on one side of the issue.

2 Review your talking points. This will help you feel more confident about delivering your oral presentation.

3 Practice delivering your presentation several times. Have your partner time your presentation.

4 Ask your partner for feedback: Did you speak clearly? Did you speak at a rate that was too fast or too slow? Did you read with expression? Did you have time to cover your talking points?

Podcast: Storm Shelter App Helps Pinpoint People Amid Tornado's Rubble

Background on the Moore, OK, Tornado

On May 20, 2013, a powerful tornado struck the city of Moore, Oklahoma. The tornado destroyed more than 1,000 homes, injured hundreds, and killed 24 people. It flattened and damaged businesses, schools, streets—even a hospital.

It was extremely difficult for emergency responders to rescue people immediately. Streets, buildings, and landmarks were completely unrecognizable. People were also trapped under heavy wreckage, so they were not visible to responders.

The tornado lasted approximately 40 minutes, but its impact remains significant today. The people of Moore are still trying to find ways to cope with the massive damage the tornado left behind. One of these people, a firefighter named Shonn Neidel, came up with a solution to fix a problem that the existing storm shelter registry did not solve. He developed, or thought of and built, an app that would enable firefighters to find people more efficiently and more quickly in an emergency. This app would increase their chances of finding tornado survivors.

⏻ SETTING A PURPOSE

As you listen, think about what purpose Shonn's storm shelter app would serve. Use the Problem and Solution chart to help you determine the problems of the existing storm shelter registry.

Storm Shelter
App Helps Pinpoint People Amid Tornado's Rubble

Problem and Solution Chart

Problem 1: The existing storm shelter registry did not give firefighters enough information. They needed to know where to dig, in order to find people who needed help as soon as possible.

Problem 2: Because street signs and house numbers were gone, firefighters had a hard time locating addresses. GPS was often inaccurate.

Problem 3: The firefighters needed an app that was easy to use, and one that worked even when cell service was down.

How the app will solve the problems:

1. The app shows how many people are in a shelter.

2. It indicates what victims' medical needs are, so first responders can appropriately plan for medical equipment and workers.

3. It provides coordinates of actual storm center locations.

4. It gives physical descriptions of what's above the shelter.

⏻ **COLLABORATIVE DISCUSSION**

Discussing the Purpose Shonn Neidel came up with a creative way to solve a problem caused by a natural disaster. With a partner, discuss why you think Shonn's app would be helpful to other communities who have experienced severe tornadoes.

DOWNLOAD

Into the Burning Night

You have read and heard about some of the ways people come up with practical solutions so that they will be better equipped to respond to future disasters. Now you will read about a narrator who must react and respond to an emergency in the present.

Know Before You Go

Katherine Schlick Noe is the author of the novel *Something to Hold*. She based this story on her experience as a child growing up on the Warm Springs Indian Reservation in Oregon during the early 1960s. The Warm Springs Reservation is home to the Warm Springs, Paiute, and Wasco tribes.

Kitty, a sixth-grader whose father has started a new job as a forester on the Warm Springs Indian Reservation, is the narrator. Two of Kitty's Native American classmates are a brother and sister named Raymond and Jewel who live with their *káthla* [kaht-la], which means "grandmother."

READING TOOLBOX

External and Internal Conflict

An **external conflict** involves a character who struggles against an outside force such as a powerful storm, an animal, or another character.

An **internal conflict** takes place within a character. One kind of internal conflict can be facing a dreaded fear.

⏻ SETTING A PURPOSE

As you read, pay attention to how a frightening situation leads Kitty to do something unexpected.

Into the Burning Night

from *Something to Hold*

by Katherine Schlick Noe

I've never heard anything so loud. I stand stunned, unable to move. Pinky reaches back and yanks hard on my arm. "Kitty!" she shouts. "We gotta *go!*"

She pulls me over the ground. She is strong for such a scrawny kid. I focus on the tower steps before us. This time, I leap for them as she does, taking two at a time.

We sprint upward as the smoke chases us and snags around our heads. Pinky holds a wet towel up to her face and signals to me to do the same. I wrap the towel around 10 my nose and mouth, stumbling behind her.

We scramble toward the top, faster and faster. No time **to catch our breath** at the landings. The smoke rises faster than we can climb, but we battle upward through it. Pinky trips and goes down hard on a step, the metal grating biting into her knee. I help her up, and we keep going. Blood drips onto each step as we pass.

I don't have time to be afraid. We just climb as fast as we can through the suffocating fog. We keep going, breathing hard, not talking. Thunder booms down on us, 20 lightning photographs the mountains around us.

I've lost track of how far we've gone. When I reach up for the next railing, my hand meets strong arms. Mrs. Wesley bends down to pull me up to the last landing. She reaches out, grasps Pinky under her arms, and hefts her up onto her hip. Mrs. Wesley reaches back and **clasps** me

> The idiom **to catch our breath** means "to rest to restore normal breathing and continue an activity."

> **clasp:** to grasp, or hold firmly with the hand

Can you guess the meaning of the compound word **trapdoor** by breaking it down into the two words it is made of?

around the wrist. I don't know how she does it, but she hauls us to safety and bangs the **trapdoor** shut.

Mrs. Wesley yanks the wet towels from our faces and tucks them quickly into the cracks around the trap door.
30 Sealing out the smoke. Then she points to the wooden bucket under the fire table, where I find new cloths, already wet. "Tie a mask around your nose and mouth!" she yells.

I hold the cloth to my face while Mrs. Wesley tends to Pinky. She is a mess—her leg bleeding furiously now and her face pale.

"Is she OK?" My voice is muffled through the towel.

Mrs. Wesley nods quickly, wrapping a wet towel around Pinky's leg. Pinky starts to cry, holding tight to her mother's arm.

40 Mrs. Wesley speaks to her quickly, softly. "I need you to be strong now. You gotta stay focused. Sit here while I call in." I hear the worry in her voice.

I sit with Pinky on the wood floor, in the corner of the tower. I tie the mask securely to my face, and I help Pinky tie hers, too. I put my arm around her as she holds the towel to her knee.

Mrs. Wesley stands up and reaches for the radio next to the fire table. She clicks the microphone. "Station One— Sidwalter . . . Station One—Sidwalter . . . Come in, Station
50 One," she repeats.

This time there is no static.

"We can't raise them," she says quietly as her hands scramble over the radio, checking wires, pushing buttons. Trying to get it to work. "*Come on*," she says.

Suddenly, we catch the tail end of Dad's transmission.
". . . you there?" *Oh, I wish I'd let him come for me yesterday.*

"Station One—trouble with the radio," Mrs. Wesley responds, and it goes out again.

I hear something underneath the storm—the frenzied
60 honking of a horn. Mrs. Wesley looks down through the window, her face reflected in the strange orange glow.

"Oh, no," she says. "They didn't get out!"

I'm scared to look, but I go to the window. *Káthla*'s truck hurtles up the road, right through the tunnel of flames, and skids to a stop at the cabin. My whole body starts to shake as Raymond jumps out from behind the wheel and pounds on the cabin door. Jewel helps her grandmother out of the pickup. *Káthla* leans heavily on her.

Mrs. Wesley turns to me. "Kitty," she says, "you've got to go down and help them get up here."

My heart catches. *"Me?"*

She takes both of my shoulders in her hands and leans down to face me head-on. "I have to stay here, get the radio to work so they know what's going on."

My shoulders shake under her hands. I know Pinky can't be the one to go. But I'm not sure I can, either. Mrs. Wesley holds me firmly, looks right in my eyes. "You have to help them. And you have to do it right now."

She grabs two more wet cloths, ties one around my nose and mouth and the other over my head. She thrusts the bucket into my hands. "Take all of these. Make them cover up. Then get them up here as fast as you can."

Mrs. Wesley scrapes the towels from around the trap door and lifts it. "You can do this," she says firmly.

Smoke boils into the tower. I'm shaking so hard, I can barely grip the bucket handle, but I take a deep breath, clamp my mouth shut, and start the long climb down. Above me, the trapdoor bangs shut. I hear Mrs. Wesley slide open a window. She leans out, yelling, *"Up here! Up here!"*

Smoke and sparks swirl around the tower steps, and I can't see anything down below.

I cling to the railing with one hand, feel for each stair with my foot. Concentrate on one step at a time, counting the turns I remember from yesterday. Six steps down to a landing, turn, six steps to the next landing. Take short breaths. Ignore the heat that blasts in my face. Don't drop the bucket. Don't think about anything else.

Usually, **Howl** refers to the sound an animal makes, but here it refers to the loud sound of the fire.

I don't see any more lightning, and the thunder has moved off to the east. What's left is the **howl** of the fire.

100 Through the smoke, I finally hear a voice not far below me. "One more, *Káthla*. That's it." Strong, no hint of urgency. *Raymond?* "Now another. Keep going."

Then Jewel. "It's OK. Hang on to me."

I can't see them, but I grip the bucket tighter, slide my hand more quickly down the railing, and call out, *"Jewel! Keep coming up!"*

I find the next landing and hang there, breathing hard. The smoke is so thick, I feel it seep into my lungs even through the mask. It's all I can do to keep my balance.

110 A hand reaches up and seizes my wrist. Raymond pulls himself and his *káthla* up to the landing. I reach out to grasp her arm and help him ease her down onto a step.

I grab wet cloths out of the bucket and thrust them at Raymond. "Quick! Tie this around *Káthla*'s face!" I order. "And these are for you and Jewel!"

He carefully covers his grandmother's face. Jewel coughs as she pulls herself up to the landing, breathing hard, and hugs her grandmother.

"Jewel!" I say sharply. "You've got to get this on your 120 face!"

slump: to sink heavily

She just **slumps** down at *Káthla*'s side.

The flames below have grown, and the roar builds and spreads up toward us. It's oven hot here on this landing, and the sparks and embers fly around our heads.

I tug on Jewel's arm. *"Move!"* I scream.

Raymond looks at me, lifts his grandmother off the landing, and starts to carry her up the stairs. I grab Jewel's sleeve, and she reacts with the strength I know she has in her. Together, we stumble up the long steps, grasping the 130 rails one after another.

Smoke and sparks lick at our feet. We work our way upward, pulling each other, until at last we reach the open trapdoor. Mrs. Wesley has helped Raymond boost his grandmother inside. Jewel and I scramble up until we're on the solid floor of the tower and Mrs. Wesley can slam the door shut against the fire.

Mrs. Wesley helps *Káthla* settle down onto the floor. Raymond and Jewel gather her between them. I stuff the towels back into the cracks around the trapdoor, then sneak a peek at the window to catch the pulsing reflection of fire in the trees below.

⏻ COLLABORATIVE DISCUSSION

Discussing the Purpose There are many ways to deal with a dangerous crisis. In this story, Kitty has to overcome her fear, as well as a threatening time constraint. With a small group, discuss how Kitty was able to rescue Raymond, Jewel, and *Káthla*. Cite details from the text to support your answers. When you speak, follow rules for classroom discussion. Remember to speak loudly, clearly, and at a normal speed.

Analyzing the Text ▸Cite Text Evidence◂

1. **Summarize** Restate the most important ideas and details about the story.

2. **Analyze** What are the external and internal conflicts in this story? How are Kitty's external and internal conflicts related?

↻ Performance Task

Writing Activity: Author's Influence Chart An **author's influence** is an important factor that affects his or her writing. For example, an author may be influenced by a historical event that happened during his or her lifetime, or a current event that recently happened. Another instance of an author's influence may be a cultural aspect, such as where he or she was raised or lived, what language he or she speaks, or any culturally significant traditions he or she observes.

Copy the chart below. Use the chart to record information about the story and the author.

Author's Influence Chart		
Time and Place	**Cultural Aspect**	**Historical or Current Events**

Vocabulary Strategy: Figurative Language

In this story, the author uses many examples of figurative language, or descriptive words or phrases, to appeal to a reader's senses. Examples from the story are:

Thunder booms (line 19)	*oven hot* (line 123)
Smoke boils (line 85)	*pulsing reflection* (line 140)

These words and phrases describe Kitty's battle with a strong and powerful force of nature: fire. They also create a sense of intense loudness, illustrate the thickness of the smoke, and help describe the immediacy of the fire. These words and phrases heighten, or intensify, the urgency and the tension of the scene.

Write On! Find other examples of figurative language in the story. Think about how these words and phrases contribute to the tension of the scene. Also, think about how these words and phrases are significant in understanding Kitty's fear. Write down the examples you find.

Back on the Board: Bethany Hamilton

You've read a fictional story about a girl who refuses to let her fear stop her from rescuing her friends. Now you will read a real-life account of a girl who refuses to give up on her dreams when she is the victim of a terrifying shark attack.

Know Before You Go

"Back on the Board: Bethany Hamilton" is an example of **narrative nonfiction**. Narrative nonfiction stories tell you about real-life events that happened to real-life people in a way that seems like fiction. Because the story that is told is a real-life account, the facts in the story must match the actual details of the event. The characters, setting, and events are real, rather than imaginary.

READING TOOLBOX

Tone

An author's **tone** is the overall attitude toward his or her subject. Adjectives are used to describe the tone of the text, such as *funny, serious,* or *respectful.* You determine the author's tone by analyzing the author's choice of words.

⏻ SETTING A PURPOSE

As you read, pay attention to how the actual details of the events and the setting are developed and how the real-life people are described.

Back on the Board:
Bethany Hamilton

from
Real Kids, Real Stories, Real Change

By Garth Sundem

Have you ever heard the saying, *When **a horse bucks you off**, get right back on and ride again?* Have you ever been in a situation like that?

> When a horse **bucks you off,** it rears up and shakes you off.

Bethany Hamilton has, but for her the horse was actually a surfboard. And instead of getting bucked off, a 14-foot-long tiger shark bit off her arm.

Bethany was born on the North Shore of Kauai, Hawaii, and started surfing before she could walk. She won her first surfing competition when she was four. At the age of seven she placed first in the 7 to 9 age division in both the short and long board events at the
10 Quicksilver surfing contest. In 2001, she won both the under-14 and under-17 girls divisions of the Volcom Puffer Fish competition. Bethany was sponsored by Rip Curl, a surfboard company, and was making plans to become a professional surfer. She was a surfer girl, born to surfer parents, living in a surfer's paradise. What could be better?

On Halloween morning of 2003, Bethany paddled into the waves of Makua Beach near her home with her best friend, Alana, and Alana's dad and brother.

There was nothing unusual about this—in fact, this is how Bethany
20 spent most mornings. Usually her mom and dad were there, too, but Bethany's dad was scheduled for knee surgery that day and was already at the hospital.

The sky was as clear as the water, and the waves were relatively gentle. Bethany surfed for about half an hour and caught maybe 10 waves. Everybody knew each other at Makua Beach, and Bethany, Alana, and about eight other surfers chatted and joked as they **straddled** their boards in the gentle swells, waiting for the next set of waves to roll in. Bethany dangled her left arm in the water.

straddled: sat with one leg on each side

From below, Bethany and her board must have looked like a lazy
30 sea turtle—which many sharks enjoy eating for breakfast.

The tiger shark rose out of the depths and tore into Bethany's board. "We never saw it, or anything, before it bit me," Bethany recalled. "It shook me. It lasted about three seconds long. All I saw was, like, a gray blur. It let go and I just looked at the red blood in the water."

tiger shark

The other surfers pushed Bethany to shore and her friend's dad tied a surfboard leash around what was left of her arm to help slow the bleeding. Alana noted that Bethany stayed "really calm." As Bethany lay on the beach wrapped in towels, she was thinking, 40 *That ambulance should hurry up.*

It was 30 miles to the hospital. When the ambulance arrived there, doctors were preparing Bethany's dad for his knee surgery in the operating room. The doctors quickly went to work on Bethany instead of her father.

Bethany lost 70 percent of her blood. She also lost her left arm, just below the shoulder. Bethany's surgeon said that without her athletic conditioning she probably would have died.

Two weeks later, Bethany and her father both had their stitches removed. Her doctors were sure that the loss of an arm wouldn't 50 **hold** Bethany **back** physically, but they warned that getting over the mental and emotional shock of a shark attack would be hard— maybe impossible. Though her wound healed within a month, her friends and family worried that Bethany might never again get back on her surfboard.

To **hold** someone **back** is a phrasal verb meaning "to prevent someone from doing something."

Imagine what it must have been like for Bethany Hamilton to sit on her surfboard, less than a month after her injury, waiting to catch that first wave. What do you think was going through her mind? Would you have been afraid if it had been you? Others wanted to give her a push to make sure she could still get up, but Bethany 60 said, "I want to make sure I catch the first wave myself, then they can help me."

Finally a good wave came and Bethany paddled as hard as she could. When she felt the wave start to push her board, she jumped up and planted her feet wide. "When I got up on my first wave," she said, "I just had, like, tears of happiness. . . . I was so stoked to be out there."

But Bethany didn't stop with catching a wave or two. In the same year, she placed fifth in the National Surfing Championships. She competed against professionals with many more years of

70 experience—and both their arms! She also won an ESPN award for Best Comeback Athlete and a special courage award for showing courage at the 2004 Teen Choice Awards. Most importantly to Bethany, she secured a spot on the U.S. Surfing Team. Since her injury and amazing recovery, Bethany has been featured in dozens of newspaper and magazine articles and has appeared on talk shows including *20/20, Good Morning America,* and *The Oprah Winfrey Show.*

77 Bethany also has her own website, www.bethanyhamilton.com.

How has all the attention changed her?

"People I don't even know come up to me. I guess they see me as a

80 symbol of courage and inspiration. One thing hasn't changed—and that's how I feel when I'm riding a wave. It's like, here I am. I'm still here. It's still me and my board."

⏻ COLLABORATIVE DISCUSSION

Discussing the Purpose When you read the details of the events, setting, and people, what paragraphs or sections did you find especially interesting and exciting? With a partner, identify specific details (such as direct statements) and the reasons you found them memorable. How does using Bethany's real-life experience and details of the events give you a clear understanding of what happened?

Analyzing the Text   Cite Text Evidence

1. **Predict** Reread the title and the saying in the first paragraph. How do the title and the saying give you clues to the author's feelings about Bethany?

2. **Interpret** What is the author's tone toward Bethany's response to her injury? Use what you analyzed about the title, saying, and other details in the text to determine what the author thinks about Bethany's response. Does he consider Bethany to be an inspiration?

3. **Evaluate** The author includes direct statements and experiences of people who were with Bethany at the time of the accident. However, he could have written the facts about Bethany's accident as an informational article, rather than a piece of narrative nonfiction. How is this text different from an informational article? Is the author's telling of the event effective? Explain why.

Speak Out! With a small group, discuss the challenges that Bethany might have faced when she surfed for the first time after her injury. What skills would Bethany have needed to relearn? When you speak, make eye contact with other members of your group. Try not to distract others by tapping your pencil or shaking your leg. Remember to use a friendly, confident tone when you speak.

A Monument to Victory — And Disaster

Bethany Hamilton triumphed over her injury. Read to find out about the ancient Athenians, who survived years of constant war and multiple invasions led by the Persians.

Know Before You Go

As a small Mediterranean peninsula, Greece traded and communicated with much of the ancient world. The Greeks considered themselves one civilization, but individual cities were independent and even went to war with each other. The city of Athens was one of the most powerful Greek city-states, as was its rival Sparta. However, the Persian Empire was much larger than Greece itself. While Greece was flourishing locally, the Persian Empire was a true world power.

READING TOOLBOX

Chronological Order

Chronological order is a pattern of organization in which the events are arranged in the order in which they happened. This structure is used in historical writing, autobiographies, biographies, and fictional narratives.

⏻ SETTING A PURPOSE

As you read, pay attention to the sequence of events that occurs during the Persian Wars. To understand the order of events that occurred in ancient times, look at the date. An event that occurred in 494 BCE happened earlier than an event that occurred in 482 BCE.

A Monument to Victory —And Disaster

by Won Kwan

The enormous statue of the goddess Athena stood high above the city of Athens. Covered in ivory and gold, the 40-foot statue was inside the glorious new building called the Parthenon. In 432 BCE, Athenians had just completed the Parthenon. It was a temple on the **Acropolis**, the highest point in Athens. The city's residents could see the glowing white marble building from anywhere in their city. The Parthenon was built to thank Athena for the city's survival of a tumultuous era. The Athenians had weathered many disasters, and the Parthenon was a symbol of their prosperity. Unfortunately, it

10 would also be a symbol of disasters yet to come.

> The Greek **prefix acro-** in *Acropolis* means "top" or "summit."

◀ *The Parthenon on the Acropolis, Athens, Greece*

121

Athenians had been building on the Acropolis for thousands of years. But in 480 BCE, an invading army had burned the city to the ground. The Athenians and the other Greek cities were at war with the Persian Empire. In those days, Greece was not a single nation. Instead, individual cities were independent. Each city-state governed itself, often in different ways. However, they all considered themselves to be Greek, and identified as one people. Although they often went to war among themselves, they were united against outside forces. In 500 BCE, Athens had supported a **revolt** against the Persian Empire in what is now Turkey, which had failed disastrously. The Persian king Darius responded by invading Greece itself. This invasion was the first stage of the Persian War.

Use **context clues** to figure out the meaning of *revolt*.

20

The First Stage of the Persian War

At the time, the Persian Empire was the mightiest empire in the world. In order to fight the Persian Empire, Athens founded the Delian League. Smaller city-states that joined the League would pay Athens **tribute** to **fund** the Athenian army. Athens used this tribute to fight the Persian Empire. Some cities, such as Sparta, did not join the League, but fought alongside Athens against the invaders.

tribute: payment of money or valuables

fund: to provide money for something

30

The first great battle of the Persian War, in 490 BCE, was almost a disaster for the Greeks. The Persians landed an army of 25,000 men on the east coast of Greece near the Plain of Marathon. The Spartans, however, were celebrating a religious festival, and could not join the fight. An Athenian army of 10,000 soldiers led by General Miltiades faced the Persians—and won. This surprising victory marked the end of the first Persian invasion.

The Second Stage of the Persian War

However, the second stage of the Persian War began in 480 BCE. The Persians returned with an immense army, led by their new king, Xerxes. Once again, the Greeks triumphed. Many died in fierce battles

at Thermopylae, and the Persians burned Athens. But the Persians
40 at last **gave up**, and left in 479 BCE. Peace was restored. The Delian
League, however, continued to exist—and Athens continued to
demand tribute from the cities it had protected. The Delian League
became the Athenian Empire.

Read ahead to find a synonym for **gave up.**

The Athenian Empire was a new disaster. From 461 BCE to 446
BCE, Athens and Sparta were at war. The two city-states were
competing to be the most powerful in Greece. After this war,
Athens began to use the Delian League's tribute to make itself
wealthier, rather than to make the League stronger. In 431 BCE, the
year after the Parthenon was finished, Sparta led the rest of Greece
50 against Athens. While Athens had been the driving force in the
defeat of the Persian Empire, the city at last surrendered to Sparta
in 404 BCE.

The Athenians turned the disasters of the Persian Wars into
victory, again and again. With the Delian League, they became the
most powerful city in Greece. The only problem they couldn't deal
with was the one they caused themselves. The Parthenon survives to
this day, reminding us of the victories— and disasters—of Athens.

UPLOAD

⏻ COLLABORATIVE DISCUSSION

Discussing the Purpose The author describes the circumstances leading from the first Persian invasion in 480 BCE to the surrender of Athens in 404 BCE. With a partner, point out the events of the Persian Wars in chronological order. How does listing the events in chronological order help you understand the effect of the Persian Wars on the city of Athens?

READING TOOLBOX

Determine Main Idea and Details

If you want to find the main idea of an informative article, the usual place to look is its first paragraph, called the **introduction**. If you're looking for the main idea of one paragraph, you'll probably find it in the first sentence.

Supporting details of an article are found in the paragraphs after the introduction. These paragraphs are called the **body** of the essay. The supporting details of a particular paragraph are in the sentences after the first one.

The last paragraph of an article, the **conclusion**, brings together the most important details given in the body and restates the main idea of the essay.

Write On! What is the main idea of this informative article? Cite text evidence that supports the main idea.

LISTENING TOOLBOX

Monitoring Listening

Ask yourself the following questions:

▶ Did I know most of the words?

▶ Were the words and sentences mostly clear or confusing?

▶ When I didn't understand, did I ask for help?

↻ Performance Task

Writing Activity: Small Group Research With a small group, conduct research to find more about how the Athenians constructed the Parthenon. Look for relevant facts and concrete details to help you form a clear idea of any obstacles that they might have faced, such as constant warfare and invading armies.

- Individually, take notes and record the sources of your information.

- Take turns telling each other about the information that you've gathered. Follow the Monitoring Listening tips when you are listening to your group members.

- Work together to compile your group's notes into one list. If you find that two of you gathered the same piece of information, make sure that you don't repeat the information twice in your list.

- Organize the information into a summary.

The Last Days of Pompeii

In real life, the city of Athens has survived through many years of war and invasion. Now you will read a fictional story about how a few citizens of Pompeii stay alive when faced with a deadly volcanic eruption.

Historical Background

"The Last Days of Pompeii" is a historical romance story that is based on a novel written by Edward Bulwer-Lytton in 1834. The love story of a historical romance is often set against the dramatic events of a specific time period to make the story more exciting. In this case, the devastating eruption of Mount Vesuvius in 79 AD provides the setting for the love story in "The Last Days of Pompeii."

GEOGRAPHICAL NOTE Mount Vesuvius is located in the Gulf of Naples, Italy. It is the most heavily populated volcanic region in the world. It has erupted many times since its eruption in 79 AD.

CHARACTERS The characters in "The Last Days of Pompeii" are:
Glaucus, a young man
Clodius, Glaucus's friend
Ione, whom Glaucus loves
Apaecides, Ione's brother
Arbaces, an Egyptian priest and sorcerer who is Apaecides' and Ione's uncle and guardian
Nydia, who is friends with Ione and Julia
Julia, who loves Glaucus

⏻ SETTING A PURPOSE

As you read, pay attention to the order of events leading up to the disastrous Mount Vesuvius eruption.

The Last Days of Pompeii

Edward Bulwer-Lytton's

retold by Dede Mack

THIS IS A TALE ABOUT LOVE AND LOSS IN THE CITY OF POMPEII.

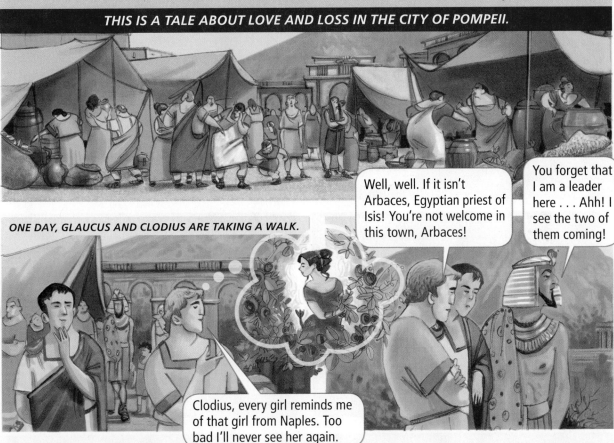

ONE DAY, GLAUCUS AND CLODIUS ARE TAKING A WALK.

Well, well. If it isn't Arbaces, Egyptian priest of Isis! You're not welcome in this town, Arbaces!

You forget that I am a leader here . . . Ahh! I see the two of them coming!

Clodius, every girl reminds me of that girl from Naples. Too bad I'll never see her again.

ARBACES HAS BEEN WAITING FOR APAECIDES AND IONE TO ARRIVE. APAECIDES AND IONE ARE TWO SIBLINGS WHO HAVE COME TO POMPEII TO LIVE WITH ARBACES, WHO IS THEIR UNCLE AND GUARDIAN.

LATER, AT A BIG PARTY . . .

It's the girl from Naples!

Nonsense, Glaucus. That's Arbaces's niece.

. . . GLAUCUS MEETS IONE.

It is you!

IN THE DAYS THAT FOLLOW, ARBACES USES HIS GUARDIANSHIP OVER IONE AND APAECIDES TO CONTROL THEM. HE FIRST PERSUADES APAECIDES TO JOIN HIS FAITH.

Worship of Isis is the only true religion, my boy!

ARBACES THEN EXPRESSES HIS LOVE FOR IONE, BUT IONE LOVES GLAUCUS.

No, no, a thousand times no!

ARBACES HOLDS HER TIGHTLY, BUT THEN THE GROUND STARTS TO TREMBLE. PEOPLE ARE PANICKING.

Help!

It's an earthquake!

Help!

Run for your lives!

It's a sign from Vesuvius.

LUCKILY IONE ESCAPES UNHARMED, BUT ARBACES IS STRUCK ON THE HEAD BY A STATUE OF ISIS. HE IS HURT BUT ALIVE.

AFTER THE EARTHQUAKE ENDS, ALL IS WELL UNTIL GLAUCUS SEES SOMETHING THAT UPSETS HIM.

Don't treat her that way!

It's only Nydia. She works for me. I paid a lot of money for her work.

Ow! Ow!

I'll pay twice that amount if you let her go.

Deal.

MY HERO!

NYDIA DEARLY LOVES HIM. SHE'S HAPPY TO RUN AN ERRAND FOR HIM.

Please give this letter to Ione.

NYDIA CAN'T HELP READING IT.

It's a love letter from Glaucus!

Ione, I love you with all my heart. I am the luckiest man in the world because you love me, too.

BUT THAT'S NOT ALL THAT'S IN THE LETTER . . .

I have to get this to Ione FAST!

me, too.

And my love, don't trust Arbaces—he wants to separate us. Be careful!

NYDIA DELIVERS THE LETTER TO IONE.

129

IONE READS THE LETTER. SHE IS HORRIFIED THAT HER UNCLE PLANS TO SEPARATE HER FROM GLAUCUS. SHE DECIDES TO CONFRONT HIM AT HIS CASTLE. GLAUCUS AND APAECIDES TRY TO STOP HER.

BUT BEFORE GLAUCUS LEFT TO STOP IONE, HE WAS NOT IN A CLEAR STATE OF MIND.

A YOUNG WOMAN NAMED JULIA ALSO LOVED GLAUCUS. SHE WANTED TO TRICK GLAUCUS INTO FALLING IN LOVE WITH HER. SHE SCHEMED TO HAVE HIM DRINK A LOVE POTION TO MAKE HIM LOVE HER.

JULIA BOUGHT A VIAL OF LOVE POTION FROM ARBACES. SHE ASKED NYDIA TO GIVE IT TO GLAUCUS.

BUT ARBACES FILLED THE VIAL WITH POISON INSTEAD OF A LOVE POTION!

FORTUNATELY, GLAUCUS ONLY DRANK ENOUGH TO MAKE HIM TEMPORARILY INSANE. HE HAS RECOVERED BY THE TIME HE SEES ARBACES AT THE CASTLE.

AT THE CASTLE, APAECIDES THREATENS TO EXPOSE ARBACES' PLAN TO SEPARATE IONE AND GLAUCUS. IONE MANAGES TO ESCAPE.

Heh, heh! After Glaucus drinks some of this, he won't be love-struck. He'll be dead!

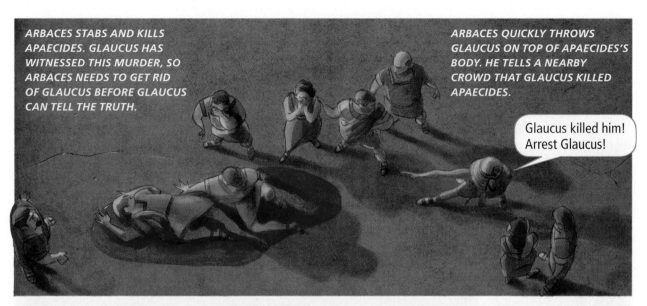

ARBACES STABS AND KILLS APAECIDES. GLAUCUS HAS WITNESSED THIS MURDER, SO ARBACES NEEDS TO GET RID OF GLAUCUS BEFORE GLAUCUS CAN TELL THE TRUTH.

ARBACES QUICKLY THROWS GLAUCUS ON TOP OF APAECIDES'S BODY. HE TELLS A NEARBY CROWD THAT GLAUCUS KILLED APAECIDES.

Glaucus killed him! Arrest Glaucus!

GLAUCUS IS ARRESTED AND CONDEMNED TO FIGHT WILD ANIMALS IN AN ARENA.

IONE AND NYDIA ALSO KNOW THAT ARBACES IS THE KILLER. ARBACES LOCKS THEM UP IN HIS CASTLE SO THAT THEY DON'T TELL ANYONE ELSE.

NYDIA HAS A PLAN.

I'll smuggle a letter to Glaucus's friend Clodius! He'll help us!

GLAUCUS'S BATTLE WITH A LION IS ABOUT TO BEGIN. THE CROWD BOOS AND HISSES. THE CROWD EXPECTS TO WATCH A SAVAGE FIGHT.

BUT THEN SOMETHING STRANGE HAPPENS. THE LION REFUSES TO FIGHT. THE CROWD BOOS.

JUST THEN, SOMEONE JUMPS INTO THE ARENA. CLODIUS HAS ARRIVED TO SAVE THE DAY!

Good people of Pompeii! You're putting an innocent man to death! The real murderer is . . . is . . .

Arbaces!

THE CROWD GOES WILD, AND A RIOT ENSUES, PITTING NEIGHBOR AGAINST NEIGHBOR .

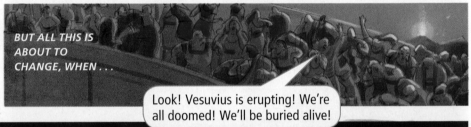

BUT ALL THIS IS ABOUT TO CHANGE, WHEN . . .

Look! Vesuvius is erupting! We're all doomed! We'll be buried alive!

AS THE GIANT VOLCANO ERUPTS, ASH AND STONE RAIN DOWN UPON THE CITIZENS OF POMPEII, CAUSING MASS PANIC AS THEY TRY TO GET AWAY.

NYDIA ESCAPES, BUT IONE IS STILL LOCKED IN THE CASTLE. AFTER GLAUCUS LEAVES THE ARENA, HE FINDS NYDIA.

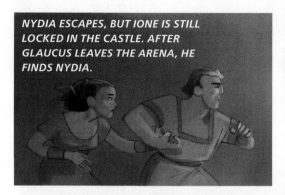

THEY RUSH TO RESCUE IONE BEFORE IT'S TOO LATE.

Stand back, Arbaces. Ione's coming with us.

ARBACES GRABS IONE AND TRIES TO MAKE A RUN FOR IT, BUT IN THE PROCESS HE GETS STRUCK BY LIGHTNING AND DIES!

GLAUCUS AND IONE KNOW THEY HAVE TO LEAVE POMPEII — BUT HOW?

We'll go to the coast! I know a boat we can use!

THE THREE OF THEM SAIL TO THE BAY OF NAPLES, FAR AWAY FROM VESUVIUS.

BUT ON THE NEXT DAY, GLAUCUS AND IONE LEARN THAT NYDIA HAS DIED.

GREATLY SADDENED, GLAUCUS AND IONE SAIL TO ATHENS.

THEY LIVE HAPPILY FOR MANY YEARS, NEVER FORGETTING THE GIRL WHO MADE THEIR ESCAPE FROM POMPEII POSSIBLE.

UPLOAD

⏻ COLLABORATIVE DISCUSSION

Discussing the Purpose With a small group, describe the order of
events that leads to the eruption. Consider these questions:

1. How does the time constraint affect the decisions that the
   characters make?

2. Do the characters find ways to help one another, or do the
   characters present significant obstacles?

3. How do the characters' actions help them survive?

↻ Performance Task

Writing Activity: Compare-and-Contrast Essay **Compare-and-
contrast order** is one pattern of organization in which you present
information about similar and different traits between two people
or things.

Write an essay in which you compare and contrast Ione and Nydia. How
do Ione and Nydia show bravery when danger strikes?

1 Prewriting Reread the text and view the art carefully, looking for
details that describe each woman's personality, behavior,
and motivation.

2 Organizing Copy the graphic organizer below, and record
your information. Use precise language from the story.

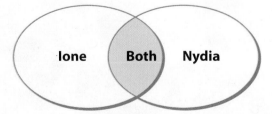

Ione   Both   Nydia

3 **Drafting** Using the information from your graphic organizer, draft your essay. First, select a strategy for organizing your ideas. Most compare-and-contrast essays follow either a **point-by-point** structure or a **subject-by-subject** structure. When you organize your information in a point-by-point structure, you first describe one point of comparison for both characters, and then you describe the next point of comparison. When you organize your information in a subject-by-subject structure, you first arrange all points of comparison for one character, and then you arrange all points of comparison for the second character. Decide which structure you will use to write your essay.

4 **Editing and Revising** Reread your essay. Be sure that you've explained the women's similarities and differences. Use transitional words or phrases such as *also, however, in contrast, in the same way,* or *similarly* to connect your ideas. Check for any spelling, grammatical, or punctuation mistakes. Finally, make sure that you've provided a strong conclusion.

Speak Out! Now that you've written your compare-and-contrast essay, work in a small group to take turns presenting your essays to one another. When you are presenting, have another group member keep track of time. Use the following helpful tips for presenting to your listeners.

SPEAKING TOOLBOX

Presentation
▶ **Make and maintain eye contact with your listeners.** If they look confused or bored, try speaking slower and louder.
▶ **Make sure to pause.** Use a slight pause after important key points for emphasis.
▶ **Remember to use body language.** Stand up straight, and don't slouch. Your listeners will not pay attention to you if you don't seem interested in telling them about your essay.

Performance Task

Speaking Activity: Informative Presentation

In this unit, you've learned how people respond in times of crisis. Your task is to plan, write, and give an informative presentation based on the theme of how people respond to a natural disaster.

Planning and Prewriting
Connect to the Theme

You've read about an ancient city that survived years of war, a young woman who triumphed over an injury, a community that is suffering from a significant water crisis, and fictional stories about individuals who rescue friends and loved ones from natural disasters such as forest fires and volcanic eruptions. In this activity, you will be delivering an oral presentation about how people prepare for a natural disaster. But first you need a main idea—your topic. What will it be?

Choose a Topic

The topic is the "big idea," or the message you want to emphasize. To find a topic statement for your presentation, think about the selections you read. What did you learn about emergency preparedness from what you've read? Consider these questions:

- Why might it be difficult to locate people after a tornado strikes?

- What can you do before, during, and after a flood?

- What safety tips should you follow when a forest fire occurs?

- How can you prepare and plan for a possible drought in your area?

Choose one of these questions, or think of one of your own, to explain in a presentation. Write a topic statement that can be supported with facts, details, and examples from these selections. This topic statement is your main idea.

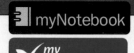
Decide the Basics

You have a topic, or main idea, that reflects the theme of the unit. Now you need to plan and give your informative presentation.

Develop Your Topic

Support your topic with relevant facts and concrete details.

- State your main idea immediately or at the beginning.
- Find examples from the selections to support your topic.
- Facts provide better support than opinions, but opinions can be valuable, too.
- You may also use additional credible print and digital sources.

Determine Your Talking Points

Determine the most important ideas. These ideas are the talking points that you will present.

- Write down the most important points.
- Find and use an interesting, thought-provoking quote from one of the selections.
- Present facts that will surprise listeners or make them curious.

Think About Language, Style, and Tone

- Use time-order words (*first, next, finally*) to show a logical order of events.
- Include transitional words and phrases (*however, for example,* and *as a result*) to connect ideas clearly.
- Use precise words and phrases to describe ideas accurately.
- Define any technical words that your listeners may not know.
- Use a friendly, confident tone.

Prepare for Speaking Aloud

Practice delivering your presentation aloud several times to a family member or a friend.

- Review your talking points. You will feel more confident about your presentation.
- Time yourself. Did you cover all of your talking points?
- Speak clearly and loudly enough to be heard. Speak at a normal speed.
- Read with energy and expression, or strong feeling.
- Use hand gestures, facial expressions, and eye contact to emphasize your points and to express emotion.

Performance Task

Finalize Your Plan

You've got the basics down. You have a topic statement based on the selections, and the evidence to support it. Now you need to organize the information—in other words, create a structure. Having a clear, logical structure is important when it comes to organizing and presenting your information. Follow the structure of the diagram in the Speaking Toolbox.

SPEAKING TOOLBOX

Elements of an Oral Presentation

There are three parts to your presentation: an introduction, a main body, and a conclusion.

Introduction	Present your topic. "Hook" your audience with an interesting detail, question, quotation, or observation that relates to your topic. Your main idea should be in the first sentence, or almost immediately.
Body (supporting details)	The body of your presentation should include your talking points, which are the examples, definitions, and details that develop your topic. Use supporting details from the selections and additional print and digital sources. Make sure to present your ideas logically. Your information should be organized so that your listeners can follow your ideas clearly. Your information must be specific and accurate, as well as clear and straightforward. Do not include text that isn't relevant to the topic.
Conclusion	End your presentation with a strong conclusion that emphasizes the most important ideas. You can restate the main idea, offer an insight of your own, or ask a question that will make your listeners think.

Don't forget to refine your Personal Toolboxes with strategies that work for you.

Speaking Before an Audience

As you prepare your informative presentation, consider your delivery, or the way you speak. Think about:

- **Audience** Remember to make direct eye contact with your listeners. Speak at a volume so that they can hear you. Enunciate, or pronounce, your words clearly. Speak at a rate that isn't too fast or too slow. Do not distract your listeners by playing with your hair or fidgeting.

- **Purpose** Think about the effect you want your presentation to have. What do you want your audience to learn?

- **Vocabulary** Use specific words and phrases that are appropriate to the presentation. Consider vocabulary that is important for your listeners' understanding.

- **Structure** Use the Elements of an Oral Presentation diagram to organize your information logically and clearly for your audience.

- **Emphasis** Remember to pause after making important points and to stand up straight. Your audience will be actively listening to your presentation if they know that you are speaking to them, not yourself.

- **Listening** Think ahead about questions that your listeners may ask after you finish your presentation. Prepare answers that will give them more specific information about your topic. If your listeners do ask questions, remember to treat them the way you would like to be treated.

Revise

Self Evaluation

Use the checklist and rubric to guide your presentation.

Peer Review

Use the checklist to comment on your classmate's presentation.

JOBS FOR ALL NOW!

fyi
hmhfyi.com

Making Your Voice Heard

Words mean more than what is set down on paper. It takes the human voice to infuse them with shades of deeper meaning.

— **Maya Angelou, Writer**

Essential Question

Why is it equally important to listen and to be heard?

The Language of Expression

The voice is a powerful communication tool. You make your voice heard when you express an opinion, share an idea, describe a feeling, or explain through example. You communicate when you speak and when you write.

You use your voice to declare what is important to you. Sometimes when you communicate your opinions or belief in a cause, you want things to change for the better. You make your voice heard so that you can make a difference for others.

You use your voice to teach others. Sometimes you want to share your knowledge. Your voice will be heard if you communicate with conviction while still being respectful and polite.

You use your voice to show how you feel about others. Using your voice to express compassion, gratitude, and appreciation are all ways of showing others how you feel about someone or something.

Sometimes making your voice heard is challenging. It can be scary, but having the courage to speak up is an important step in making your voice heard. Your words have meaning. Your words have worth. The power of your words—your voice—is important.

In this unit, you will explore how people make their voices heard. You will read about people who use their voices to improve living conditions for other people or animals. You will learn how characters express their thoughts through writing and speaking. You will discover how the power of a voice can truly be an inspiration to others.

> **What are the different ways of making your voice heard?**

Express Yourself: Suffixes That Form Nouns

Since there are many ways to make your voice heard, there are many words that express how to share and communicate ideas.

The word *expression* is formed by adding a suffix to the base word *express*. When you see an unfamiliar word, look for any suffixes that you may recognize. A **suffix** is a word part that appears at the end of a base word to form a new word. The suffix *–ion* means "the action of" or "the process of." The word *expression* means "the action of making your feelings known."

The following chart contains words with suffixes that form nouns.

Word	Suffix	Base Word	Meaning of Suffix	Meaning of Word
demonstration	*-ion*	demonstrate	action or process	the process of showing how something is used
activism	*-ism*	active	action or practice	the act of being directly involved in a cause
consciousness	*-ness*	conscious	quality or state	the state of being awake and aware of surroundings
difference	*-ence*	differ	state or condition	the condition of being unlike something else
supporter	*-er*	support	one that performs or causes an action	one who encourages or promotes

↻ Performance Task

Express how you feel. Choose one of the words listed above or in **Browse** magazine. Write a short speech about why this word is important. Use the supports in your **Activity Book**.

➡ *Browse magazine*

DOWNLOAD

Sharing knowledge is one way of making your voice heard.

 SETTING A PURPOSE

As you read this blog, think about the order of events that the blogger follows to deliver an oral presentation. Pay attention to how he prepares his information and practices his delivery.

ClassPrez

Enter your email address:

Subscribe me!

SEARCH

Comments 0

January 28

Tips for Preparing an Oral Presentation

Since I'm Class President, my classmates ask me for help with all kinds of things. Recently, I was asked for tips on giving oral presentations. That's something I have to do a lot! I've developed my own way of getting ready. I'm happy to share these ideas with you in the hope that they help you with YOUR next big oral presentation. Good luck!

Oral Presentations and Written Ones Are Different

An oral presentation does not mean just reading your written essay aloud. An oral presentation is different. It takes more preparation.

There's No Substitute for Preparation

♦ The more prepared you are, the more confident and relaxed you'll feel. This lets your audience know that they can trust you.

♦ Make sure you know what you're talking about. Do enough research. Get lots of facts. Know the material well. You should be on solid ground with the information you are presenting.

Write an Outline

◆ Go through your research and decide on the most important points. Figure out what order they should be in, and write an outline. Your outline can be a series of bulleted points. If you prefer to write out a draft of the presentation, and then make the outline from the draft, that's OK. Just remember you'll be speaking from the outline, and not simply reading your presentation out loud.

◆ Don't forget to include an introduction and a conclusion!

Visual Aids and Handouts

◆ An oral presentation goes better when the audience has something to follow—either a handout with the main points you are covering, projected slides, or both.

◆ If you are using projected slides, practice using the equipment. A slide projector or laptop that isn't working can be distracting.

Practice

The most important thing is to practice!

◆ Practice making eye contact with the audience.

◆ Practice giving the whole presentation from your outline.

◆ Practice the opening and closing sentences of the presentation several times so you know them by heart.

Delivery

◆ Say your first line with confidence. Don't start with "Okay so. . . ."

◆ Slow down and speak up! If you're nervous, you're probably rushing. The audience will follow better if you speak slowly and loudly.

◆ Don't end with "so yeah. . . ." Say the last line you practiced.

◆ Don't fiddle with your hair, scratch your nose, or do anything else distracting!

◆ Make eye contact with your audience. THIS IS VERY IMPORTANT!!

◆ Don't apologize for, or call attention to, things you have skipped or messed up.

My last piece of advice? Relax! Have fun! If you have fun, your audience will, too.

ARCHIVES

January

December

November

October

September

August

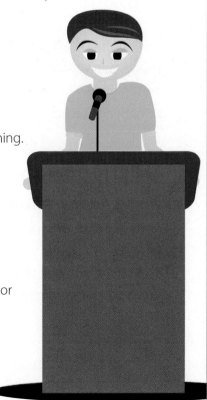

UPLOAD

⏻ COLLABORATIVE DISCUSSION

Discussing the Purpose In this blog, ClassPrez's tips are given in sequential order—a pattern of organization that shows the order of steps or stages in a process. With a partner, find the headings in the blog that state the order of events, and describe how these headings help the reader understand the steps of delivering an oral presentation.

Exploring the Topic Have you ever run for a class office? Would you like to? Tell a partner what office you would want to have, and why you would want to run.

Staying Safe It is a good practice not to write about where and when you will be away, especially if your home will be empty for a period of time. Always remember that *anyone* can see information published on a blog. A blog is public!

Write On!
Write a short comment on ClassPrez's post. State your opinion about his tips for preparing for and delivering an oral presentation. Then exchange comments with a partner and write something in reaction to his or her comment. 🗨 Comments 0

↻ Performance Task

Writing Activity: Schedule Your Calendar Many bloggers like to write posts ahead of when they want to publish them. For instance, if you will be away on a school trip or a family vacation, you can set up blog posts on a calendar to be published later. This way, your blog automatically sends posts and continues to update your readers.

Write three posts in advance. Your blog software will have a scheduling feature that allows you to set up your editorial calendar for future publication.

1 Write an entry about a favorite book or movie that you wish to publish at a later date.

2 Send a reminder about an upcoming event, such as a science fair at a local museum. Make sure that your blog post gives the accurate date and time of the event. You don't want to invite readers to an event at the wrong location or day!

3 Create a blog post to celebrate a good friend's or family member's birthday or any special day. Add a special design for fun!

Language Cam video

Watch the video to learn more about making your voice heard.

Running for President

Blue Jasmine

Building the strength to speak up takes courage and confidence.

Know Before You Go

Twelve-year-old Seema and her family have moved from India to Iowa City, IA. She misses her cousin and her grandmother, Dadima. Before she left, she and her cousin used to tease their classmate Mukta, whose family is poor. Mukta continues to be Seema's friend, despite Seema's teasing.

Seema makes friends at school, but she faces mistreatment herself when a new girl named Carrie makes fun of her. Now that Seema feels ostracized, she begins to see that her treatment of Mukta was no better than Carrie's bullying.

READING TOOLBOX

Identifying the Theme

Narrative texts are made up of elements that create the mood and action of the story. These elements are the plot, the characters, and the setting. Stories also have a **theme**, or big idea, that the author is trying to convey. The theme is implied, rather than stated directly. The reader has to infer what the theme is from the other elements. When determining the theme, follow these steps:

▶ **Think about the plot.** What is the story mainly about?

▶ **Analyze what the characters do and say.** Why do they act the way they do? Do they change?

▶ **Consider the setting.** Does the location have any meaning?

⏻ SETTING A PURPOSE

As you read, think about the elements of the story.

As you work through this unit, remember to create your Personal Toolbox with strategies that work for you. It's available from Student Resources or from your teacher.

Blue Jasmine

by Kashmira Sheth

"I wish we were done already. Tomorrow will be so boring. We should have a rule to only present people we know. Who cares about a bunch of strange people from some foreign country?"

Danny didn't answer Carrie. She went on, "Don't be surprised if I **call in sick** tomorrow or if I *s-e-e-m* to get sick just before someone's presentation." She stretched out the "seem" so long that Danny gave me a quick glance. This fueled Carrie. "You seem to know what I am saying. Maybe
10 I'll show up. It'll be fun!" she snickered.

I got up to leave for my ESL class.

"Good luck getting rid of your accent. Seem-a," Carrie pressed each sound as if she were sipping a delicious drink.

I stopped. Say something. I urged myself, anything. But nothing came to my lips.

She laughed. I don't know if anyone laughed with her. I fled.

All through English I was too upset to learn a word. As soon as the bell rang I left without waiting for Jennifer or
20 Ria. I had a problem and had to work it out myself.

It had snowed about an inch that afternoon, which made the sidewalks slick. I was still not used to walking very fast on snow, and suddenly someone tugged my braid. As I turned to look I lost my balance, slid, and fell flat on my back. My right elbow was scraped and my right hand hurt, but I managed to get up. When I looked back all I saw were the masses of chick pea-colored hair bouncing away.

> When people say they will **call in sick**, they mean they are going to telephone, email, or text to excuse themselves from work or school because they are ill, or sick.

Mommy bandaged my elbow and rubbed some almond oil on my hand. She didn't ask how I fell and I didn't tell her, not until that night, after Mela went to bed. "Mom, can you listen to my speech one more time?" I asked.

"Yes," she said.

"You've done good work," she said when I'd finished.

"Thanks," I said, looking away from her.

"Seema, why are you so upset?"

All evening long I'd been thinking about Carrie.

"I don't want to go to school tomorrow."

"Why? What's the matter? Your speech is perfect, and now you wrap your sari as well as I do."

"It's Carrie..." I began and told her about my whole day.

"Are you sure she pulled your braid?"

"I think so," I said. "No one else would do that."

"Why would she do such a thing?"

"Mom, that's how she is. You don't know her. You don't have to go to school with her," I said.

"Even if she's unpleasant, remember what Dadima used to say."

"What did Dadima used to say?" I asked.

"That an **unpleasant** person is like a tiny boil. If you keep thinking about it and keep feeling it with your hands it gets bigger and bigger. The best way to get rid of it is to ignore it."

"She's in my class. There's no way to ignore her," I said.

"Do you want me to talk to Ms. Wilson?"

"No." I didn't want Mommy to come and talk to Ms. Wilson. *"Padeshe ava devashe*, I'll deal as it comes. I'll be fine," I mumbled.

"By the way, this came for you today," Mommy said, handing me an envelope.

Before I saw the sender's name I knew by the oil spots that it was from Mukta.

Learning the meaning of prefixes will help you understand new words. The **prefix *un*-** means "not," or "the opposite of."

Dear Seema,

You must've received my letter because Raju gave me your message that you would write me a letter soon. Every day I wait for it and wonder if it got lost in the mail. School is going all right for me. I am not doing that good because I have no time to study. Since Kaki is sick Mommy and I take care of my little cousin and keep him and my sister away from Kaki as much as
70 possible.

In the last two weeks Mommy and I have been making **flower garlands** for the temples. Since I help the tailor in the shop next to us, I've learned to be quick with needles and thread, and I like to work with flowers. Every day we get a basketful of roses, jasmine, chrysanthemums, and marigolds. When I sit next to the baskets and make garlands I don't smell the smoke of Pappa and Kaka frying snacks. When the fragrance of roses fills our house, I imagine that our home is a
80 garden. We have planted a rose in an empty oil can, but I don't know when it will bloom.

All the garland-making work leaves me no time for studies, but we're making good money so we can send Kaki to a **sanitarium** for a rest. Kaka is taking her there next week. I hope she comes back healthy.

How's school for you? Have you made a friend in your class? Is Iowa City as big as Vishanagar, or smaller? I heard Raju saying to someone that you have your own room. Is that true? Do you walk to school?
90 Does everyone have a car? Do roses and jasmine grow there?

Say hello to your family. Write soon.

Mukta

Look at the picture above to see what **flower garlands** are.

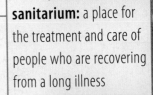

sanitarium: a place for the treatment and care of people who are recovering from a long illness

Trouble is like the head of the cobra, always looking bigger and scarier than it really is. Like Mukta, I have to be brave and capture the cobra and make it dance, I thought as I finished reading her letter.

100 I reread Mukta's letter, folded it, and slipped it in my backpack with my speech and my sari.

Courage was with me.

⏻ COLLABORATIVE DISCUSSION

Discussing the Purpose Talk with a partner about the plot, characters, and setting of *Blue Jasmine*. What do you think the theme of this story might be?

Analyzing the Text   Cite Text Evidence

1. **Explore Language** Identify words and phrases that the author uses to tell you about how Seema may be feeling and how Mukta's letter may have affected her.

2. **Make Predictions** Will Seema deliver her speech in class the next day? How do you think it will go?

↻ Performance Task

Writing Activity: Review What is your opinion about the story and the characters so far? Would you recommend this selection to a friend? Would you like to keep reading to find out what happens to Seema and her new life in America? Write a short review of the selection. Cite appropriate details from the story to support your opinion.

- Remember that an **opinion** is your personal view about something. You can support your opinion with facts and examples.

- Let readers know your opinion of the selection at the beginning of your review. Then restate your opinion again at the end.

DOWNLOAD

In *Blue Jasmine*, you read about Seema's struggle to build courage as a new student in America. Next, find out about Confucius and the wisdom and courage he shared with the world.

⏻ SETTING A PURPOSE

As you read, pay attention to the events in Confucius's life and the order in which they happened.

Confucius: Words of Wisdom

by Tomás Prado

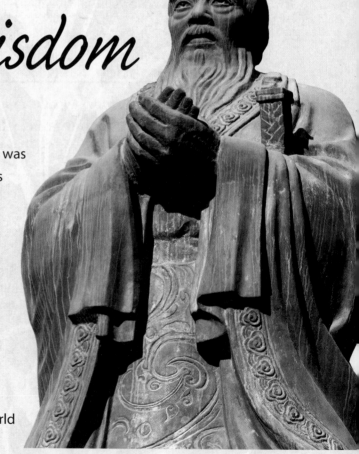
a statue of Confucius

More than 2,500 years ago a baby boy was born in eastern China. His name was Kong (the family name) Qiu (his personal name). We know him as Confucius.

Confucius lived for 73 years. He spent much of his time studying, thinking, and talking. Confucius's ideas were unusual for his time. Important leaders and figures of authority of his day believed wealth and power were
10 the most important things in life. His ideas about thoughtfulness and self-control were unpopular. Yet today, people around the world follow the teachings of Confucius. How did this happen?

A 1989 stamp from China shows Confucius with his students; it commemorates the 2,540th anniversary of Confucius's birth.

Confucius as a Teacher

From the time he was a teenager, Confucius believed that education was the secret to a noble life. He thought the way to be wise was to study the wisdom of the past. Whenever he met scholars or others who knew Chinese traditions, Confucius asked questions. Learning was the way to become a good person, he said.

20 By the time Confucius was in his 30s, he had become a teacher. In fact, historians say Confucius was the first to see teaching as a career. (Today, Chinese people celebrate September 28 as Confucius's birthday. Some call it "Teachers' Day.") Teaching was one way to share ideas with others—an important goal for Confucius. Another way was through **public service**. When Confucius was in his 40s and 50s he held political jobs. He was a judge and later an adviser to a king. By the time he was 56, however, Confucius was **disillusioned**. He did not feel that people were listening to his ideas. He did not think he was making a difference.

The *Analects*

30 For the next 12 years, Confucius traveled around China teaching his ideas. A group of students and followers traveled with him. By the time Confucius died, at 73, he had thousands of followers. In the century after his death, followers collected his teachings into a book. It is called the ***Analects*** of *Confucius*. Because of the *Analects*, we know what Confucius taught.

> Which words help you figure out the meaning of the phrase **public service**?

> In the word **disillusioned**, The prefix *dis-* means "to do the complete opposite." Read ahead to find another word that shares the same prefix.

> In the word **analects**, the Latin root *lect* means "to read." A related term is *lecture*.

At the time, the many kingdoms of China were at war almost constantly. Every king wanted to seize whatever he could, through strength or trickery. Consequently, they felt that a ruler should do whatever he wanted to ensure his own success. As the *Analects* show,
40 Confucius disagreed. He believed that every individual should try to be the best, most moral person possible. People should honor their ancestors. They should respect their families and the institutions of society such as schools and communities. He taught that being a good and honorable person was the most important goal for anyone. To bring order to a troubled and uneasy world, each individual should try to be the best he or she could be.

The Influence of Confucianism

Over the past 2,000 years, the teachings of Confucius have become a philosophy called Confucianism. In ancient China, Confucianism became not just important, but the official government philosophy.
50 For centuries, one had to pass an exam on Confucian thought in order to hold a **position** in the Imperial Chinese government. Confucianism is not a formal religion such as Buddhism. But for millions of people in China, Japan, Korea, and other Asian countries, it is a way of life.

> The term **position** has more than one meaning. It can mean "location," "rank," or "job." Use the context clues to determine which meaning is correct.

⏻ COLLABORATIVE DISCUSSION

Discussing the Purpose Informational texts often describe a sequence of events, or the order in which the events happened. In a small group, discuss the significant events in Confucius's life.

Analyzing the Text `Cite Text Evidence`

1. **Analyze** Why did Confucius want to share his ideas and make his voice heard?

2. **Explore the Theme** Which character traits indicate that Confucius was courageous?

Speak Out! Should people share their opinions even when their ideas are unpopular? Work with a small group to share your opinion. Justify your argument with facts and examples.

Vocabulary Strategy: Identifying Prefixes

The author uses the words *unusual* (line 7) and *unpopular* (line 12) to describe Confucius and his teachings. These words start with the prefix *-un*. A **prefix** is a word part added to the beginning of a base word. Prefixes often change the meaning of a word. Identifying prefixes can help you figure out the meaning of unfamiliar words.

Prefix	Meaning	Example
un-, dis-	not	unhappy, disapprove
mis-	wrongly	misunderstand
re-	again	replay

Practice and Apply Use the prefixes above to change the meanings of the words below, and then write the meanings of the new words.

    do   organize   interpret

DOWNLOAD

Podcast: After WWII, A Letter Of Appreciation That Still Rings True

The *Analects of Confucius* had a powerful effect on many. A letter can be powerful, too.

Background on World War II

World War II was one of the deadliest wars in United States history. The Allies (the U.S., Great Britain, France, the Soviet Union, and China) fought the Axis powers (Germany, Italy, and Japan). The Allies won the war in 1945, but thousands of American soldiers had died. When the surviving soldiers returned home, they had been forever changed by their experience.

Every Memorial Day, Americans honor the people who sacrificed their lives and who currently serve our country. We appreciate the efforts of those who have been public servants. We feel compassion for those who lost loved ones because of war.

In this podcast, Maureen Corrigan talks about her father, who had served in the Navy during WWII. He received a letter of thanks that deeply touched not only him, but also others.

⏻ SETTING A PURPOSE

As you listen, think about the main idea: how meaningful a simple thank-you letter can be. Use the chart to help you follow along.

After WWII, A Letter Of Appreciation That Still Rings True

Main Idea Chart

Topic

Gratitude toward veterans

Main Idea

The speaker found a letter that the Secretary of the Navy sent to her father after he was discharged from the Navy. The letter thanks veterans for their service. The speaker reflects on the letter's message that the whole nation appreciates her father and the other veterans who served with him.

Supporting Detail

It is a form letter, but it is compassionate.

Supporting Detail

The letter meant a lot to the author's father.

Supporting Detail

The letter says the nation will remember veterans with gratitude.

⏻ COLLABORATIVE DISCUSSION

Discussing the Purpose With a small group, discuss how the supporting details support the main idea. What important ideas about expression and reflection does the letter show? What is the significance of this letter of thanks?

DOWNLOAD

Saving Animals with Compassion

You've heard how a letter can be a powerful tool for expressing thoughts and reaching out to others. Find out how interviews help people reach out to a wide audience of readers.

Know Before You Go

The Galápagos Islands are located off the coast of Ecuador in the Pacific Ocean. In the mid-1800s British naturalist Charles Darwin visited the islands. Later, he wrote about the many unique animals he saw there. Today much of the Galápagos is protected as a national park and a UNESCO World Heritage Site.

READING TOOLBOX

Interpret Information: Interviews

Interviews are question-and-answer conversations between two or more people. One of these people is a reporter, whose job is to draw statements, facts, and comments from the other person. Those statements are recorded and then published. Interviews are a direct way of finding out information from:

witnesses   experts   researchers   athletes   celebrities

Writers and reporters follow a **5Ws and H** outline for writing a story. By asking these 5W and H questions, reporters hope to get the key pieces of information needed to tell a complete story.

Who   What   When   Where   Why   How

⏻ SETTING A PURPOSE

As you read, see if you can answer the 5W and H questions.

Saving Animals with Compassion

An Interview with Tod Emko

As a conservationist, Tod Emko wants to conserve, or protect, the environment. Animals in need are his special focus. In 2008 Emko went to the Galápagos Islands on a **mission** to protect the islands' rare animals. In the Galápagos, Emko was fascinated by wildlife seen nowhere else. But he was also shocked. All over the islands he saw dogs, cats, and horses in terrible shape. Today, Emko is the president of Darwin Animal Doctors. This program helps the "companion animals" of the Galápagos and their owners.

> Look in a dictionary to find the multiple meanings of the word **mission**. Use context clues to determine which meaning fits in this sentence.

Recently, *The City Daily Globe* interviewed Tod Emko about Darwin
10   Animal Doctors.

NYCDG: What led you to start Darwin Animal Doctors (DAD)?

TE: I was horrified by what I saw on the streets in the Galápagos. There were dogs and cats everywhere, and they lived short, harsh lives. There were no veterinarians to take care of them.

Shortly after that trip, I was on another volunteer mission. While there, I found a very, very sick puppy. He'd been injured in an accident. The little dog was so sick that he looked like a hairless piglet. So I named him Piggy. I brought Piggy home, and he is still part of my life. It was Piggy that got me thinking. There are wonderful, beautiful animals all
20   over the world that deserve to have happy lives. But this would never happen if the animals could not get critical veterinary care. My friend Andrea Gordon and I decided we wanted to start a permanent year-round veterinary hospital. It would be someplace without veterinary services. That's when I thought about the countless animals in need in the Galápagos!

The word **vet** is used here as the short form of *veterinarian*. A veterinarian is an animal doctor.

Which meaning of the word **mission** fits in this sentence?

NYCDG: How did you start DAD?

TE: In 2010 we started with one Ecuadorian **vet**. We paid him ourselves. Our **mission** was daunting but clear. We wanted to start giving veterinary services to the animals of the Galápagos any way we could. Our vet went door-to-door. He treated animals for everything from ticks to car accidents.

30

The government of Ecuador was very happy when they learned what we were doing. So they invited us to bring vets to treat companion animals on the populated islands. (There are more than 20 islands in the Galápagos but people live on only five of them.) We reached out online to find veterinary volunteers. The response was immediate and worldwide. Soon we had experienced, eager vets, vet students, and vet techs (assistants) from North America, South America, Europe, and Australia!

40 A nonprofit group on one of the islands decided to help us. They set up our clinic in a huge space next to theirs, and soon we were up and running.

NYCDG: Tell us about DAD's work today.

spay/neuter: to sterilize animals by surgically removing their reproductive organs

TE: Now we have a two-floor clinic on the most populated island of Galápagos. It is staffed with veterinary volunteers year round. We treat thousands of animals per year. We do intense **spay/neuter** campaigns to limit the population of animals. We teach **humane** animal practices—how to care for your animals in the best, kindest way possible. And we give emergency care wherever we are needed.

humane: gentle, compassionate

50 **NYCDG:** What message would you like to send to our readers?

TE: Compassion is a true super power, and it's all you need to start making the world a better place. Be a hero. Be kind to animals and anyone who can't fight back. You'll be amazed at how much you can make the world better for everyone!

⏻ COLLABORATIVE DISCUSSION

Discussing the Purpose With a small group, discuss why the interview is an effective format for presenting the information about Tod Emko and his work with DAD. Follow rules for appropriate classroom discussion as you consider the following questions:

- Did the reporter answer *who, what, when, where, why*, and *how*?

- How might you describe Tod Emko? How did the reporter use Emko's story to convey this image of him?

READING TOOLBOX

Interpret Information: Interviews

Reread the article, looking carefully for answers to the 5Ws and H questions. Copy the chart below and use it to keep track of the information you read. Charts are useful tools for taking notes and making sense of texts. They can help you to remember and understand what you've read.

The chart has been partially completed for you.

Who?	Tod Emko
What?	Started a veterinary clinic called Darwin Animal Doctors (DAD)
When?	
Where?	
Why?	
How?	

Write On! Write a letter to Tod Emko to share your opinion about his work with DAD. Cite precise examples from the interview to support your opinion. Include any questions you would like to ask him. Use a formal style throughout the letter.

DOWNLOAD

Saying Yes to 100 Hours

You just read an interview about Tod Emko and the work he is doing to help animals. Now read an argument to find out why one student supports a new community service requirement at school.

READING TOOLBOX

Features of an Argument

An argument is an essay that states and defends an opinion. Authors often use arguments to inform readers about a topic. They may also use them to try to convince readers that their opinion about a topic is "right." Arguments usually contain the following elements:

▶ **Claim** This is the author's opinion about the topic or question. It is what he or she is arguing for.

▶ **Reasons and Evidence** These are the explanations, facts, and examples the author uses to support his or her opinion.

▶ **Counterclaims** These are arguments against the author's opinion. Often authors address counterclaims to make their argument stronger and to show a full understanding of the topic.

⏻ SETTING A PURPOSE

As you read, pay attention to the author's claim and reasoning. What is his opinion about the new community service requirement? What reasons and evidence does he use to support his claim?

SAYING YES TO 100 HOURS

Why Community Service Is Important for Graduation

by Luis Alba

Should middle school students be required to complete 100 hours of community service in order to graduate? That's the question that the administrators of Rayne Middle School are considering. I am a sixth-grade student here at Rayne. To me, community service should mean more than a responsibility to learn in school. It is appropriate for us to be aware of the challenges that face our world. It is also important that we contribute to the greater good. Therefore, a requirement of community service is in our
10 best interests and should be necessary for graduation.

By setting the number of required hours at 100, the middle school is creating a standard that is fair for all of us students. This standard number of 100 hours may seem like a lot of time, but it is spread out over the course of the school year. And 100 hours total equals less than four hours per week. Four hours per week takes less time than many students spend watching TV or playing video games. Many of us can find four hours to serve after school each week or during weekends. Some of us already help our families by
20 doing chores or baby-sitting our younger siblings. Other students already serve the community by taking part in community activities or helping in their local centers.

Identify the suffix in the term **meaningful** to help you understand its meaning.

The term **assistance** is another word for *help*.

For our community service to be **meaningful** to ourselves and to those we are helping, we should ideally commit to more than a single day. But what if one student is able to complete only 20 hours? Does that make his or her contribution less valuable than that of someone who is able to easily contribute 100 hours? Additionally, some students might have extra homework or need 30 extra tutoring or academic **assistance** after school or during weekends. These academic activities take priority over community service. As a result, these students would have very little time left for fulfilling hours of community service. There are also students who would need transportation to the volunteer site after school or during weekends. Additional transportation to and from the volunteer site can be time-consuming and expensive. These are issues that absolutely need to be addressed.

What are the **logistical obstacles**, or coordination challenges, mentioned in the previous paragraph?

For these students who face **logistical obstacles** after 40 school or during weekends, there should be other community service options available. One idea would be for those students to fulfill their community service during summer vacation or school breaks. Another idea is allowing those students to complete their community service in a series of one-day opportunities, such as local neighborhood cleanup days. A third idea is letting students volunteer to complete a simple service in their local neighborhood at times convenient for them. For example, they can gather clothing, food, or toys for

50 local hospitals or shelters. That way, there would be no consequences for those students who do not have any free time after school or during weekends.

The middle school should not make community service difficult for some students to complete. After all, the most important goal is that we become good citizens in our community. Our middle school years are a time when we are beginning to understand ourselves, our families and friends, and our world. Studies have shown that students who volunteer in their communities are better informed.

60 Studies have also shown that students learn valuable skills for the future, and often follow a path of service that continues into adulthood. Finally, students who volunteer grow into involved citizens who can set the best path forward for society. All students at Rayne Middle School should be encouraged to serve their community, not for graduation, but in order to become good citizens.

UPLOAD

⏻ COLLABORATIVE DISCUSSION

Discussing the Purpose With a small group, talk about the author's claim. Was he able to persuade you to agree with his opinion?

Comparing Texts

Interviews and arguments are different types of texts that can be used to share ideas and opinions. How did you feel reading the interview? How did you feel reading the argument? Discuss with a partner how the two text types differ and the different impacts they have on readers.

Analyzing the Text   Cite Text Evidence

1. **Make Inferences** Why does the author state in paragraph 1 that "community service is in our best interests"?

2. **Make Inferences** Why does the author include counterclaims toward the end of the essay rather than at the beginning? Does the author address the counterclaims effectively?

READING TOOLBOX

Features of an Argument

Arguments often follow a format, or outline.

▸ **Beginning: Claim** The author introduces the topic and clearly states his or her opinion.
▸ **Middle: Reasons and Evidence** The author supports his or her claim with facts and reasons throughout the body of the essay. The author lists and refutes counterclaims.
▸ **End: Restate Claim** The author restates his or her opinion in a conclusion. Reread "Saying Yes to 100 Hours," paying close attention to the format. Take notes about the claim, reasons, and evidence to help you understand what you've read.

Speak Out! Work with a partner to debate the 100 hours of service requirement discussed in the reading selection. Take turns supporting the requirement and opposing it. Remember that the most convincing arguments are made with facts and details.

LISTENING TOOLBOX

Listening to an Argument

Listen with an open but sensible mind.

▶ **Listen for evidence.** Identify the speaker's position and follow his or her argument.

▶ **Listen for persuasive tricks.** Don't let yourself be flattered by the speaker, and watch out for empty but important-sounding words. Don't fall for faulty logic.

▶ **Respond to the speaker.** Challenge facts and ask for explanations at suitable times in the argument.

↻ Performance Task

Writing Activity: Argument Choose a topic you feel strongly about, but that has many sides. It could be a school requirement, the importance of sports and physical activity for young people, the use of tablets and computers in school, or some other topic of your choosing. Write a short argument explaining your views on the topic.

● Introduce the topic and clearly state your claim.

● Support your claim with facts and examples. The best arguments do more than restate the author's opinion and feelings. They use information to justify, or prove, the argument.

● Discuss and respond to counterclaims.

● Include a conclusion that restates your opinion.

Helen Keller

Writing an argument is one way to state your opinion. Read to find out how Helen Keller didn't let her disability stop her from voicing her opinion and making a statement.

Historical Background

Helen Keller helped change our way of thinking. She told her story to change expectations for people who were blind and deaf. Before Helen raised awareness, they were often sent away from their homes. Some people felt that those who had vision or hearing impairments could not be productive people in their communities. However, Helen pushed for greater opportunities for those with vision and hearing loss and other physical disabilities.

Helen was also instrumental in campaigning for literacy for the blind community. Because people who were blind had several systems of reading, there was much confusion. Helen Keller worked to make one of these systems of reading—Braille—the standard.

⏻ SETTING A PURPOSE

As you read, pay attention to specific events in Helen Keller's life that enabled, or allowed, her to express her ideas and communicate with others.

Helen Keller

by Jessica E. Cohn

IN THE SUMMER OF 1880, HELEN KELLER IS BORN IN TUSCUMBIA, ALABAMA.

WHEN JUST 19 MONTHS OLD, SHE BECOMES SERIOUSLY ILL.

It's brain fever.

Can we do anything?

THE UNKNOWN ILLNESS AFFECTS HELEN'S SIGHT AND HEARING. SHE BECOMES BLIND AND DEAF.

There is nothing we can do.

Oh no!

YOUNG HELEN IS UNABLE TO COMMUNICATE MUCH BEYOND NODDING "YES" OR "NO." HER LIFE IS FILLED WITH FRUSTRATIONS.

HARRGH!

MISS SULLIVAN, WHO IS 21, ENTERED PERKINS AT AGE 14. SHE HAS HAD SEVERAL EYE OPERATIONS. THEY HAVE BROUGHT BACK SOME OF HER SIGHT.

It's clear she sees well enough.

If only there were an operation to help Helen.

MISS SULLIVAN HAS STUDIED REPORTS ABOUT THE TEACHING OF STUDENTS WHO ARE BOTH DEAF AND BLIND. SHE HAS BECOME AN AUTHORITY ON THE CHALLENGES.

SHE IMMEDIATELY TRIES TO TEACH HELEN SIGN LANGUAGE. SHE BEGINS TO SPELL OUT SIMPLE WORDS ON HELEN'S OPEN HAND.

D-O-L-L. This is a D-O-L-L.

SOON, THE YOUNG TEACHER SEES HOW HELEN'S BEHAVIOR UPSETS EVERYONE.

YAYYYY!

SHE CAN ALSO SEE THAT, BY FOLLOWING HELEN'S INTERESTS, SHE CAN INTRODUCE THE WORDS HELEN NEEDS TO CONNECT WITH OTHERS.

F-L-O-W-E-R

MISS SULLIVAN IS FIRM IN HER BELIEF THAT HELEN CAN LEARN TO BEHAVE APPROPRIATELY. SHE BELIEVES THAT HELEN CAN LEARN BOTH WORDS AND MANNERS.

TO BETTER DISCIPLINE HELEN, MISS SULLIVAN ASKS TO WORK WITH HER ALONE. THE KELLERS ALLOW THEM TO MOVE TO THE COTTAGE BEHIND THE MAIN HOUSE.

We need to work without distractions.

HELEN IS BRIGHT. SOON, SHE CAN REPEAT THE CORRECT ORDER OF LETTERS FOR WORDS THAT MISS SULLIVAN INTRODUCES.

That's right, Helen. M-U-G.

HELEN DOES NOT, HOWEVER, CONNECT THE HAND SIGNS TO THE ITEMS THEY NAME. SHE CONFUSES NOUNS WITH VERBS.

Do you understand?

THE YOUNG TEACHER WORKS TIRELESSLY, SIGNING THE NAMES OF EVERYDAY THINGS.

Now, if only you would, on your own, spell MUG after holding one.

M-U-G.

DESPERATE TO REACH HER PUPIL, MISS SULLIVAN TAKES HELEN TO A WATER PUMP OUTSIDE. SHE HOLDS HELEN'S HAND UNDER THE RUNNING WATER.

This is WATER.

SHE WANTS HELEN TO UNDERSTAND THAT W-A-T-E-R IS THE COOL LIQUID.

W-A-T-E-R.

AS WATER FLOWS THROUGH HER FINGERS, HELEN SUDDENLY UNDERSTANDS.

W-A-...

EXCITED, HELEN SIGNS THE LETTERS FOR WATER. THEN, SHE RUSHES TO TOUCH THE GROUND.

Yes! G-R-O-U-N-D.

BY NIGHTFALL, HELEN HAS LEARNED NUMEROUS WORDS AND UNDERSTANDS WHICH ITEMS THEY NAME. HER LIFE HAS BEEN CHANGED FOREVER.

T-E-A-C-H-E-R.

MISS SULLIVAN, ALSO KNOWN AS ANNIE, HELPS HELEN FOR MANY YEARS. EVENTUALLY, HELEN ATTENDS CLASSES AT PERKINS. SHE ALSO BECOMES THE FIRST BLIND AND DEAF PERSON TO COMPLETE COLLEGE.

When she graduates from Radcliffe College in 1904, Helen has already started writing her biography. It will be called The Story of My Life.

SHE BECOMES A WELL-KNOWN AUTHOR. TO WRITE HER BOOKS, SPEECHES, AND ESSAYS, SHE USES A SPECIAL TYPEWRITER.

HELEN ALSO BECOMES KNOWN FOR HELPING THE BLIND. SHE WORKS TO GUARANTEE THE LEGAL AND NATURAL RIGHTS OF ALL PEOPLE.

SHE MEETS WITH WORLD LEADERS. WHEREVER SHE GOES, SHE ENCOURAGES PEOPLE.

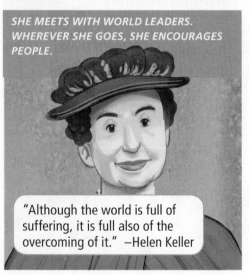

HELEN MAKES FRIENDS WITH MANY FAMOUS PEOPLE, SUCH AS ALBERT EINSTEIN, THE SCIENTIST.

HER AUTOBIOGRAPHY IS TRANSLATED INTO MANY LANGUAGES. FROM 1946 TO 1957, HELEN VISITS 35 COUNTRIES ON FIVE CONTINENTS.

I am honored, Helen...

BY HOLDING HER HANDS OVER A SPEAKER'S THROAT AND MOVING LIPS, HELEN CAN UNDERSTAND SPOKEN WORDS.

SHE SPEAKS WITH EVERY U.S. PRESIDENT IN HER LIFETIME, FROM GROVER CLEVELAND TO JOHN F. KENNEDY.

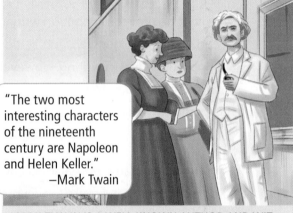

"The two most interesting characters of the nineteenth century are Napoleon and Helen Keller."
–Mark Twain

MARK TWAIN IS A WELL-KNOWN AUTHOR AND WIT. HE COMPARES HER TO THE FRENCH EMPEROR WHO TRIED TO CONQUER THE WORLD IN THE EARLY 1800S.

HELEN WINS THE RESPECT OF PEOPLE EVERYWHERE WITH HER ABILITIES, HER OUTLOOK, AND HER STORY.

Alone we can do so little. Together we can do so much.

⏻ COLLABORATIVE DISCUSSION

Discussing the Purpose With a partner, discuss the key events in Helen's life. What were the pivotal, or significant, moments that changed the way she was able to communicate?

READING TOOLBOX

Identifying Facts versus Opinions

A **fact** is a statement that can be proved, or verified. An **opinion** is a statement that expresses a belief, feelings, or thoughts; it cannot be proved. Nonfiction writing can contain both facts and opinions. In general, facts serve as dependable evidence for supporting ideas in writing. However, an opinion may provide support if it comes from an expert with extensive knowledge of a particular subject.

To identify which statements are facts and which are opinions, ask yourself which statements can be proved with evidence and which cannot.

Statement	Fact or Opinion?	How Do You Know?
In the summer of 1880, Helen Keller was born in Tuscumbia, Alabama. (p. 171)	Fact	You can check reliable reference sources.
"The two most interesting characters in the nineteenth century are Napoleon and Helen Keller." (p. 177)	Opinion	This expresses someone's personal belief.

Write On! Reread the story to find one additional fact and one additional opinion. Copy the chart above, and write your examples.

SPEAKING TOOLBOX

Formal and Informal Language

The audience to whom you are speaking should influence how you choose to speak.

▶ **Formal language** is a polite, precise way to speak to someone. You use formal language when you are speaking to an adult of authority such as a school principal or a teacher. You also use formal language when you are speaking to your whole class or when you are presenting.

▶ **Informal language** refers to the casual, everyday words that you use with your friends or speaking one-on-one with a person your own age. Examples of informal language include idioms and slang. Idioms are expressions whose meanings are different from the literal meanings. Slang is informal language used by a specific group.

Formal Language	Informal Language
I don't agree with you.	No way!
What did you mean when you said —— ?	Huh?
I don't understand.	I don't get it.

Speak Out!   Helen Keller spoke with many important people during her lifetime. She met with U.S. presidents, foreign dignitaries, and famous authors and celebrities. When speaking to distinguished people or figures of authority, you must speak politely and respectfully. With a partner, discuss why it is important to speak formally with someone you do not know and why you might not speak as formally as you would with your friends and classmates.

Performance Task

Writing Activity: Argument

In this unit, you read about people who made a difference by voicing their opinions. You read about how an ancient scholar's unpopular ideas were eventually adopted by millions, how a young girl writes a speech and finds her "voice," how principled veterinarians turn their passion for helping animals into a concrete solution, and how a student supports his argument for mandatory community service by addressing the opposite point of view. Your task is to write an argument, or an opinion piece, about making your voice heard using evidence from the selections to support your ideas.

Planning and Prewriting

Connect to the Theme

You use your voice to tell others what you think and why. Sometimes—especially if your opinions are not widely shared—it means taking a risk. And when you take a risk, you want to be heard, even if others don't agree. So you need evidence to support your opinion. Your activity will be writing an argument based on the theme of making your voice heard.

Make a Claim

First, choose a topic you feel strongly about. Then, make a claim, or the argument you make. Write your claim in the form of a statement. Here are some examples:

- Voicing an unpopular opinion makes people respect you.

- Letter writing is the best way to get your voice heard.

- Every great idea starts with someone speaking out.

Decide the Basics

Now that you have a claim, you'll have to find reasons that back it up. You'll have to decide whether those reasons are strongly supported by facts or opinions. And you'll need to structure your essay so your argument is clear.

Make a Claim

When you make a claim, you're stating your position on an issue.

- Write your claim in the form of a statement.
- State your claim at the beginning. Try to grab the reader's attention with the first sentence.
- Your claim can take the form of an interesting line of text, or a thought-provoking question.

Know Your Sources

Claims are supported by facts and examples from a variety of sources.

- Using more than one selection makes your case stronger.
- Make sure your sources are credible.
- You're not limited to informational sources—fiction can be used to support an argument, too.
- Recognize that every source, no matter how "objective," has a point of view.

Find Reasons

Support your claims with evidence, or relevant facts and examples from the text.

- Use only those examples that relate to your topic.
- Make sure your reasons are presented in logical order.
- Facts provide better support than opinions, but opinions can be valuable.
- Identify and address counterarguments.

Think About Style

Pay attention to vocabulary, tone, and word choice.

- Use transitional words and time-order phrases to show how ideas are related.
- Choose words that clearly support your claims. These words should appear in logical order.
- Use a neutral, formal style.
- Explain technical words, or words a reader may not be familiar with.

Performance Task

Finalize Your Plan

You've got the basics down. You've developed a claim based on the selections you read. You have evidence to support it. Now you need a way to present the information—in other words, a structure.

Use the diagram in the Writing Toolbox to help you.

WRITING TOOLBOX

Elements of A Written Argument

Introduction	**The introduction** should make a claim about an issue, or a problem that needs to be solved. Stating your claim at the beginning allows your readers to follow the rest of your argument. Also think about what effect you want your argument to have on readers.
Reasons	**Provide reasons** that support your claim. (Facts are best, but opinions can be valuable, too.) **Respond to opposing viewpoints** with evidence from the text. This shows you really understand your subject.
Conclusion	**The conclusion** follows from and supports your claim. It restates your argument and summarizes the evidence. You can also offer a comment of your own or ask a thought-provoking question.

Don't forget to refine your Personal Toolboxes with strategies that work for you.

Draft Your Argument

You've made a claim. You have evidence and counterarguments. You've organized your ideas. Now start writing! As you write, think about:

- **State Your Claim** What is your opinion? State it at the beginning.
- **Your Audience** Who are you writing for? Think about your readers.
- **Present Strong Evidence** Make sure your reasons support your claim, and that they're strong and based on fact.
- **Use Connecting Words** Use words like *consequently, for example*, and *however* to clarify related ideas and make your ideas flow.
- **Opposing Point of View** Anticipate the other side of the argument, and refute it with evidence.
- **Elements of a Written Argument** Use your Elements of a Written Argument diagram to give an introduction, reasons, and a conclusion.
- **Conclusion** Refer to your original claim and sum up your argument. Tie your ideas together at the end.

Revise

Self Evaluation

Use the checklist and rubric to guide your analysis.

Peer Review

Exchange your argument with a classmate. Use the checklist to give feedback on your classmate's work.

Edit

Edit your argument to correct spelling, grammar, and punctuation errors.

Publish

Finalize your argument and choose the way to share it with your audience.

Stream to Start

fyi
hmhfyi.com

Decisions That Matter

You can't make decisions based on fear and the possibility of what might happen.

— **Michelle Obama**

Essential Question

What factors are involved when people have to make important decisions?

The Language of Decisions

You make decisions every day. Sometimes, making a decision can be easy. For example, it might be easy to decide what to eat for lunch. Other times, it might be very difficult to make a decision, such as choosing an after-school activity. You may wonder if you made the right choice.

Decisions can be small. An example of a small everyday decision would be taking the bus to school instead of walking to school. By taking the bus, you might reach school earlier. This extra time at school might allow you to review your homework before class starts. Having to make this decision might not have been difficult, but it is important nonetheless.

Decisions can be big. An example of a big decision would be deciding to move to a new city after living in one place for many years. Making the decision to move to an unfamiliar location from a place where you are already content can be very difficult. Big decisions can be terrifying because you don't know what to expect.

Whatever decision you make, it is your choice. It is a choice that matters. It is important because you realize that you want to change the current or existing status, or state of things. Sometimes other people may not agree with your decision. That's OK. You stand by your decision with conviction. Believe in your decision.

In this unit, you will discover how decisions, no matter how big or how small, can be significant. You will explore how important historical decisions change the lives of citizens and communities. You will read and hear stories about events and actions that lead individuals to change the course of their lives. You will look into how much thought and effort it took to make these decisions.

> **How do the decisions that individuals make affect communities?**

Making **Choices:** Connotation and Denotation

When you speak or write about making a choice, you have to use words that would accurately describe and convey what your decision is. Finding and using precise words is important when making yourself clear.

Our words have meaning because of **denotation** and **connotation**. *Denotation* is the word's literal dictionary meaning. *Connotation* is the meaning imparted by the ideas and feelings associated with the word. When you share your decision with others, you purposely choose words that will describe your decision in an accurate way. Your readers or listeners will understand what you mean because of your specific word choice.

Authors use connotation to communicate positive or negative feelings. Each connotation creates a different tone in the writing and creates different feelings in the reader. Two words that have a very similar definition—like *remove* and *snatch*—can convey very different feelings. The context of surrounding words and phrases can help you determine the connotation of a word.

> When delivering a speech, you have to be **prepared**, not just **ready**.
>
> Choosing to play a game after school instead of studying for an exam is **foolish**, not just **impulsive**.
>
> To answer this difficult essay question, you have to think **thoughtfully**, not just **carefully**.
>
> The extreme train delay means that our arrival at the event will be **inevitable**, not just **certain**.

↻ Performance Task

It's Your Choice! Choose one of the sentences above, or in **Browse** magazine. Which bolded word expresses the meaning of the sentence better? Use a print or online dictionary to help you with unfamiliar words. Then tell a partner the reason for your choice. Use the supports in your **Activity Book**.

→ *Browse magazine*

DOWNLOAD

Making a significant decision requires thoughtful reflection.

⏻ SETTING A PURPOSE

As you read this blog, think about how the blogger examines a tough problem and finds a way to solve it.

I ♥ Basketball

Enter your email address:

Subscribe me!

SEARCH

💬 **Comments** | **3**

Saturday, April 2nd

I'm not sure what to do. If you know me, you know how much I love basketball! I was a starting player last year, and that was a big part of what made 5th grade so awesome. But, this year is different. Now that I'm 12, I've started wearing the *hijab*. My clothing has to be modest: long sleeves and long skirts, nothing tight, see-through, or form fitting. I don't think I can join the team and stay in these boundaries. I'll talk to my mom and see what she says.

Sunday, April 3rd

My mom says that if I want to play basketball, it's up to me. She says she doesn't mind if I have to get into uniform, and even take off my headscarf. That's what she says, but I don't know. I think she's just saying that to make me feel better. I know that following our religion's traditions is important to her. She was so proud when I decided to wear the *hijab*—even though I knew it might be awkward at first at school. But it's a matter of pride and identity for me. I just wish I didn't have to give up basketball . . .

Monday, April 4th

I ran into Jessie and Shanaya today. They asked if I was going to the basketball tryout Friday. "Probably not," I said, but when Jess asked why, I felt awkward. Of course I want to play, but I don't think I can keep to both *basketball's* rules and *my own*. I'm not sure what to do.

Tuesday, April 5th

Today some people were making shots outside after school. I went over and joined them for a while. No harm in that! My 3-pointer is still pretty hot, even if I am modestly dressed! I think my dad saw me, because when I got in the car, he asked if I was going to play this year. I said no. He asked why not. I said, "I can't!" He said, "Are you sure? Maybe you can. We can think of a way." He doesn't understand.

Wednesday, April 6th

I saw Coach Walker in the hall today. I guess Jess and Shanaya said something to him about me not coming out for the tryout. He wanted to know the deal. I explained about not being able to wear the uniform, about covering my head, arms, and legs. He just said, "Huh."

Thursday, April 7th

After school, both of my parents surprised me by meeting me outside. Instead of heading home, we went to Coach Walker's office. He wanted to talk with us about me playing basketball. He said that as far as he was concerned, I could modify the uniform in any way I wanted—wear leggings under the shorts, add in a long-sleeve shirt and keep on my headscarf. As long as I drink plenty of water and don't overheat, it's OK with him. My parents agreed. Now the decision is up to me. Should I play or not? Is it worth the hassle of maybe getting teased by players from other teams? Is it worth looking different from everyone else? I'm not sure.

Friday, April 8th

I'm going to the tryout! Who cares about what I'm wearing? I'm excited to show that I can play basketball well. I hope I make the team! Wish me luck!

ARCHIVES

April

March

February

January

December

November

October

September

UPLOAD

⏻ COLLABORATIVE DISCUSSION

Discussing the Purpose Making a decision to play basketball while wearing a modified uniform was very difficult, but it made the blogger very happy. With a small group, discuss how talking to her coach, her parents, and her friends helped her make this choice. Cite evidence from her blog that details her dilemma, or problem.

Exploring the Topic Why did the blogger think that her dad wouldn't understand her dilemma? Why did she feel that he wouldn't understand her principles? Share your opinion with a partner.

Staying Safe Make sure to use language that is respectful. Use appropriate language that shows that you can share meaningful and thoughtful content. Do not call anyone names and always maintain a polite tone.

Write On!

"I♥Basketball" gives readers the opportunity to add a comment to the blog. Add a short comment to one of the posts. State your opinion about what happened to the blogger and how she responded. Then exchange comments with a classmate and write something in reaction to his or her comment. 💬 Comments | 0

↻ Performance Task

Writing Activity: Helpful Tips When Writing Blog Posts When you are writing blog posts, think about the tone of your blog and your audience.

1 Do you want your blog to be informative, educational, or entertaining? Think about your topic. For instance, if you are providing tips and resources for the newest technology tool, the tone of your blog should be informative. Similarly, if you are blogging about your move to a new city, your tone can be more conversational.

2 Think about your audience. Some bloggers consider their readers to be a community. They might think of blogging as an email format and introduce their posts with "Hi, readers!" Other bloggers use a more formal style. Even if your tone is conversational, be sure to proofread your blog posts. Pay attention to your spelling and grammar. Your readers might not take your blog seriously if you show that you do not take the time to write well.

3 If your blog entries are time-sensitive, or need to be read right away, consider using software that allows your readers to subscribe to, or sign up for, your blog. They will automatically be updated when you publish a new entry. For blogs that provide daily or weekly updates about scheduling events, this is a handy tool so that your readers do not miss any of your posts.

Language Cam video

Do you want to learn more about how people make important decisions? Watch the video.

Why I Run

Revolutionary Rope

The blogger made a decision after thoughtful reflection. Now, read about why an engineer made some unusual—and very precise—design decisions.

Know Before You Go

The Brooklyn Bridge is located in New York City and spans the two boroughs, or areas, of Manhattan and Brooklyn. These two areas of the city are separated by the East River. To this day, people cross this bridge on foot, on bicycles, and in cars and buses.

READING TOOLBOX

Researching Information Critically

Nonfiction, as in an article or a report, tells about real people, places, and events. The purpose of nonfiction is to convey factual information. To present this information, writers must conduct research and find sources for that information. A **source** is a person, a book, or an organization that gives information about a topic. There are two main types of sources:

▶ **primary sources** materials written by people who witnessed or took part in an event. Examples: letters, diaries, autobiographies, or speeches
▶ **secondary sources** materials written by people who were not directly involved in an event or present when it occurred

As you work through this unit, remember to create your Personal Toolbox with strategies that work for you. It's available from Student Resources or from your teacher.

⏻ SETTING A PURPOSE

As you read, think about potential sources for the information that is presented. Pay attention to the clues that indicate sources. Can you tell anything about the sources the author used?

REVOLUTIONARY ROPE

by Natalya Konrad

John Augustus Roebling was an engineer with an individual dream. Roebling wanted to build the largest **suspension bridge** in the world. In the 1860s he designed the Brooklyn Bridge to fulfill that dream. When it opened in 1883, many people said it wasn't just an engineering achievement: it was truly a miracle. That miracle happened because John Roebling made some very smart decisions.

You will learn the definition of the term **suspension bridge** later in the text.

John Roebling was born in Germany and immigrated to the United States in 1831. Soon he was building canals in western Pennsylvania. Roebling was a good observer. For instance, he saw that the
10 hemp cables used to pull the canal boats **wore out** very quickly. Roebling decided to try something new. According to an article by the American Society of Mechanical Engineers, Roebling had seen cables made of iron wire in Germany. There, people twisted the wire together to make a strong wire rope that could be used as cables. Roebling decided to make a similar wire rope for pulling boats. Many canal boat owners bought Roebling's wire rope, so he opened a factory to make it.

The phrase **wore out** is a phrasal verb that means "deteriorated or destroyed through use."

Designing the Bridge

In the 1850s and 60s, Roebling used his iron rope to design and build suspension bridges. Suspension bridges are designed so that
20 the roadway hangs suspended from cables. But when it came time to build his greatest bridge, the Brooklyn Bridge, he decided to do something different. It was so different that people said it was "revolutionary." Roebling decided to make his rope cables out of steel. Steel is "the metal of the future," he said.

The word *turbulent* is a Spanish **cognate**. Use cognates to guess the meaning of similar words.

At the time, the bridge Roebling was designing would be the longest bridge in the world, for it would cross the East River from Brooklyn to Manhattan. To make such a long bridge, Roebling had to come up with new engineering ideas. The steel cables were one of the most important of these. The East River is very **turbulent**, so a suspension bridge was the best kind of bridge to design. It does not require any supporting piers in the river itself. The bridge would hang between two towers, one on each shore. This meant the entire weight of the bridge would depend on the cables. By using steel cables, Roebling could build a very long bridge—almost 1,600 feet across the river.

John Roebling had created a brilliant design, but he did not live to see the bridge built. In the process of choosing the exact site for the bridge, Roebling was injured in an accident. He died of an infection three weeks later. His son, Washington Roebling, took over and supervised the building of the great bridge.

The Brooklyn Bridge, New York City

Constructing the Bridge

40 The first step was to build the two towers. This was dangerous work, because the towers had to be sunk into the shores about 45 feet on the Brooklyn side and 75 feet on the Manhattan side. Many workers suffered serious physical problems caused by the extreme conditions of working underground.

The towers supported the cables, which supported the roadway across the river. Once the towers were complete, workers began the complex job of **spinning** steel wire for four huge cables. First, a boat from Brooklyn carried a wire across the East River. Then, workers lifted the wire over the two towers. They joined it to another wire to create
50 a continuous loop. This continuous loop was called a "traveler." Using these travelers, workers spun steel wires to create incredibly strong steel cable. Like spiders, men worked high above the river to spin the wires for the cables. Historian Robert McNamara explains that the bridge company specifically found sailors to do this work because they were already used to climbing high in the rigging of ships. The job took 18 months to complete. Each cable was made of 5,434 steel wires in 19 strands. It took 6.8 million pounds of steel wire to make these cables.

> **spinning:** rotating or twisting rapidly

When the Brooklyn Bridge was finally completed in 1883, it opened to
60 much fanfare. Indeed, it was a momentous occasion. Thanks to John Roebling's sound decisions, the Brooklyn Bridge was an engineering marvel. It has since been designated a National Historic Landmark.

UPLOAD

⏻ COLLABORATIVE DISCUSSION

Discussing the Purpose In a small group, discuss the information you read. Brainstorm possible sources that the author might have used. When reflecting and commenting on each other's ideas, follow the useful phrases below to build on the ideas shared before yours.

SPEAKING TOOLBOX

Useful Phrases for Group Discussions

Group discussions let you exchange your thoughts with a few (or more) people at one time. They can help you understand ideas and help you think about things differently.

> **Useful Phrases**
>
> ▷ I agree with María's answer, but Frank also suggested that ____.
>
> ▷ What I believe Lola means is ____.
>
> ▷ Henry, would you please repeat that?
>
> ▷ In my opinion, Catalina's idea was good because ____.

Recognizing Source Information

There are three ways to include research materials, or sources, in either an informative essay or research report:

- **Paraphrase**—the writer states in her or his own words specific material from a source:

  Historian Robert McNamara explains that the bridge company specifically found sailors to do this work, because they were already used to climbing high in the rigging of ships. (lines 53–55)

- **Summary**—the writer takes information from a source and summarizes it:

  According to an article by the American Society of Mechanical Engineers, Roebling had seen cables made of iron wire in Germany. (lines 11–13)

- **Direct quotation**—the writer takes the exact information used in a source and states it word-for-word with quotation marks around those words in the sentence:

  Roebling decided to make his rope cables out of steel. Steel is "the metal of the future," he said. (lines 22–23)

No matter the method of including sources, you must indicate where your information comes from. If you don't document your sources, you will commit **plagiarism**, the unauthorized use of someone else's words or ideas.

↻ Performance Task

Writing Activity: Paraphrase When you paraphrase, you do not change the author's meaning. You restate the author's ideas and cite evidence using your own words. Paraphrasing helps you check your understanding and better remember what you have read. It will also stop you from accidentally copying or taking credit for another person's ideas. Follow the steps below for paraphrasing:

1 Identify the main idea of the selection or paragraph. Ask yourself, "What is the author trying to tell me?"

2 Look up words and phrases that are unfamiliar to you. Use a dictionary or online source.

3 Restate ideas and details using your own words. Don't just rewrite the words in a different way. Ask yourself, *How can I use my own words to restate what the author is saying?*

Rewrite the following direct quote from "Revolutionary Rope" into a paraphrased citation.

At the time, the bridge Roebling was designing would be the longest bridge in the world, for it would cross the East River from Brooklyn to Manhattan. (lines 24–26)

DOWNLOAD

Looking for Me

Roebling's decision to fulfill his dream revolutionized engineering. Find out how one "ordinary" girl's decision to declare an ambition changes her world.

Know Before You Go

Looking for Me by Betsy R. Rosenthal is set in 1930s Baltimore. Edith is the eleven-year-old daughter of Jewish parents. As one of twelve kids in the family, Edith feels left out. Between caring for her younger siblings and working at her father's diner, she does not have any free time for herself. She is resigned to, or has accepted, a future that only involves working at the diner. Edith is the first-person narrator of this story.

READING TOOLBOX

Analyze Poetic Form

Poetry is a form of literature in which words are carefully chosen and arranged to create certain effects. **Form** is the way words are arranged in the poem. The two basic elements of form in poetry are **line** and **stanza**. Line is the main unit of all poems. A **stanza** is a group of two or more lines that form a unit in a poem.

Two kinds of poetry are **free verse** and **narrative**. Free verse does not have a regular rhyme, length, or rhythmic pattern. Much like a short story, a narrative poem tells a story and contains characters, a setting, and a plot. *Looking for Me* is written as narrative free verse poetry.

⏻ SETTING A PURPOSE

As you read, pay attention to narrative elements such as characters, setting, and plot. How do the individual events in each poem help you determine the narrative structure?

from
Looking for Me

by Betsy R. Rosenthal

An Inspiration

I try to rush out after class
like I always do,
but today Miss Connelly
tells me to stay.

5 All I can think about
is how she's going to give me detention
for falling asleep in class again,
and how Dad is going to kill me
for being late to work.

10 But instead,
she asks me in a voice so gentle
it feels like a hug,
"Where do you race off to after school
every day?"

15 And suddenly the words
start pouring out of me like rain
and I find myself telling her
all about the burgers and diapers
and long days
20 and late nights
and crowded beds.

> The phrase **pouring out** usually refers to liquids. In this instance, it refers to telling someone everything that you are feeling.

Then she says,
"I have seen what you can do
when your eyes are open, Edith.
25 You're a smart girl and a fast learner, too.
You should go to college someday."

College? Smart? Fast learner?
No one has ever said words
like these to me.
30 No one.

But then I remember
the girl in my class with the big vocabulary,
and I say, "I don't think I'm so smart,
Miss Connelly.
35 I don't even know
what any of those big words mean
that Helen Krashinsky uses."

"Neither does she," Miss Connelly says
with a wink.

Floating

I am a bubble
blown full
with Miss Connelly's words,

floating out of the classroom,
5 bobbing across the grassy lot,
drifting by Levin's Bakery,

letting the breeze carry me to the diner.
"WHERE HAVE YOU BEEN!?"
Dad yells when I come in,
10 but I just float right by him.

bobbing: to move up and down repeatedly, as by floating on water

The word **lot** has multiple meanings. In this instance, it means a small piece of land.

Even Bubbles Have to Work

But at least
I don't have to work the late shift tonight.
So I serve my last hot roast beef sandwich
and float home.

5 I glide into the parlor.
Do they notice my feet
aren't touching the ground?
"I'm going to college someday,"
I announce,
10 "and I'm going to be a teacher."

Dad grunts.
"We don't have money for college,
and girls don't need to go anyways,"
he says.
15 "You'll work at the diner
until you get married."

His words pierce me,
and I burst.

Bubby Comfort

I go over to Bubby Etta's house
to tell her about my future,
the one I had for a little while,
until Dad smashed it into a million pieces.

5 And even her golden brown knishes
filled with creamy potato
that she's just taken out of the oven
don't help me feel any better.

knishes: baked or fried dough, usually stuffed with potato

But then she cradles my cheeks in her hands,
10 forcing my eyes to look straight into hers,
and says, "Don't worry, *bubbelah*,
you *will* go to college,
and I will help you."

I throw my arms around her
15 and squeeze her hard,
feeling as if she's just reached
into her shopping bag of gifts
and pulled my dreams out
whole again.

Our Secret

I'm having a late-night ironing talk
with Mom
when I tell her
what Miss Connelly said
5 about me being smart
and about college
and how Bubby said she'd help.
"That Miss Connelly is a sharp lady,"
Mom says.
10 Then she leaves the room
and comes back
with something cupped in her hand.
She opens my hand,
drops a wad of dollar bills into it,
15 and then closes it up tight,
holding her shushing finger
up to her lips.
"For college," she says,
and goes back
20 to her ironing.

The term **shushing** comes from the verb *to shush* which means "to order to be quiet or silent." It is used as an adjective here.

I Have to See for Myself

So I don't tell anyone
where I'm going,
and I take two quarters
(two days' wages)
5 that I've stashed away
and use them to pay the fare
each way
for two buses
and a trackless trolley.

10 It takes me
more than an hour
to get there,
but when I do,
it's better than I imagined—

15 tall brick buildings
with ivy clinging to them,
packed with classrooms and dormitories,
boys and girls
sitting on the grass
20 in small groups, chatting,
others hurrying down the walkways
hugging their books.

On the way home
I think about how it was definitely
25 worth two days' wages,
two buses,
and one trolley
to see Towson State Teachers College,
where someday
30 I'll be going to school.

The phrase **stashed away** is a phrasal verb that means "to store in a secret place."

trolley

ivy

UPLOAD •

⏻ COLLABORATIVE DISCUSSION

Discussing the Purpose In a small group, talk about the narrative elements that appear in this text. Identify the characters, setting, and plot. What is the resolution?

READING TOOLBOX

Understanding Poetic Style

A poem is usually written in a particular **style**. Style involves *how* something is said rather than *what* is said. These elements contribute to a poem's style:

▶ **structure** or **form** — line lengths, breaks, rhyme scheme, punctuation
▶ **figurative language** — words and phrases that express ideas in an imaginative way
▶ **sound devices** — ways of using words for the sound qualities they create

Figurative Language: Similes and Metaphors

The poet made specific word choices to emphasize Edith's emotions. To identify Edith's feelings, look for similes and metaphors, or examples of figurative language that make comparisons between unlike things. A **simile** is a comparison between two unlike things using the words *like* or *as*. A **metaphor** is a comparison of two unlike things, and does not contain *like* or *as*.

> *And suddenly the words / start pouring out of me like rain*
> ("An Inspiration," lines 15–16)

These lines contain a simile because *like* is used. Edith's sudden outburst of feelings is compared to a sudden downpour of rain. This simile expresses the intensity and heartache of Edith's feelings.

I go over to Bubby Etta's house / to tell her about my future, / the one I had for a little while, / until Dad smashed it into a million pieces.
("Bubby Comfort," lines 1–4)

These lines contain a metaphor. Edith's future dream of becoming a teacher is compared to something being crushed and broken into many tiny little pieces. This metaphor conveys how deeply hurt Edith feels after her father ridicules her dream. The image of something being violently smashed creates feelings of shock and despair.

Practice and Apply   What is the example of figurative language in the poem "Floating" and in the poem "Even Bubbles Have to Work"? What effect does this language have on each poem?

↻ Performance Task

Writing Activity: Poem   Edith expresses her aspiration to become a teacher. She comes to this decision after talking with three important figures: Miss Connelly, her Bubby, and her mother. Write a poem in which you describe a time when you had to make an important decision.

- Choose the topic, or main message, that you want to convey. This topic has to be clear and specific.

- Ask yourself what you want the outcome to be.

- Decide who will be the speaker in your poem.

- Carefully choose vivid adjectives that show how you feel about your topic. These words express the tone, or attitude, that you want to create in your poem.

- Create comparisons that help express your ideas.

Podcast: A Kind of Wisdom

You just read about one girl's decision to go to college. Now you will listen to decisions a father and daughter make about a business.

Background on Chinatowns in the U.S.

Some major cities in the United States have a neighborhood known as Chinatown. People from mainland China, Hong Kong, Taiwan, and other places in Asia emigrated, or moved from their native countries, and settled in these neighborhoods. Some of these families have lived in these neighborhoods for generations. In Chinatown, you can find all kinds of businesses catering to the Chinese-speaking customers. People who don't live in their city's Chinatown might also visit it to see friends and family, buy groceries, or go out to eat.

This podcast is about a market in Boston's Chinatown that became very important to its Chinese American community. Ellie Lee makes the important decision to stand up for the business that her father built.

 SETTING A PURPOSE

As you listen, think about the decisions Ellie's father makes. Why do you think she doubts her father's decisions? Do you agree with her?

A Kind of Wisdom

Point of View in the Podcast

Claim: Ellie's father showed that he cared for the Chinatown community more than most anything.

Reasons	Evidence
He knew that customers could not afford such high prices.	He set low prices at his store. He made less of a profit on what he sold compared to someone who would have marked the prices up higher.
He knew that many families and friends gathered at the store.	After the store was completely destroyed in a fire, he chose to rebuild it because the community valued it.
Mr. Lee took risks when he rebuilt his store after the fire. First, he did not have much money. Second, the location he chose was unsafe.	He and his longtime employees pooled their resources. The new location did not discourage people from coming to the store. The store once again became vital to the community.
He knew that some of his customers were hungry and did not have money for food.	He once caught a little boy shoplifting, but chose to excuse the boy.
He created a loyal following of customers and employees that he could rely on.	When he received the eviction notice, Ellie organized the community to fight for him and for the store.

⏻ COLLABORATIVE DISCUSSION

Discussing the Purpose Throughout the story, Mr. Lee's personality is described through his decisions. Ellie decides that her father had a kind of wisdom. With a partner, discuss Mr. Lee's business decisions. Do you think the decisions were wise? Or was Ellie right to be unsure from the beginning?

Caesar at the Rubicon

You've been listening to and reading about how making a decision requires much consideration. Now you will read about one of the most world-changing decisions in history.

READING TOOLBOX

Identifying Topics and Research Questions

For nonfiction, whether it is an informative essay or a research project, the first step is developing a topic. The author of "Caesar at the Rubicon" followed these steps:

1. First he decided on a general subject to write about. He chose an ancient Roman politician named Julius Caesar. He realized that for a short article like the one you will read, Caesar's entire life was too broad a topic, so he narrowed his focus to Caesar's monumental decision to cross the Rubicon River.

2. Once the author determined his topic, he formulated questions to guide his research. A good research question:

   ▶ is open-ended—doesn't have fixed answers; isn't restrained by definite limits, restrictions, or structure.
   ▶ requires investigation.
   ▶ cannot be answered in just one word or short phrase.

⏻ SETTING A PURPOSE

As you read, think about what question the author might have asked himself to guide the research that underlies the information he presents.

Caesar at the Rubicon

by Dario Valdez

On a January day more than 2,000 years ago, the Roman leader Julius Caesar made a decision that changed history. Caesar was already a powerful man—one of the leaders of the Roman government. But Julius Caesar was a very ambitious man. He wanted to be the most powerful leader in Rome. What he decided on January 10, 49 BC, caused that
10 outcome to happen.

Decision to Conquer

By 49 BC Julius Caesar had spent about ten years away from Rome. During that time Caesar had conquered the Roman province, or **colony,** of Gaul. Caesar was one of the individual consuls who controlled the Roman Republic. He had larger ideas, however. In order to **take over** the government of the Roman Republic, Caesar needed to bring his army to the center of power—Rome itself.
20 For many years, the Rubicon River had marked the frontier of Rome. It was a border between Rome proper and outer territories

> What word in the sentence helps you understand the meaning of **colony**?

> The phrasal verb **take over** means "to take control."

like Gaul. A law said that no general could lead an army across the Rubicon and into Rome. To do so was treason; the punishment for treason was death. If Caesar decided to lead his army across the Rubicon, he faced death. But if he did not cross the river, he could never take control of the Roman Republic.

Decision Day

A Roman historian, Suetonius, wrote an account of what
30 happened that day in 49 BC. Caesar's army approached the Rubicon. Caesar led them, and at the **banks** of the river he stopped to think. To cross the Rubicon would be simple—but once he had done it, there was no turning back. He would be at war with the rest of Rome.

According to Suetonius, Caesar spent a long time trying to figure out what he should do. He could not calculate the answer.

Eventually, rather than think it out further, Caesar decided simply to do it, and face the consequences. He cried out: "*Let us go where the omens of the Gods and the crimes of our enemies summon us! THE DIE IS NOW CAST!*"

40 Caesar meant that he had made his decision, and however the dice landed—he had made up his mind. He advanced his army over the bridge and into Rome.

According to historians G.R. Stanton, E.S. Gruen, and K.A. Raaflaub, Caesar crossed the Rubicon because he had been forced into war by his opponents' threats of his elimination from political and military life. The historian C. Meier also suggested that Caesar chose to cross the river because by crossing the Rubicon, Caesar committed himself and his army to an irrevocable—unchangeable—course of action. When Caesar reached Rome, he was able to take control of
50 the Republic. He became its dictator, and his son Augustus was the first Emperor of Rome. The course of history was changed by Caesar's decision to seize power.

The word *banks* is a **multiple meaning word**. Here, it means "the land on the sides of a river."

This statement is a **metaphor**. It refers to dice being rolled. Can you guess what Caesar meant here?

⏻ COLLABORATIVE DISCUSSION

Discussing the Purpose In a small group, brainstorm possible questions the author might have asked when he was researching facts and details. Then, evaluate the questions. Are they broad or narrow? Are they open-ended? Do they require investigation?

RESEARCH TOOLBOX

Using Search Terms

When you research a topic, you first decide on **search terms**, or words that describe your topic. Use these terms to search reference materials. In the library catalog or a search engine, use **advanced search features** to help you find information.

Add a **minus sign** (–) before a word that should not appear in your results. Use an **asterisk** (*) in place of unknown words or to find all words that share a word stem. Use **quotation marks** (" ") to search words as exact phrases in the order that they appear.

Keep a list of the name and location of each possible source, adding notes about its possible usefulness.

↻ Performance Task

Research Activity: Search for Information Choose a topic to research.

- Write down all the words and phrases you know about the topic.

- Using a search engine, type these in as search terms.

- Based on what your search terms yield, use the minus sign, asterisk, or quotation marks to bring up information that is most relevant to your topic.

Spider Boy

You've read how Caesar made an important decision that would affect the course of history. Now, find out about an important decision a boy makes in "Spider Boy."

Know Before You Go

Bobby, who has started at a new school, has an unusual hobby. He cares for his pet spiders, and is very knowledgeable about arachnids. Because his individuality sets him apart, he has a difficult time making friends. Bobby does gradually become friends with a couple of classmates. However, others in his class continue to make fun of him and refer to him as "Spider Boy."

READING TOOLBOX

Mood and Tone

Mood is the feeling or atmosphere that the writer creates for the reader. Mood is closely related to **tone**, which is the writer's attitude toward the subject of the text. Authors achieve mood and tone by purposely choosing words to describe the setting, characters, and plot. Look carefully for vivid, descriptive words and phrases that express what and how the characters feel, think, and do. Also, look for examples of **dialogue**, a text treatment an author uses to show a realistic conversation between characters. Mood and tone can be described by adjectives such as *sympathetic, peaceful, annoyed*, or *humorous*.

⏻ SETTING A PURPOSE

As you read, pay attention to the author's choice of words. How do his words about Bobby and Chick help set a mood?

from **Spider Boy**

by Ralph Fletcher

"Clear your desks for the test," Mr. Niezgocki said at the beginning of science class. Groans. Mr. Niezgocki stood at the front of the room holding a thick pile of test papers.

"As you all know we've just begun a new honor system, and that's going to mean a few changes in the way we do things around here. I will no longer act as a policeman during a test. You're too old for that, and so am I. I trust you to behave yourselves. I may leave the room for a few minutes while you're taking the test. Under the honor
10 system you'll have more freedom, but there is also more responsibility put on you to be honest and to ensure that your peers are being honest."

Somebody **snickered** from the back of the room. Mr. Niezgocki glared at him.

"Do you find that funny, Mr. Carroll?"

"No," the boy said.

"This is an experiment. I think it's important. It's not very often you get to shape the kind of school you go to. It's up to you. If it doesn't work, if people abuse it, we'll go back
20 to the old way of teachers babysitting students. I hope that doesn't happen."

snickered: laughed quietly but disrespectfully

GEOLOGY TEST

Name _____

1. Describe at least three different . . .

The geology test packet came to Bobby. Question number one: *Describe at least three different terrains a river might pass through from its source water to the ocean. Describe the **interplay** between the river and this terrain. Specifically, how does the river affect the terrain? In what ways does the terrain affect the river?* Question number two: *Name three ways glaciers permanently changed the landscapes through which they passed.*

30   Bobby gulped.

He started to write, **dredging up** from memory the answers he knew or thought he knew. After about ten minutes he realized that Mr. Niezgocki had left the room. Other kids looked up, realized they were alone, and went back to work. It felt weird to be sitting in a roomful of kids his age with no adult around. And nobody talking.

Then Bobby spotted Chick Hall at the front of the room, leaning to his left and furiously copying off Scott Shanahan's test paper. Scott's paper was pushed all the way
40   to the right so Chick could get a good look at the answers.

Bobby felt a flush of anger. Scott was one of those popular, tough kids who still managed to get high grades. Chick Hall would ace this test simply by copying Scott's answers.

The term **interplay** is a compound word that means "interaction."

dredging up: digging up

Cheating. And no teacher around to see it, let alone stop it.

Bobby glanced over at Lucky. She met his gaze and rolled her eyes at him, but he realized she only meant how hard the test was. From her seat she probably couldn't see Chick at all.

When Mr. Niezgocki returned to the room, Chick's gaze snapped back to his own test. Mr. Niezgocki stayed for five minutes, but when he left again Chick's eyes flew back to Scott's test. He started copying some more, his pencil moving even faster than before. Nobody else seemed to notice it.

Bobby glanced up and saw that he'd already wasted at least ten minutes. *Forget about Chick,* he told himself. *You can't do a thing about that. Concentrate! Think rock! Faults and folds. Plate tectonics. Sedimentary rocks are made in layers. Fossils are often found in sedimentary rocks.* **Igneous** *and metamorphic rocks—one made from fire, the other through pressure. Which is which?* He worked hard to catch up, moving **swiftly**, trying not to make careless errors.

"Time's up," Mr. Niezgocki announced. Kids looked up, blinked, groaned. Bobby still had two questions to go.

"That was *hard*, Mr. N," one boy said.

Chick Hall stretched and loudly cracked his knuckles.

"Before you pass in your test, there's something you need to read on the bottom of the last page," Mr. Niezgocki said. "It says, 'On my honor I know of no cheating on this test.' Under the new honor system, whenever you take a test you must read that and sign your name below it. If you are aware of cheating on this test, you should sign your name and *draw a line through your signature.* Is that clear? Sign your name no matter what. You may hand me your test on the way out of the room."

> **igneous:** formed from an intensely heated liquid, usually volcanic lava, into a solid

> Reading what is before and after the word **swiftly**, can you guess what it means?

On my honor I know of no cheating on this test.

_____

On my honor I know of no cheating on this test. On my honor I know of no cheating on this test. On my honor. Bobby read and reread those words. Each time they brought back the picture of Chick copying off Scott's paper.

80   He signed his name. And drew a dark line through it.

"That was a bear!" Lucky whispered outside the room.

"It was easier for some people than for others," Bobby said.

"Meaning you?" she asked.

"Forget it."

"I'm depressed," Lucky told him.

"The test?"

"Look," Lucky said. She pointed to a window through which they could see rain **spattering** the dark asphalt

90   outside the **cafetorium**. "No race. Like I said, when I can't run, I get **glum**."

After school Bobby found Mr. Niezgocki waiting for him in the lab, a serious expression on his face.

"Sit down," he said. "I just saw your test paper."

"How'd I do?" Bobby asked.

"You know what I'm talking about."

"Yeah." Bobby lowered his eyes.

"You know, Bobby, I was one of the people here who really pushed for this honor system," Mr. Niezgocki said. He stood

100   and began pacing back and forth. "Lots of teachers thought kids in this school weren't ready for it. I argued that it was just what kids needed. I still think so. I really want it to work here. It's so important to give you young people choices here, now, where we can help you see the consequences of those choices."

Bobby looked at him.

spattering: splashing in scattered drops

cafetorium: a large room in a building that is used as a cafeteria and an auditorium

glum: sad and in low spirits

"You're *sure* you saw somebody cheating?" Mr. Niezgocki asked. "Could you possibly have been mistaken?"

"Mistaken?"

"A few weeks ago you wrote an imaginative essay about
110 your father's silk farm." Mr. Niezgocki folded his arms. "That turned out to be fiction. Just wondering if this might be another fiction."

"You think this is just another story I'm making up." Bobby looked down at the floor.

"Is it?" the man asked.

"No!" Bobby replied sharply. "You don't have to believe me. But I'm telling the truth."

"I do believe you," Mr. Niezgocki said **glumly**. "I wish I didn't, but I do."

120 "Did anybody else cross out their names?"

"No." Mr. Niezgocki sighed. "I have to admit I'm curious about who it is you saw cheating. But I should tell you that you don't have to name the person. You've already done everything you're supposed to do."

"I'd rather not say," Bobby said after a moment.

"I see."

"I guess maybe I shouldn't have crossed out my name,"
130 Bobby said.

"No," Mr. Niezgocki said. "You did the right thing, young man. But sometimes doing the right thing puts other people in a tough spot."

Look at the callout on the previous page for the word *glum*. Recall what you know about suffixes. What do you think **glumly** means?

Next morning on the way to science class, Bobby heard a familiar cry.

"Hey, Spider Boy!" It was Chick Hall with a gang of three. "How's the spider business? Eat any good bugs lately?"

140

Raucous laughter. Bobby tried to move around him, but Chick blocked his way.

Raucous: harsh, rough, unpleasant in sound

"**C'mon**, Spider Boy, don't be like that," Chick said. "You know, I'm your biggest fan! I got all your comics!"

C'mon is a colloquial abbreviation of the expression "come on."

All at once Chick lurched forward and pushed Bobby in the chest. Bobby could see himself as if in slow motion, falling backward over someone who had knelt behind him, his books and notebooks spilling all over the place.

"Nice trip?" Chick asked, extending his hand. Bobby ignored it. He gathered his books and got up, **flustered** but unhurt.

flustered: nervous or confused

150

"Hey, Chick," he said, motioning him closer. When Chick drew close enough Bobby whispered, "I got a new nickname for you. Chick the Cheat."

Chick stepped back like he'd been struck.

"What'd he say?" Scott Shanahan asked Chick as Bobby turned and walked into Mr. Niezgocki's class.

⏻ COLLABORATIVE DISCUSSION

Discussing the Purpose The author uses words and phrases, such as "dredging up from memory" (line 31), "furiously copying" (line 38), and "a flush of anger" (line 41), to tell what is happening in the classroom. With a small group, discuss this question: How do these word choices impact the mood and set a tone for this part of the story? Use the tips below to aid your discussion.

LISTENING TOOLBOX

Active Listening
Ask yourself the following questions:

▶ Were the key ideas and details clearly expressed?
▶ Did I understand what my group members said?
▶ Do I know of other facts or examples from the text to contribute?

Analyzing the Text   Cite Text Evidence

1. **Make Inferences** When discussing the new honor system, Mr. Niezgocki says, "I will no longer act as a policeman." What does this choice of words imply about Mr. Niezgocki's feelings about both the new honor system and the previous system?

2. **Make Inferences** How do the rest of Mr. Niezgocki's words on page 213 help set the mood for the events that happen next?

3. **Analyze Character** How do Bobby's feelings evolve through the selection? What evidence in the text supports your ideas?

Speak Out! Think about a time you've made an important, but difficult, decision like Bobby. Tell a partner about the decision. Explain why it was a difficult decision to make and how it turned out.

The Strange Case of Dr. Jekyll and Mr. Hyde

In the last story, Bobby considered the consequences of telling his teacher about the cheating he'd witnessed. Now read about the consequences of one man's strange identity.

HISTORICAL CONTEXT Robert Louis Stevenson set *The Strange Case of Dr. Jekyll and Mr. Hyde* in England during the Victorian era, which was the mid-1800s to about 1900. One character, Dr. Jekyll, is very fascinated with vice, or wicked and shameful weakness, and crime. Dr. Jekyll's fascination mirrors Victorian England's fascination with crime.

GENRE *The Strange Case of Dr. Jekyll and Mr. Hyde* is an example of Gothic fiction. A Gothic novel may include one or more of these elements:

- **An ominous, or menacing, setting.** Look for old castles, empty buildings, or broken-down areas.

- **An eerie and mysterious mood.** Look for events that take place during nighttime or stormy weather.

- **A character's extreme physical transformation**. This physical transformation indicates an internal conflict that the character must resolve.

⏻ SETTING A PURPOSE

As you read, pay attention to how elements of the Gothic novel are developed in the story.

Robert Louis Stevenson's

The Strange Case of DR. JEKYLL AND MR. HYDE

retold by
Dina McClellan

TWO ENGLISH GENTLEMEN—A MR. UTTERSON AND HIS GOOD FRIEND MR. ENFIELD—ARE TAKING THEIR EVENING WALK WHEN MR. ENFIELD BEGINS TO TELL A STRANGE STORY . . .

It was late at night . . . I was coming home from a dinner party. Suddenly a man leaps out of nowhere and tramples a young girl!

THOSE OF US WHO WERE THERE CORNERED THE MAN AND FORCED HIM TO GIVE MONEY TO THE VICTIM. THE MAN PRODUCED A CHECK, DRAWN FROM THE BANK ACCOUNT OF "DR. JEKYLL." BUT THE MAN WAS NOT DR. JEKYLL. THE MAN WAS MR. HYDE!

UTTERSON IS BAFFLED—DOUBLY SO, SINCE HE HAPPENS TO BE DR. JEKYLL'S LAWYER!

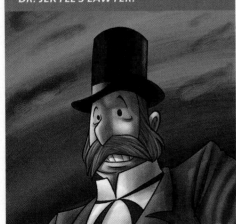

UTTERSON CANNOT GET ENFIELD'S STORY OUT OF HIS MIND. HE STARTS HAVING NIGHTMARES ABOUT A MAN WHO STALKS THE STREETS OF LONDON.

He's coming to get me!

221

UTTERSON BECOMES MORE AND MORE ALARMED AS TO THE WELL-BEING OF DR. JEKYLL—ESPECIALLY SINCE, AS HIS LAWYER, HE KNOWS THAT JEKYLL HAD RECENTLY CHANGED HIS WILL, TURNING OVER HIS ENTIRE ESTATE TO HYDE IN THE EVENT OF HIS DEATH OR DISAPPEARANCE.

MR. UTTERSON ASKS A MUTUAL FRIEND, DR. LANYON, FOR MORE INFORMATION ABOUT DR. JEKYLL.

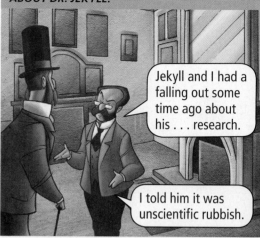

Jekyll and I had a falling out some time ago about his . . . research.

I told him it was unscientific rubbish.

UTTERSON IS EXTREMELY SUSPICIOUS ABOUT ALL OF THIS. HE FEARS THAT HYDE IS BLACKMAILING JEKYLL.

I'll get to the bottom of this mystery if it's the last thing I do!

MR. UTTERSON STAKES OUT A BUILDING HYDE VISITS —WHICH, IT TURNS OUT, IS A LABORATORY ATTACHED TO THE BACK OF JEKYLL'S HOME— AND LOOKS THROUGH A WINDOW . . .

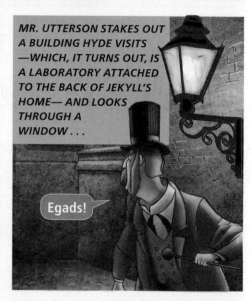

Egads!

This is a very strange sight!

I don't understand!

UTTERSON DECIDES TO CONFRONT THE MATTER HEAD ON. AT ONE OF DR. JEKYLL'S DINNER PARTIES, UTTERSON STAYS BEHIND TO TALK . . .

You can tell me, Jekyll— I'm your friend as well as your lawyer . . .

There's nothing to tell, Utterson—everything is quite in order. I suggest you leave the matter alone.

A YEAR PASSES UNEVENTFULLY. BUT THEN ONE DAY, A MAN NAMED SIR DANVERS CAREW IS FOUND DEAD.

I saw him, officer! It was that horrible Mr. Hyde!

SIR CAREW HAD BEEN CARRYING A LETTER ADDRESSED TO UTTERSON WHEN HE WAS KILLED . . .

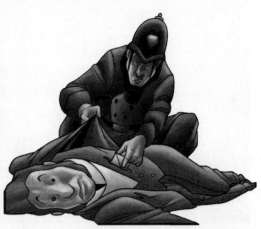

. . . WHICH LEADS THE POLICE TO UTTERSON.

The culprit has been identified, sir—he goes by the name of Hyde. We think you may know where to find him.

Hyde! Why, yes, I do. Allow me get my hat and coat.

WITH A SENSE OF FOREBODING, UTTERSON LEADS THE OFFICER TO HYDE'S APARTMENT.

BUT WHEN THEY ARRIVE . . .

He's gone!

Vanished!

MEANWHILE, DR. JEYKLL IS DOING WELL. HE HAS BEEN VOLUNTEERING, THROWING DINNER PARTIES FOR HIS FRIENDS—

—AMONG THEM DR. LANYON.

Good to see you again, Jekyll. It's been too long!

BUT TWO MONTHS AFTER ONE OF JEKYLL'S PARTIES, DR. LANYON BECOMES ILL AFTER RECEIVING INFORMATION ABOUT DR. JEKYLL.

I can't believe this . . . This is too horrible . . .

Oh no!

DR. LANYON DIES. BUT BEFORE HE DIES, HE SENDS A MYSTERIOUS LETTER TO MR. UTTERSON.

"From Dr. Lanyon, to be opened only in the event of Dr. Jekyll's death or disappearance . . ."

DR. JEKYLL REMAINS IN SECLUSION, REFUSING TO SEE HIS FRIENDS . . .

I'm terribly sorry, Mr. Utterson, Sir, but Dr. Jekyll is not accepting visitors at this time . . .

A FEW WEEKS LATER, AS UTTERSON IS ENTERTAINING HIS FRIEND MR. ENFIELD AT HOME, THERE'S A KNOCK AT THE DOOR.

Isn't that Jekyll's butler, Poole?

I wonder what he wants . . .

THE BUTLER BRINGS A MESSAGE OF CONCERN.

I'm terribly worried, Sir! Jekyll's locked himself in his laboratory and won't come out! It's been weeks since I've seen him!

THE TWO MEN DECIDE TO GO TO DR. JEKYLL'S LABORATORY AND SEE FOR THEMSELVES.

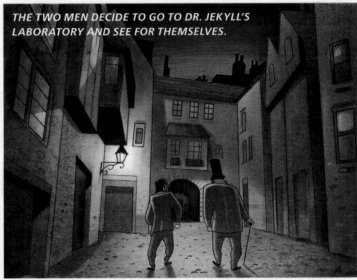

THEY WALK THROUGH EMPTY, WINDSWEPT STREETS AND ARRIVE AT THE LABORATORY . . .

. . . WHERE THEY FIND THE SERVANTS HUDDLED OUTSIDE THE DOOR, TERRIFIED.

L-l-l-l-listen! D'you hear that voice coming out of the laboratory? It's not his!

And those aren't his footsteps either!

UTTERSON AND ENFIELD TRY THE DOOR, AND FINDING IT LOCKED—

Let's break in!

BAM!!

JEKYLL WAS NOT THERE!

BUT SOMETHING ELSE WAS —A BODY!

It's Hyde! Lying dead on the floor!

And he's wearing Jekyll's clothing!

THEN ENFIELD NOTICES SOMETHING POKING OUT OF HYDE'S POCKET—A LARGE ENVELOPE.

It's addressed to you, Utterson!

I'll go through this at home. Perhaps it will explain everything.

BACK HOME, UTTERSON RIPS OPEN THE ENVELOPE AND FINDS TWO LETTERS—ONE FROM DR. LANYON, THE OTHER FROM DR. JEKYLL—WHICH, IT TURNS OUT, ARE TWO PARTS OF THE SAME STORY.

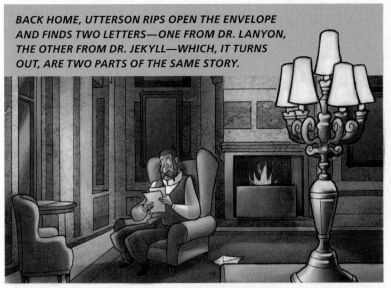

IN THE FIRST LETTER, DR. LANYON DESCRIBES HIS OWN DETERIORATION RESULTING FROM THE SHOCK OF SEEING HYDE DRINK A POTION, THEN TURN INTO DR. JEKYLL.

IN THE SECOND LETTER, DR. JEKYLL EXPLAINS HOW HE DECIDED TO SEPARATE HIS GOOD QUALITIES FROM HIS SHAMEFUL WEAKNESSES BY DRINKING A POTION HE HIMSELF HAD CONCOCTED.

THIS POTION ALLOWED HIM TO PERIODICALLY TRANSFORM HIMSELF INTO A HEARTLESS KILLER, FREE FROM CONSCIENCE.

I cannot believe that Dr. Jekyll behaved this way!

AS TIME WENT ON, JEKYLL'S EVIL SIDE BECAME HARDER AND HARDER TO CONTROL —

—UNTIL HE BECAME HYDE!

IN THE LETTER JEKYLL WONDERS IF HYDE WILL FACE EXECUTION FOR HIS CRIMES—OR KILL HIMSELF. WITH THAT, THE LETTER ENDS. MR. UTTERSON LOOKS OUT THE WINDOW AND SIGHS.

And so ends the strange, sad life of Dr. Jekyll!

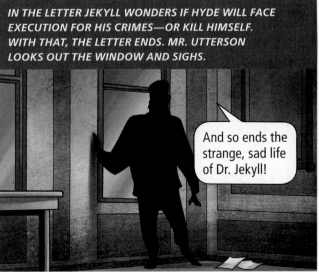

227

⏻ COLLABORATIVE DISCUSSION

Discussing the Purpose Think about the elements of the Gothic novel that appear in this story. With a partner, discuss the following questions, and cite evidence to support your answers:

- How do specific words and phrases in this story contribute to the setting or the mood?

- How do the events and the setting build suspense, add drama, and provide excitement for you as a reader?

- How might the characters' reactions to Jekyll's extreme transformation and Hyde's crimes reflect what the English believed about proper social behavior at the time?

Vocabulary Strategy: Idioms

I'll get to the bottom of this mystery if it's the last thing I do! (p. 222)

The phrase *I'll get to the bottom of this* is an **idiom**, which is an expression that cannot be understood from the words' individual meanings. *I'll get to the bottom of this* means "I'll find out the truth of the matter."

Write On!   Find another idiom in the story. If you don't know what it means, look it up in an online or print dictionary. Write the idiom and its meaning.

Analyzing the Text   Cite Text Evidence

1. **Summarize** How does Mr. Hyde end up in Dr. Jekyll's clothes?

2. **Analyze** What kind of individual is Dr. Jekyll? Describe his character traits.

3. **Make Inferences** Why does Dr. Jekyll have trouble controlling Mr. Hyde's moods and actions?

↻ Performance Task

Speaking Activity: Small Group Oral Report When Robert Louis Stevenson first published *The Strange Case of Dr. Jekyll and Mr. Hyde* in 1886, it was an immediate success. Thousands of copies were sold all over Britain. People were excited to read this new book.

With a small group, prepare an oral report that compares and contrasts the success of the story over time. You might consider the following questions: How successful is this novel now? Has the novel been adapted for a TV show or a movie? If so, how were those received?

- First, take turns paraphrasing the events that happened in the story.

- Decide how to divide the responsibilities of each group member.

- Gather information from an online or print encyclopedia, journal, newspaper, or another reliable source.

- Collaborate to discuss what you learned about the novel's modern-day reception.

- Take notes of the key points, or central ideas, that you've discussed. Be sure to cite examples.

- Decide if you want to include visual aids such as graphs, charts, or images.

- Decide how each group member presents a part of the report.

- Practice speaking your part with your group before presenting to the rest of the class.

Performance Task

Writing Activity: Research Project

In this unit you have read about some notable decision makers of the past—unusual thinkers who lived and dreamed on a grand scale. Your task is to write about a real-life figure who made an important, well-considered—and possibly risky—decision.

Planning and Prewriting

Connect to the Theme

How did the great decision-makers of the past make their decisions? In this research project, you'll be researching a historical figure who made a decision that had significant consequences. Who will you write about?

Choose a Research Topic

Consider one of the informational selections you've read. You've learned why John Augustus Roebling decided to use a new engineering design to build a bridge. You've read about Julius Caesar's monumental decision to cross the Rubicon. But what if you want to know about *others*?

You can use the library or the Internet to do your research. Decide on key words to search for information in the library catalog or a search engine. If you need more help finding things, use the advanced search features. Using these search terms or the advanced search features will lead you to interesting individuals you might not have known. As you search, list the name and location of each possible source, adding notes about its potential usefulness. It is an important step in the research process to evaluate your sources. Your goal is to use sources that are credible, reliable, and trustworthy.

Once you've chosen your topic, make sure it is focused for the scope of your research project. Is there an aspect of your subject's, or this figure's, life you'd like to focus on, such as why he or she decided to do something differently? Or maybe you'd like to research a particular event in your subject's life, such as how the outcome of one decision affected others?

Decide the Basics

Now that you have a topic, assemble your sources of information, read information critically, take notes, and make an outline. Use the notes below to help guide your research.

Gather Your Sources

The two main types of sources are:

- **Primary sources** are materials written by people who witnessed or took part in an event.

- **Secondary sources** are materials written by people who were not directly involved in an event, or present when it occurred. Make sure that your sources are reliable. There's a difference between an opinion posted on a website and an online article written by an expert in the field. All sources are not the same!

Check Your Facts

Since you'll be conducting research on an actual person, you'll be dealing with facts.

- Facts have to be correct.

- Using more than one source will help you double-check your facts. It will also give you the benefit of multiple viewpoints.

- An encyclopedia entry, a news article, and a biography all give you different kinds of information. If you're having trouble finding a certain fact in one place, you might find it in another.

Take Notes

- Date your notes. Note the page numbers where you find key information. That way, you can easily find it again. Summarize information from your sources.

- Paraphrase sections of text, or restate them in your own words. This avoids plagiarism, or copying the author's sentences.

- Write a direct quotation from a source by stating it word-for-word with quotation marks at the beginning and end of the passage.

Make an Outline

An outline keeps you focused on the points you're trying to make and establishes your message.

- An outline lists all your ideas and puts them in order.

- It shows which facts are most important and which facts are details.

- When you start to write, an outline will help you organize and structure the information you want to present.

Performance Task

Finalize Your Plan

You've got your outline. Now you need to decide how to present the information. Follow the structure in the Writing Toolbox.

WRITING TOOLBOX

Elements of a Research Report

Introduction	In the **introduction**, present your topic. Introduce the person and why you've chosen him or her to write about. "Hook" your readers with an interesting detail, or a quotation.
Main Idea and Details	You can have one paragraph or more than one. If you have more than one, each paragraph should include a **main idea** and supporting **details**.
Conclusion	The **conclusion** should follow and sum up how the details support your main idea.
Bibliography	A **bibliography** is a list of sources that you have consulted or cited in your report. It is a separate page at the end of your report. For print sources, include the author's name, the title of an article or a book, the title of a periodical such as a journal or magazine, the edition (if a periodical), and the city and date of publication. For online sources, include the author's name, the name of the website, the date of access, and the complete URL. Make sure to follow a style manual so that you are correctly documenting your sources.

> Don't forget to refine your Personal Toolboxes with strategies that work for you.

Draft Your Research Report

Now start writing! As you write, here are some things to think about:

- **Audience** What effect do you want your research report to have on your readers? Will it give them a better understanding and appreciation of the subject you wrote about?

- **Purpose** Tell why you chose this person early on in your report so readers can follow the points you make. Is it clear why you made that choice?

- **Title** The title of your report should identify your subject or refer to him or her in a way that provokes the reader's interest.

- **Structure** Use the diagram on the opposite page to help you organize your information.
  Be sure to link your paragraphs together in a way that makes sense.

- **Vocabulary** Use a formal tone. Make sure your sentences flow smoothly. Use words like *first, next*, and *at the beginning* to show the sequence of events.

- **Conclusion** Use a concluding paragraph to tie your ideas together. Restate your main idea. You may want include comments of your own, based on the research you did.

Revise

Self Evaluation

Use the checklist and rubric to guide your work.

Peer Review

Exchange your report with a classmate. Use the checklist to give feedback on your classmate's work.

Edit

Edit your report to correct spelling, grammar, and punctuation errors.

Publish

Finalize your report and choose the way to share it with your audience.

Stream to Start

fyi
hmhfyi.com

What Tales Tell

"My father used to say that stories are part of the most precious heritage of mankind."

— **Tahir Shah, writer**

Essential Question

How can stories set in different places and different times express similar ideas?

235

The Language of Storytelling

When authors write narrative tales, or stories, they want to provide some kind of insight, or idea about life.

Stories come in many forms. They can be traditional tales, classic epics, myths, legends, fables, folk tales, mysteries, historical romances, or adventure stories.

Stories relate to a specific time period, a specific setting, or a specific culture. When these stories are related to specific times, settings, or cultures, the themes of these stories may reflect these specific ideas and the customs.

Stories may be told differently. A long time ago, people told stories. Because people did not always write down their stories, the stories may have been changed as they were passed down from generation to generation. This oral, or spoken, sharing of stories is called the oral tradition.

While stories might have changed over time from culture to culture, the insights that are expressed remain the same. For instance, authors might tell about a struggle to be good. These insights are universal, or common.

In this unit, you will hear and read about stories that span different time periods, different settings, and different world cultures. You will read about stories that reveal characters' internal conflicts and personal discoveries. You will explore how characters change and grow throughout from the beginning to the end.

> **How can stories from different places help us understand different times and cultures?**

Let's Tell a Story: Latin and Greek Affixes

There are many words related to stories, storytelling, or the process of writing a story. Some of these words have Latin or Greek **affixes**, or word parts that are added to the beginning or the end of a base word to form a new word. Here are examples of words with Latin and Greek affixes.

Affix	Latin or Greek	Meaning	Examples
-scrib, -script	Latin	to write	describe, manuscript
omni-	Latin	all	omniscient
techno-	Greek	craft, skill, or art	technique, technology
lingua-	Latin	language, tongue	bilingual
liter-	Latin	letter	alliteration, literary
pro-	Latin	for, forward	protagonist
ant-, anti-	Greek	opposite, against	antagonist
vid-, vis-	Latin	to see	evident, revise
auto-	Greek	self, same	autobiography

↻ Performance Task

What's in a story? Choose one of the example words above, or one from **Browse** magazine. Use a dictionary to confirm the meanings of unfamiliar words. With a partner, take turns telling how this word can be used to describe stories, storytelling, or the process of writing a story. Use the supports in your **Activity Book.**

→ **Browse** *magazine*

DOWNLOAD

Sharing a story is one way of sharing an idea.

⏻ **SETTING A PURPOSE**

As you read this blog, consider how CharmingHood's conversation with his blog readers helps him expand his knowledge about a familiar story.

Charming Hood

Enter your email address:

[   ]

Subscribe me!

SEARCH

[🔍]

💬 **Comments** 17

June 4th *Cinderella, Anyone?*

Hey! How's it going? I hope you are all doing GREAT.

If you've had fun reading about my silly, funny, exciting adventures and if you appreciate the time I put in to pass them along to you, then maybe you'll do me a favor in return. *I need help with an assignment!*

We've been discussing *Cinderella* stories in class. We read the original one and two versions from around the world: *Adelita* from Mexico and *The Golden Sandal* from Iraq. Now I need to do a presentation on Cinderella-type stories.

What Cinderella-type books have you read and loved? It could be a picture book, a novel, movie, or play. I'm interested in the plot, and the themes, too—like stepmothers, magical helpers, and "slipper" tests to find the right person.

Please respond! I'm here waiting.

Posted by **CharmingHood**, 2:45 pm

👍 Like 2   👎 Dislike 0   REPLY

COMMENTS

I liked Mufaro's *Beautiful Daughters*. *Cindy Ellen* is pretty funny!

Posted by **TrueBeliever**, 3:17 pm   👍 Like 2   👎 Dislike 0   **REPLY**

Read *Prince Cinders* and *Chickerella*!

Posted by **StillClucking**, 3:39 pm   👍 Like 2   👎 Dislike 0   **REPLY**

My class read *The Gift of the Crocodile*, *Raisel's Riddle*, and *Cendrillon*.

Posted by **MooMadHatty**, 4:12 pm   👍 Like 5   👎 Dislike 0   **REPLY**

TrueBeliever, StillClucking, MooMadHatty: These are ALL great suggestions so far! Thanks! I appreciate it.

Posted by **CharmingHood**, 4:35 pm   👍 Like 5   👎 Dislike 0   **REPLY**

CharmingHood, *Cinder* is set in a future time period. Cool!

Posted by **IHeartApplePie**, 5:44 pm   👍 Like 7   👎 Dislike 0   **REPLY**

I love *The Higher Power of Lucky!* It's about a girl and her stepmother/ guardian. It's my favorite book!

Posted by **QueenRulz,** 6:48 pm   👍 Like 8   👎 Dislike 0   **REPLY**

QueenRulz, I liked that book, too. But it's not a *Cinderella* story, really. The stepmother isn't cruel. Maybe we can make a list of our favorite books later, and you can add *The Higher Power of Lucky*.

Posted by **BumpyGuppo,** 7:02 pm   👍 Like 5   👎 Dislike 0   **REPLY**

Thanks, all of you! Heading to the library tomorrow!

Posted by **CharmingHood,** 9:01 pm   👍 Like 5   👎 Dislike 0   **REPLY**

Leave your comment

ARCHIVES

June

May

April

March

February

January

December

November

October

UPLOAD

⏻ COLLABORATIVE DISCUSSION

Discussing the Purpose You've read the responses written by CharmingHood's blog readers. With a partner, discuss how each blogger's response to CharmingHood's post allows him to reflect on new ideas for books that are similar to the *Cinderella* fairy tale.

Exploring the Topic Do you know another story that is related to the *Cinderella* fairy tale? Why do you enjoy reading it? Tell a partner about it.

Staying Safe Notice how CharmingHood and his readers avoid mentioning their specific names. Instead, they refer to each other by their blog names. Discuss ways to talk about using names without giving specific information.

Write On! One of CharmingHood's readers suggested that the readers compile a list of their favorite books. Draft a list of your favorite books, and write a brief description of what you like about them. For example, if you like *Cinderella* because of the magical setting, you may write a description about it. Make sure to cite evidence from the stories to support your descriptions

↻ Performance Task

Writing Activity: Share and Interact with Other Blogs Now that you have successfully started a blog, brainstormed ideas, chosen a design, scheduled posts, and are being mindful of respectful blogging rules, you are ready to share your blog with others! Interacting with other bloggers is one of the most exciting activities about blogging.

1 Participate with bloggers you may know by leaving comments or asking questions about their blog posts. If a blogger replies to your comment, you can then continue the conversation. Additionally, by leaving a comment, you have the chance to promote your own blog. Many blog forms allow you to include your blog website.

2 Find new blogs that are similar to yours. Leave comments on these blogs and join the conversation! You might learn something new, or you might be asked to explain something further. Either way, participating in an online community is beneficial!

3 Ask your readers if they have questions or comments about one of your blog posts. For example, if you write about a cultural tradition that's important to your family, invite your readers to share their own cultural traditions of significance.

4 Request your readers to suggest future topics.

Language Cam video

Do you want to learn more about how stories are shared? Watch the video.

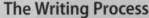

The Writing Process

The Ramayana

Classic literary themes have captured the hearts of many readers. Now you'll read a retelling of one of the most important literary works of ancient India.

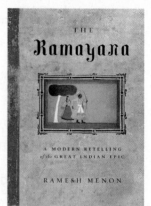

Know Before You Go

The Ramayana, or Rama's journey, is one of the most important epics of traditional Indian literature. It tells the story of the hero Rama as he rescues his wife Sita, who has been captured and taken to the city, Lanka. Rama asks the monkeys and bears of the forest for help. The strongest of these creatures is the monkey Hanuman, who is the son of the wind god. Hanuman vows to help Rama find Sita.

READING TOOLBOX

Features of an Epic: The Hero's Journey

The Ramayana is a narrative that follows the pattern of an epic called the **hero's journey.** It is the story of a hero, who is usually the main character, who sets out on a quest to achieve a goal for the community.

▶ In the hero's journey, there are certain stages that a hero follows. In this chapter from *The Ramayana*, Hanuman has answered the call to adventure, or has accepted the challenge of making the leap across the wide, expansive ocean to Lanka.

▶ An important element of a hero's journey is that it must be completed alone. Accomplishing this challenge alone is a test of individual courage and strength.

> As you work through this unit, remember to create your Personal Toolbox with strategies that work for you. It's available from Student Resources or from your teacher.

⏻ SETTING A PURPOSE

As you read, pay attention to story elements such as characters, setting, and plot.

from *The RAMAYANA*

by Ramesh Menon

CHAPTER 1

The Leap of Faith

Hanuman was a tremendous beast, **straddling** the Mahendra. As he craned toward the sky, the **sinews** on his neck and back stood out like cobras. Restlessly, the son of the wind paced the mountaintop. Tigers, bears, and leopards that lived near the summit scurried out from their caves and fled down the mountain: this was not a monkey they would care to contend with. Mahendra, which stood unmoved by

10 tidal wave and typhoon, shuddered beneath Hanuman's **footfalls**. Elephants blundered down the slopes. Gandharvas and kinnaras who lived in some of the caves flew into the air in flashes, or fled with the animals.

straddling: standing with one leg on each side

sinews: tendons

footfalls: the sound of footsteps

243

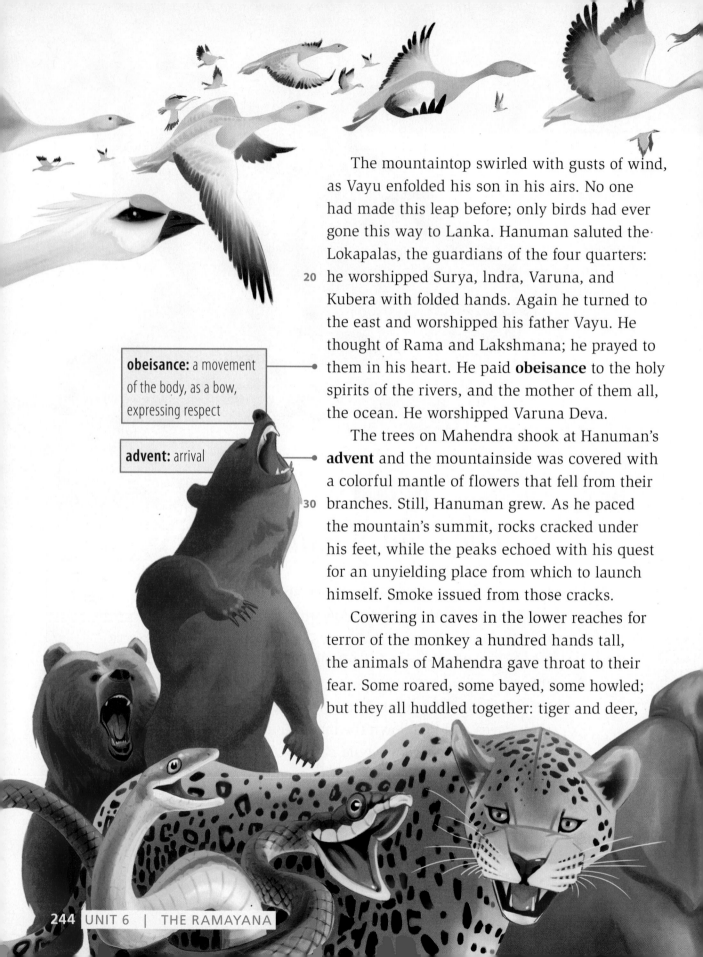

The mountaintop swirled with gusts of wind, as Vayu enfolded his son in his airs. No one had made this leap before; only birds had ever gone this way to Lanka. Hanuman saluted the Lokapalas, the guardians of the four quarters: he worshipped Surya, Indra, Varuna, and Kubera with folded hands. Again he turned to the east and worshipped his father Vayu. He thought of Rama and Lakshmana; he prayed to them in his heart. He paid **obeisance** to the holy spirits of the rivers, and the mother of them all, the ocean. He worshipped Varuna Deva.

The trees on Mahendra shook at Hanuman's **advent** and the mountainside was covered with a colorful mantle of flowers that fell from their branches. Still, Hanuman grew. As he paced the mountain's summit, rocks cracked under his feet, while the peaks echoed with his quest for an unyielding place from which to launch himself. Smoke issued from those cracks.

Cowering in caves in the lower reaches for terror of the monkey a hundred hands tall, the animals of Mahendra gave throat to their fear. Some roared, some bayed, some howled; but they all huddled together: tiger and deer,

20

30

obeisance: a movement of the body, as a bow, expressing respect

advent: arrival

40 elephant and panther, the great bears
of those hills, Jambavan's cousins, and hissing,
venom-spitting serpents. A thousand flights of
birds flew screaming from their nests in caves
and crannies, and the sky was full of their dark
wheeling alarm. On the mountain's summit,
Hanuman paced and paced, gathering himself.

It is said even the rishis of Mahendra scuttled
off that massif, and secret vidyadharas flew into
the sky and hovered there like strange birds to
50 watch Hanuman's leap. Then the awesome vanara
stood still on a spot that did not give below his
feet, as if it had once been created just for him.
He turned his face to the sky and roared like
the wild creature he was, lord of them all, while
above him the sky **recoiled** at the sound. Behind
him, longer than the longest hamadryad pulled
out of its hole by Garuda, his tail coiled and
twitched with life of its own. Far below on the
seashore, Angada's vanaras stopped their ears
60 with their hands.

wheeling: turning, rotating

recoiled: jumped or shrinked back

245

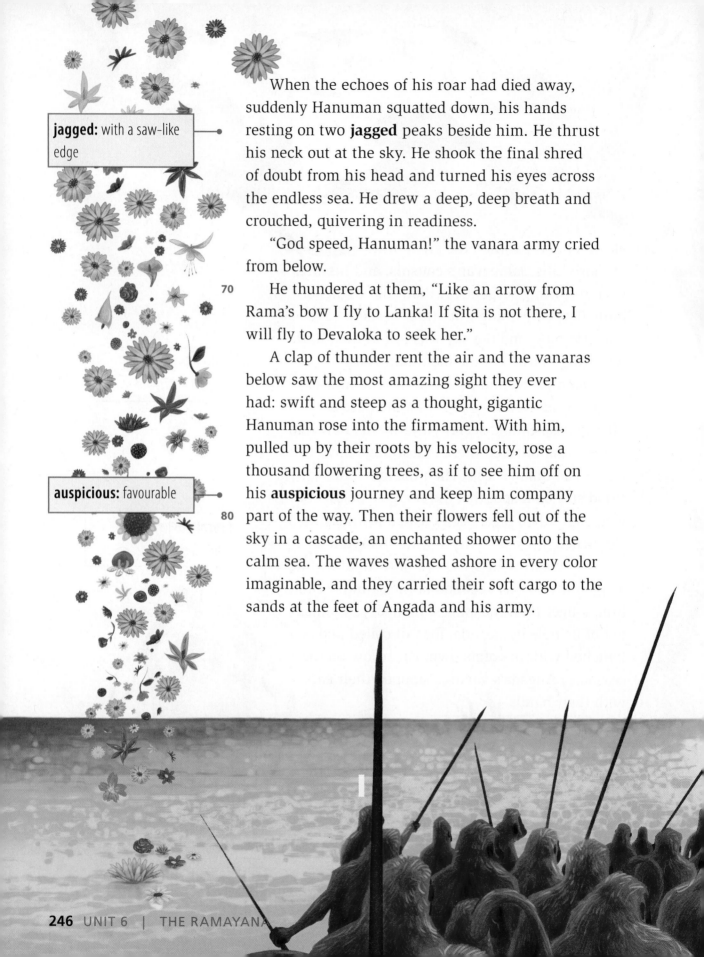

jagged: with a saw-like edge

auspicious: favourable

When the echoes of his roar had died away, suddenly Hanuman squatted down, his hands resting on two **jagged** peaks beside him. He thrust his neck out at the sky. He shook the final shred of doubt from his head and turned his eyes across the endless sea. He drew a deep, deep breath and crouched, quivering in readiness.

"God speed, Hanuman!" the vanara army cried from below.

70 He thundered at them, "Like an arrow from Rama's bow I fly to Lanka! If Sita is not there, I will fly to Devaloka to seek her."

A clap of thunder rent the air and the vanaras below saw the most amazing sight they ever had: swift and steep as a thought, gigantic Hanuman rose into the firmament. With him, pulled up by their roots by his velocity, rose a thousand flowering trees, as if to see him off on his **auspicious** journey and keep him company

80 part of the way. Then their flowers fell out of the sky in a cascade, an enchanted shower onto the calm sea. The waves washed ashore in every color imaginable, and they carried their soft cargo to the sands at the feet of Angada and his army.

But above them, Hanuman did not fall back to the earth. Up he flew and away, carried by the power unleashed by his mighty legs and arms, borne on the swift currents of his father the wind: truly like the manavastra of Rama of Ayodhya. They heard the peals of his **exhilarant** laughter, floating down like more blooms from the sky.

90

> **exhilarant:** excited and thrilled

Like a thundercloud sped along by a tempest, Hanuman flew through the air. His arms were stretched before him like two streaks of lightning. The Devas saw his flight and gathered on high to watch. On flashed the vanara, and they whispered among themselves in awe, the immortal ones. They said he might swallow the very sky with his **cavernous** mouth. Hanuman's shadow on the placid ocean was thirty yojanas long, as he flitted across the firmament like a mountain in the days before Indra sheared their wings.

100

> The term **cavernous** comes from the root word *cavern*. Can you guess what it means?

Through fleecy clouds, like a plunging moon he flew; and eager for his success, the Devas showered unearthly petal rain over him. Not wanting him burned, the sun shone softly on his back as he arrowed along. And, of course, his father Vayu held him precious in his arms, heart to heart. Never before had he felt his son so near him, so much his own, and he sped him on with a timely gust.

110

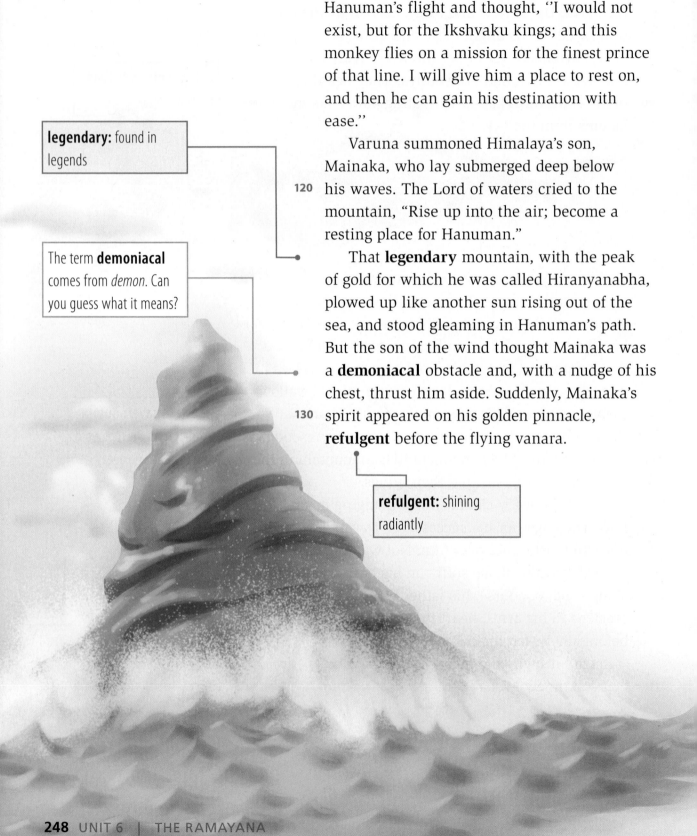

Varuna, the ocean below, watched Hanuman's flight and thought, ''I would not exist, but for the Ikshvaku kings; and this monkey flies on a mission for the finest prince of that line. I will give him a place to rest on, and then he can gain his destination with ease.''

120 Varuna summoned Himalaya's son, Mainaka, who lay submerged deep below his waves. The Lord of waters cried to the mountain, "Rise up into the air; become a resting place for Hanuman."

That **legendary** mountain, with the peak of gold for which he was called Hiranyanabha, plowed up like another sun rising out of the sea, and stood gleaming in Hanuman's path. But the son of the wind thought Mainaka was a **demoniacal** obstacle and, with a nudge of his chest, thrust him aside. Suddenly, Mainaka's

130 spirit appeared on his golden pinnacle, **refulgent** before the flying vanara.

legendary: found in legends

The term **demoniacal** comes from *demon*. Can you guess what it means?

refulgent: shining radiantly

Mainaka cried to the monkey, "Varuna bade me rise to be a resting place for you. The Lord of waves would like to be of use to you, Hanuman, and to the prince of the House of the Sun whom you serve. Your father Vayu saved me from Indra's vajra, when the Deva king severed the wings of all mountains. The wind hid me under the ocean when Indra hunted my kind. Look!" And silver

140   wings shimmered behind that **resplendent** being. Mainaka said again, "Come, Hanuman, rest a while upon me. Then you can fly to Lanka from my summit."

> **resplendent:** magnificent, glorious

Hanuman replied, "I am moved by your love and by the ocean's kindness. But my time is short and I have none to rest. Farewell, good mountain, we shall meet again someday."

Hanuman waved to the golden one. As Mainaka sank under swirling waves again, the

150   vanara streaked on through the sky.

UPLOAD ●─────────────────────────────

⏻ COLLABORATIVE DISCUSSION

Discussing the Purpose In a small group, identify the characters, setting, and plot of this chapter from *The Ramayana*. Who are the characters? What is the plot? Where does the action take place?

Analyzing the Text `Cite Text Evidence`

1. **Analyze Characters** Who is the hero of this chapter?

2. **Analyze Characters** What qualities does this hero possess?

3. **Summarize** What is this hero's challenge?

4. **Analyze** How does this hero's challenge contribute to the overall plot of *The Ramayana*?

5. **Explore the Theme** What is the theme of this chapter? How do the title, the characters' words and actions, and setting help you to determine the theme?

Imagery

This chapter of *The Ramayana* includes examples of imagery, or language that creates vivid sensory-word pictures.

> *Then their flowers fell out of the sky in a cascade, an enchanted shower onto the calm sea. The waves washed ashore in every color imaginable . . .* (lines 80–83)

Words and phrases such as *flowers fell out of the sky in a cascade, an enchanted shower onto the calm sea,* and *waves washed ashore in every color imaginable* appeal to our sense of sight.

> *Still, Hanuman grew. As he paced the mountain's summit, rocks cracked under his feet, while the peaks echoed with his quest for an unyielding place from which to launch himself. Smoke issued from those cracks.* (lines 30–34)

Words and phrases such as *rocks cracked* and *the peaks echoed* appeal to our sense of hearing. The phrase *Smoke issued from those cracks* appeals to our sense of smell.

Good writers use relevant words and phrases to describe vivid sensory images that allow the reader to visualize the setting.

Practice and Apply   Identify any examples of imagery in the sentence below. Explain your reasons.

> *Mahendra, which stood unmoved by the tidal wave and typhoon, shuddered beneath Hanuman's footfalls.* (lines 9–11)

Write On!   Consider the setting of this chapter from *The Ramayana*. Write a brief paragraph that answers this question: How is the setting significant to the story?

The Ramayana

In this chapter from *The Ramayana,* Hanuman faces challenges that seek to prevent him from crossing the ocean. Continue reading to find out what happens to Hanuman and how he responds.

READING TOOLBOX

Author's Purpose

An author has many reasons, or purposes, for writing. An author may write to inform, to persuade, to entertain, or to express thoughts and feelings. These reasons are called the author's purpose. To identify the **author's purpose**, read the details in a text. An author carefully chooses words to describe something or someone. He may provide an opinion about someone or something with concrete facts and relevant examples. Descriptive words and phrases also help to explain why the author feels the way he does.

⏻ SETTING A PURPOSE

As you read, pay attention to the words, phrases, and details that occur in this story to help you determine what the author wants you to know. What is the author's purpose?

CHAPTER 2

The Tests

But then the Devas of light are never content to leave any hero **untested** in his most difficult hour. They called Surasa, who is the mother of all serpents.

The Devas said, "We want to see how great this monkey really is. He is the wind's son; just this leap is too easy for him. But we can test his **mettle** if he finds someone dreadful in the sky barring his way. Become

10 a rakshasi in the air, Surasa. Let us see how worthy Hanuman truly is."

Soon, spread across the sky like a thunderstorm, Hanuman saw a rakshasi who dimmed the brightness of the sun. She grinned, baring fangs big as hills. She licked her lips when she saw him, and **bellowed**, "How hungry I have been! But here comes a fair feast, flying into my mouth. Come to me, little ape, and be my lunch."

20 Hanuman folded his palms to the awful one. He said humbly, "Devi, I am on a sacred mission. On my way back I will fly into your mouth. You have my word."

Identify prefixes and suffixes to understand the meaning of **untested**.

mettle: courage, strength of character

bellowed: roared

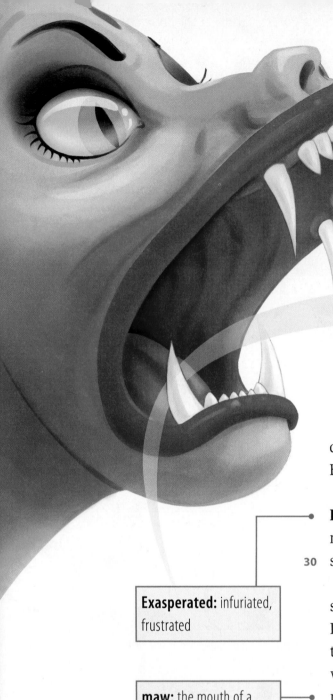

boon: gift, blessing

But she cried, "By Brahma's **boon** no one can pass me without going through my mouth! Brahma's boon shall not prove false."

She yawned her mouth wide as the horizon. **Exasperated**, Hanuman cried, "Rakshasi, your mouth is too small to contain me. Open wider, 30 so I can fit in it."

She yawned her firmament of a mouth still wider; she let it gape a hundred yojanas. In a flash, Hanuman was the size of a man's thumb and, before the demoness realized what was happening, he flashed in and out of her plumbless **maw**. Outside its darkness again, Hanuman grew vast once more.

He bowed to Surasa. "I flew into your mouth. Now let me pass."

40 Surasa laughed; she liked this clever monkey in the sky. She cried to him, "Pass in peace, Hanuman, it was only the Devas testing you. May your journey be fruitful; may all your missions succeed."

Exasperated: infuriated, frustrated

maw: the mouth of a ferocious, devouring creature

She vanished out of the sky and Hanuman
flew on. His path was many thousands of feet
high. It was the skyway of the birds he flew
along, the subtle path of rishis and gandharvas.
Vayu had **wafted** his son up to where he flew

50   as swiftly as he wished. It was damp today,
the celestial skyway, and raindrops fine as dew
moistened his face pleasantly as Hanuman
flashed along.

    Farther ahead, there was a real rakshasi
called Simhika who lived in the ocean.
Suddenly Hanuman felt himself slowing and
then coming to a **standstill** in the air. He felt
himself being dragged down, and when he
looked at the sea below he saw that a rakshasi's

60   curved claw clutched his shadow on the water.
Even as he watched, amazed, she parted the sea
like another mountain and rose, lion-faced and
terrible, out of the waves. Her mouth yawned
from horizon to sky to swallow him.

> **wafted:** carried in the air

> Break **standstill** into two smaller words to understand its meaning.

Now Hanuman lost his patience. With a roar, he plummeted down into her jaws like a fishing hawk. Down her throat he plunged, becoming tiny again so she could not find him with her fangs. Down into her belly he flew. Beginning

70 to grow again, he clutched two handfuls of her intestines and flashed back up again, dragging her stomach out through her mouth. Simhika died screaming, and her **entrails** floated like dark garlands on the waves.

entrails: intestines

Like Garuda himself, Hanuman flew on and the wind flew with him, making his passage effortless. He saw a dark speck appear on the horizon, and, at the speed at which he flew, it grew rapidly. Soon a lush island lay below him,

80 a jewel in the sea. Within its **undulating** green confines, he saw a mountain that thrust its way up toward the clouds, and the sun-dappled gardens of that Mount Trikuta. Lower and lower he circled. He saw rivers, streams, and silvery waterfalls. He wondered at the richness of this Lanka he had reached after flying a hundred yojanas through the sky.

undulating: rippling, with a wavy shape

Quickly Hanuman thought, "I cannot land here like this. I am so big the rakshasas will

90 never let me into their city without a fight. Then how will I find Sita?"

In the twinkling of an eye, he was a little monkey three feet high, and softly he set himself down on the peak of the Lamba hill. **Round-eyed** at the beauty of Ravana's island, Hanuman stood chattering approvingly at what he saw around him. He heaved a sigh of relief that his fantastic journey, his momentous crossing, was

100 accomplished. To find Sita now should be no great matter.

The term **round-eyed** means "surprised." Can you guess where this word comes from?

⏻ COLLABORATIVE DISCUSSION

Discussing the Purpose What do the chapter title and the characters' words and actions reveal about the author's purpose? With a small group, share your ideas. Cite specific words and details to support your answer.

READING TOOLBOX

Features of an Epic: The Hero's Journey

In a traditional epic, the hero must complete daring and nearly impossible obstacles, or tests, to prove that he is worthy of this journey.

▶ The hero must not allow these obstacles to keep him from completing his quest.

▶ The hero must use his intelligence and cleverness to outwit others.

▶ The hero must be brave and strong to overcome his foes successfully.

Analyzing the Text `Cite Text Evidence`

1. **Summarize** What are the tests that Hanuman faces?

2. **Analyze Characters** Why do you think Hanuman behaves and acts the way he does with Surasa and Simhika?

3. **Understand Structure** How does this chapter and the previous chapter fit in the overall structure of *The Ramayana*?

4. **Evaluate** Do you think that Hanuman will complete the quest to find Sita? Justify your reasons.

SPEAKING TOOLBOX

Active Listening

Act the way you would like listeners to act when you speak.

▶ **Give your full attention to the speaker.** You may think you know what the person is going to say next, but you may be wrong!

▶ **Let the speaker finish before you begin to talk.** You can't really listen if you are busy thinking about what you want say next.

▶ **Ask questions.** If you are not sure you understand what the speaker has said, just ask.

Useful Phrases

▷ I'm not sure what you mean by ____.

▷ I understand what you mean, but ____.

▷ That sounds right, but I still think ____.

Speak Out! Why do you think that *The Ramayana* has remained such a beloved tale? What does this epic tale reveal about Indian heroism, honor, and bravery? Share your opinions with a partner. When you listen to your partner, use the Active Listening tips as a guide.

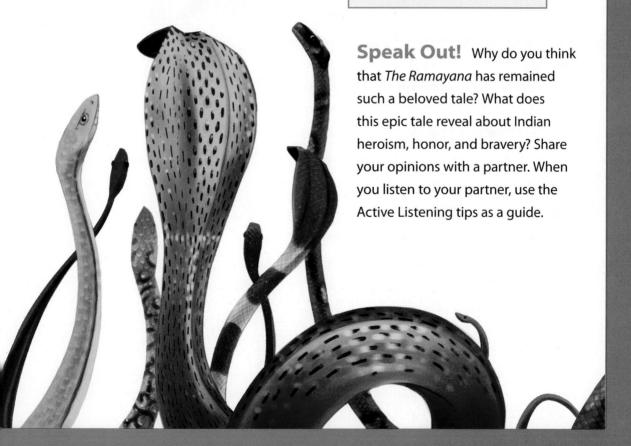

DOWNLOAD

Podcast: Madeleine, Mrs. Murphy, and Me

Storytelling can be inspiring and courageous. It can also be exciting and stimulating.

Background on New York City

New York City is the largest city in the United States. The most well-known part is the island of Manhattan, which is one of the most densely populated places in the United States.

In this podcast, Jake is the narrator. Jake and his family live near Central Park and the American Museum of Natural History. Central Park is a huge park in the heart of Manhattan that was officially opened to the public in 1876. It is home to three lakes, a zoo, and miles of paths for walking and cycling. The American Museum of Natural History was founded in 1869 and contains a famous collection of dinosaur fossils. It also has many exhibits on plant and animal life.

 SETTING A PURPOSE

As you listen, think about how Jake's opinion about Mrs. Murphy changes over the course of the story.

Madeleine, Mrs. Murphy, and Me

Sequence of Events

1. Madeleine and her parents live in Manhattan, a part of New York City.

↓

2. Madeleine begins talking to and playing with an imaginary friend, Mrs. Murphy.

↓

3. Jake and Katie get used to Mrs. Murphy going everywhere with them.

↓

4. After just a few months, Mrs. Murphy disappears.

↓

5. Madeleine's parents become worried about her.

↓

6. Madeleine begins to travel to all sorts of imaginary places on her own.

⏻ COLLABORATIVE DISCUSSION

Discussing the Purpose In a small group, discuss how Jake's opinion about Mrs. Murphy changes over the course of the podcast. How did Jake and his wife first react to Madeleine's imaginary friend and, later, to her imaginary trips by herself? Why did Jake and Katie react the way they did at each stage of the story? Cite specific words and phrases to support your answer.

Etched in Clay

You've read an influential Indian epic that has endured over centuries. Now you will read a story about the influence of words.

Historical Background

Etched in Clay is based on the true story of a slave named Dave, who lived in South Carolina during the 1830s. During this time period, slavery was legal. Slaveowners were not allowed to teach their slaves to read and write.

Dave works at a pottery factory where he creates beautiful clay pots. His days are long and difficult. His family members are sold. Yet Dave continues to fight for himself by learning how to read and write, despite chances of being caught. One day, Dave marks his words in his clay pots. Through his clay etchings, Dave tells the story of his suffering and heartache, bravery, and heroism.

READING TOOLBOX

Determining Style Elements

Style elements work together to communicate the **mood** and **tone** of a text. **Repetition** is a word pattern that repeats. **Rhythm** is a pattern of stressed and unstressed syllables in a line of poetry, like rhythmic beats in music. **Point of view** is how the writer chooses how to tell a story. *Etched in Clay* is told from several first-person points of view. This means the speaker, or the voice that tells the story, is a character in the story and uses pronouns such as *I, me*, and *we*. Mood and tone can be described by adjectives such as *intense, serious*, and *angry*.

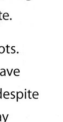

⏻ SETTING A PURPOSE

As you read, pay attention to the speaker of each poem. What event does each speaker describe? What is each speaker's tone?

from *Etched in Clay*

by Andrea Cheng

End Slave Literacy

A NULLIFIER, 1834

David Walker in Boston,
Nat Turner in Virginia,
stirring up the slaves
these past few years,
5   killing white men,
innocent women,
and children too.
It's just plain wrong,
and we have had enough!
10 People, you must understand
that when you teach a slave
to read and write,
you are giving him the tools
to send out a message
15 and plan his escape—
or worse,
to slit your throat.
Let us pass a law
here in South Carolina:
20 a slave who learns to write
will be given twenty lashes,
and his teacher will pay
a hefty fine.

stirring up: agitating or disturbing the quiet

The term **fine** is a multiple-meaning word that in this context means a sum of money imposed as a punishment. You determine the meaning by the context clue *hefty*. *Hefty* is an adjective that means "substantial or heavy."

Etched in Clay

DAVE, JUNE 12, 1834

Only me here,
turning pots, making jars,
turning words inside my head
until I'm ready to explode
5 like a jar with an air bubble
in the furnace.

Magnanimous,
sagacity,
concatenation.
10 Here, on this jar
for all to see,
I'll inscribe the date,
June 12, 1834,
and the word
15 *Concatination.*
Someday the world will read
my word etched in clay
on the side of this jar
and know about the shackles
20 around our legs
and the whips
upon our backs.

furnace: an apparatus or appliance to produce heat, sometimes used to melt metals

sagacity: wisdom

magnanimous: generous and kind

concatenation: a group of elements linked together in a series

I am not afraid
to write on a jar
25 and fire it hot
so my word
can never be erased.
And if some day
this jar cracks,
30 my word will stay,
etched in the shards.

What in the context of this sentence helps you understand the meaning of **shards**?

A Poem!

DAVE, JULY 12, 1834

The summer's so hot,
it's like we're living
in the furnace.
The clay doesn't like it either,
5 getting hard on me
too quick.
I better hurry now,
before the sun's too low to see.

Is sun's a possessive noun or is it a contraction for "the sun is"?

What words will I scrawl
10 across the shoulder
of this jar?
I hear Lydia's voice in my head.
Be careful, Dave.
Those words in clay
15 *can get you killed.*
But I will die of silence
if I keep my words inside me
any longer.
Doctor Landrum used to say
20 it's best to write a poem a day,
for it calms the body
and the soul
to shape those words.

This jar is a beauty,
25 big and wide,
fourteen gallons
I know it will hold.
I have the words now,
and my stick is sharp.
30 I write:
put every bit all between
surely this Jar will hold 14.

To shape is used as a metaphor here. Reread the sentence. What do you think "to shape those words" means?

Anti-Literacy Law

MEMBER OF SOUTH CAROLINA GENERAL ASSEMBLY,
DECEMBER 17, 1834

New law, passed today by the
South Carolina General Assembly:
Any white person
convicted of teaching a slave
5   to read or write
will be fined up to one hundred dollars
and put in prison for up to six months.
Any slave
convicted of teaching another slave
10 to read or write
will get fifty lashes.
Any informers
will receive half the money collected
from the fines.

⏻ COLLABORATIVE DISCUSSION

Discussing the Purpose With a partner, identify evidence from the text as you discuss the following questions:

- What do the speakers say and do? What effect do they have on others, if any?
- How does each speaker's voice add to the overall meaning of this narrative?
- How do the time period and setting reflect the beliefs of the slaveowners?
- How do repetition and rhythm contribute to the overall mood and tone of this narrative?
- How does the poet use line length and italics to emphasize meaning?

SPEAKING TOOLBOX

Reading Aloud with Expression

When reading poetry aloud, use your voice to convey and enhance the meaning of the words you are saying. Pay attention to the meaning of particular words, the way the words are written, and the punctuation used. This will help you to make decisions about the best way to communicate what you are reading. Modulate, or vary, your voice for different effects. Read words carefully, picking which syllables in words to emphasize.

To modulate your voice, speak:

fast or slow   high or low   loud or soft   flat or emotionally

Speak Out!   Memorize the second poem, "Etched in Clay." Practice reciting it several times to yourself. Then, recite the poem to a small group. Follow the tips above when speaking with expression.

Don Quixote

There are many ways to create imaginary worlds.

ABOUT THE NOVEL   *The Ingenious Gentleman Don Quixote of La Mancha* is often cited as the first modern novel in history. It's one of the most translated and published books, after the Bible.

Miguel de Cervantes intended for his two-volume novel to be a satire of books of chivalry, in which knights dedicated their lives to honor and chivalry, while swearing their love and loyalty for an unobtainable lady.

ABOUT THE AUTHOR   Miguel de Cervantes was born in central Spain in 1547. A poet, novelist, and playwright, he is compared often to Shakespeare, who died the day after he did in 1616.

Cervantes is one of the most renowned authors in the world, and one of the leaders of the Golden Century of Spain. This period in Spanish history from 1492 to 1659 is known for its great contributions to humanities. It starts with Christopher Columbus's first trip to the New World. It also includes the works by Velázquez and El Greco in art, and Cervantes and Lope de Vega in literature.

⏻ SETTING A PURPOSE

As you read, think about what motivates Don Quixote and Sancho Panza to behave and act the way they do. Also, consider the order of events in the story. What happens, and when?

Miguel de Cervantes'

Don Quixote

retold by Candy Rodó

IN A VILLAGE OF LA MANCHA, THE NAME OF WHICH I HAVE NO DESIRE TO CALL TO MIND, THERE LIVED NOT LONG AGO . . .

. . . A GENTLEMAN, ALONSO QUIJANO, WHO WAS CAPTIVATED BY EPIC TALES.

DAY AND NIGHT HE SPENT READING OF KNIGHTS, AND PRINCESSES, AND CHIVALROUS DEEDS, UNTIL HIS MIND WAS LOST.

HE DECIDED TO WEAR HIS OLD ARMOR AND CALL HIMSELF A KNIGHT. HE VOWED TO SUPPORT HIS OWN HONOR AND TO SERVE HIS COUNTRY.

But every knight needs his lady, and mine will be Dulcinea del Toboso.

WITH HIS HORSE, A STEED IN HIS EYES, WHOM HE CALLED ROCINANTE, HE LEFT HIS VILLAGE IN SEARCH OF ADVENTURES.

THUS, THE NAME HE GAVE HIMSELF WAS DON QUIXOTE DE LA MANCHA.

Uncle, don't go!

HE SAW AN INN, AND THINKING IT A CASTLE, ASKED THE INNKEEPER TO DUB HIM A KNIGHT.

HAVING FUN WITH HIS GUEST'S LACK OF WITS, THE INNKEEPER WENT ALONG WITH THE STORY AND AGREED.

DON QUIXOTE GUARDED HIS ARMOR ALL NIGHT . . .

. . . AND LEFT A KNIGHT IN THE MORNING.

Every knight must have several sets of clothing and a good amount of money!

Thank you, milady! I'll return home and get ready.

ON HIS WAY HOME, HE GOT INTO A BRAWL WITH TWO MERCHANTS . . .

Swear that Dulcinea is the fairest lady in the whole world!

Sure, but she's missing an arm, ha, ha!

And an eye!

HE LOST. DELIRIOUS, HE STARTED RECITING
LINES FROM THE BOOKS HE LOVES.

"Amadis is called
The Child of the
Sea, beautiful to
a wonder…"

A LOCAL PEASANT RECOGNIZED
HIM AND HELPED HIM GET HOME.

Come, Don Alonso,
let's take you back
to your niece.

Oh, uncle! How
can we stop this
nonsense?

His friend the
priest will know
what to do!

THE PRIEST CAME TO VISIT HIS FRIEND.

It's all because of
those silly books!

Let's burn
them all!

BEING HOME HELPED DON QUIXOTE
RECOVER, BUT HE STILL HAD IN
MIND TO FIND A PROPER SQUIRE.

Come with me in my
adventures and I'll make
you governor of an island!
What's your name?

Sancho Panza, sir.

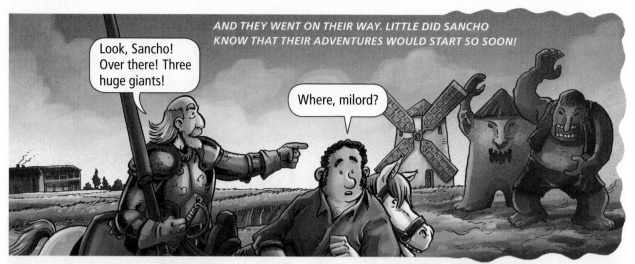

AND THEY WENT ON THEIR WAY. LITTLE DID SANCHO KNOW THAT THEIR ADVENTURES WOULD START SO SOON!

Look, Sancho! Over there! Three huge giants!

Where, milord?

Those are windmills, milord! Wait!

Windmills, milord! Those were no giants!

Ouch!

IN HIS DESIRE FOR ADVENTURE, HE SAW FOES EVERYWHERE.

A lady in distress! Those rascals have kidnapped her!

I will spare your life, most valiant man, if you command yourself to the wishes of my Lady Dulcinea!

I will, milord!

SO MANY ADVENTURES MADE SANCHO WEARY.

Milord, when will you make me governor of an island?

Soon, my dear Sancho, you will have treasures beyond belief!

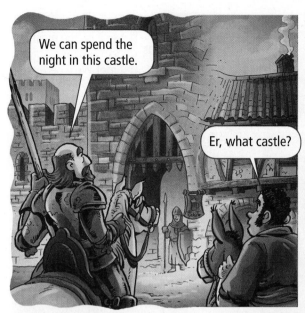

We can spend the night in this castle.

Er, what castle?

IN THE MORNING, THEY GOT READY TO LEAVE.

Ahem . . . there's the small issue of the payment . . .

Payment? Knights don't pay to stay in castles!

You will pay, then!

FINALLY, DON QUIXOTE AND SANCHO PANZA WERE ALLOWED TO LEAVE . . .

. . . BUT THEY KEPT THEIR SADDLEBAGS.

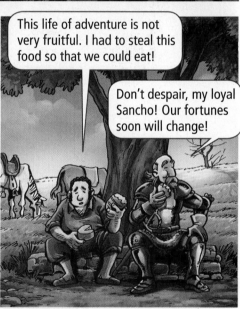

This life of adventure is not very fruitful. I had to steal this food so that we could eat!

Don't despair, my loyal Sancho! Our fortunes soon will change!

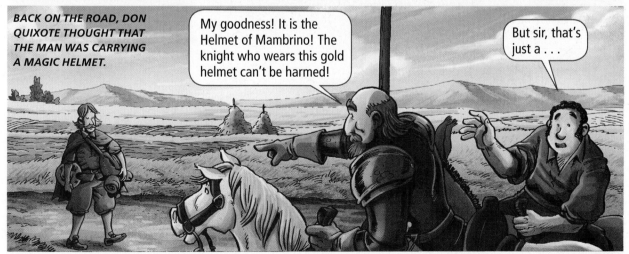

BACK ON THE ROAD, DON QUIXOTE THOUGHT THAT THE MAN WAS CARRYING A MAGIC HELMET.

My goodness! It is the Helmet of Mambrino! The knight who wears this gold helmet can't be harmed!

But sir, that's just a . . .

275

THEY DRAGGED THEMSELVES TO AN INN FOR THE NIGHT.

Master, I want to go home.

Nonsense, Sancho.

Those are the thieves who stole my basin!

Thank you for defending my honor, my most loyal esquire! I will make you a knight!

Not me, sir!

POOR SANCHO HAD HAD ENOUGH OF CHIVALROUS FEATS, BUT DON QUIXOTE WASN'T QUITE DONE. WHEN DON QUIXOTE SAW A GROUP OF WEARY TRAVELERS, HE THOUGHT THEY WERE BANDITS.

Thieves, Sancho! Let's finish with these rascals!

Don Quixote. You're hurt!

My dear friend, I think it's time to go home for a while.

AT HOME, HIS NIECE AND HIS HOUSEKEEPER WERE RELIEVED TO HAVE HIM BACK.

I leave you in good hands, milord. But I'll be ready for more adventures when you recover!

⏻ COLLABORATIVE DISCUSSION

Discussing the Purpose With a partner, discuss Don Quixote's and Sancho Panza's motivations for their behavior and actions. How do their actions affect the order of events?

Exploring Characters

Recall that character traits are the qualities shown by a character. These qualities can include physical traits, such as strength or speed. Character traits can also be expressions of personality. For example, a character may be brave. Consider the following questions. Remember to cite text evidence to support your answers.

1. **Analyze** What physical character traits do Don Quixote and Sancho Panza exhibit?

2. **Analyze** What expressions of personality do Don Quixote and Sancho Panza show?

3. **Evaluate** Do Don Quixote and Sancho Panza's character traits change throughout the story? How do they respond to events that happen? What is the resolution of the story?

Vocabulary Strategy: Degrees of Comparison

Suffixes are added to the end of words. When you add *-er* and *-est* to adjectives, you are comparing, or showing, a difference between things. These **comparatives** (*-er = more*) and **superlatives** (*-est = most*) indicate relationships.

> Swear that Dulcinea is the fairest lady in the whole world! (page 272)
>
> fairest = most fair

In this sentence, the suffix -*est* is showing a comparison. In this context, *fair* means "beautiful." Don Quixote always believed that Dulcinea was fair, or beautiful, and believes it even more now.

Be aware that adding the suffixes -*er* and -*est* to some words will require additional spelling changes. Words with one syllable ending in a vowel and then a consonant require doubling the consonant, as in *big* and *bigger*. Two-syllable words ending in –*y* require changing the –*y* to an –*i* before adding the suffix, as in *happy* and *happiest*. Some words do not get the suffix -*er* or -*est* added; instead the word *more* or *most* is added before the word, as in *more valiant*.

Practice and Apply
Find other comparatives and superlatives in *Don Quixote*. If the words are comparatives, change them to superlatives. If they are superlatives, change them to comparatives.

Speak Out!
You've now read epic tales from two different cultures: *The Ramayana* and *Don Quixote*. With a partner, compare and contrast these two texts. Are the themes alike or different? Why are these epics so important in their cultures? Do they share any customs or values?

Performance Task

Writing Activity: Literary Analysis

In this unit, you have read stories from different cultures and set in different places. Your task is to explore story elements in a literary analysis.

Planning and Prewriting

Connect to the Theme

Culture can relate to the theme; impact characters' traits, behaviors, and motivations; play a part in setting; and influence the plot. Authors use style elements such as imagery and point of view to explain cultural events or why they feel the way they do.

In this activity, you'll be writing an essay that analyzes literature. You will consider how story and style elements shape a narrative. You can investigate elements within one piece of fiction, or you can compare and contrast elements across more than one. First, decide what you will be examining. What story elements will you discuss?

Write Down Possible Questions

Consider the stories you read, and their important story elements. Write down several possible ways you can analyze the literature that you read. Choose one of these topics to write about. Here are some examples:

- What lesson does the main character in *Don Quixote* learn? How does this main character change from the beginning to the end?

- How is the main character of *Etched in Clay* like the main character in *The Ramayana*? How are they different?

- What actions does the main character of *The Ramayana* take to resolve a problem or conflict?

- How does the author of *Etched in Clay* repeat an important idea or image?

Decide the Basics

Now that you have your topic, this will become your main idea. You will support your idea with examples and details from the stories. Ask yourself these questions:

Characters

- What are your impressions of the characters?
- How are the characters described?
- What are the characters' relationships to one another?

Plot

- What are the important story events?
- What is the conflict?
- What is the resolution?

Characters' Actions

- What are the characters' motivations for their actions?
- What do the characters think or say?
- Do the characters change how they feel about something or someone?

Style Elements

- How does the author convey the theme?
- How is the setting significant to the plot?
- What details suggest the mood and the tone of the story?
- How does the author use word choice and point of view to emphasize important ideas?
- How does the title of the story fit into the theme?

Performance Task

Finalize Your Plan

You've got the basics down. You are ready to determine the main ideas of the stories you read; you know which examples you'll use to support your ideas. Now you need to present the information—in other words, a structure.

Use the diagram in the Writing Toolbox to help you.

WRITING TOOLBOX

Elements of A Literary Analysis

Introduction	"Hook" your audience with an interesting detail, question, or quotation that relates to your main idea. Identify what you will be describing, and state your controlling idea.
Main Idea and Details	Follow a framework like the one shown here to organize your main ideas and supporting evidence. Include relevant facts, concrete details, and other text evidence. Restate your ideas.
Conclusion	Summarize the key points and restate your controlling idea. Include an insight that follows from and supports your controlling idea.

Don't forget to refine your Personal Toolboxes with strategies that work for you.

Draft Your Analysis

You've got it all planned out. You've decided on your main idea, or controlling idea, and you have all the supporting evidence you need from the text. And you have a way to organize your ideas. Now it's time to start writing. As you write, think about:

- **Purpose and Audience** What effect do you want the analysis to have on readers? Demonstrate your understanding of the requirements of writing a literary analysis.

- **Clarity** Make sure your ideas are straightforward and understandable. Your sentences are clearly worded and appear in logical order.

- **Support** Include examples from the stories that support your ideas.

- **Style** Use a formal and objective tone.

- **Transition** Use transitional words and time-order phrases to show how one idea relates to another.

Revise

Self Evaluation

Use the checklist and rubric to guide your analysis.

Peer Review

Exchange your literary analysis with a classmate. Use the checklist to comment on your classmate's work.

Edit

Edit your literary analysis to correct spelling, grammar, and punctuation errors.

Publish

Finalize your literary analysis and choose a way to share it with your audience.

Student Resources

Grammar

Writing that has a lot of mistakes can confuse or even annoy a reader. Punctuation errors in a letter might lead to a miscommunication or delay a reply. A sentence fragment might lower your grade on an essay. Paying attention to grammar, punctuation, and capitalization rules can make your writing clearer and easier to read.

Quick Reference: Parts of Speech

Part of Speech	Function	Examples
Noun	names a person, a place, a thing, an idea, a quality, or an action	
Common	serves as a general name, or a name common to an entire group	subway, fog, puzzle, tollbooth
Proper	names a specific, one-of-a-kind person, place, or thing	Mrs. Price, Pompeii, China, Meg
Singular	refers to a single person, place, thing, or idea	onion, waterfall, lamb, sofa
Plural	refers to more than one person, place, thing, or idea	dreams, commercials, men, tortillas
Concrete	names something that can be perceived by the senses	jacket, teacher, caterpillar, aroma
Abstract	names something that cannot be perceived by the senses	friendship, opportunities, fear, stubbornness
Compound	expresses a single idea through a combination of two or more words	jump rope, paycheck, dragonfly, sandpaper
Collective	refers to a group of people or things	colony, family, clan, flock
Possessive	shows who or what owns something	Mama's, Tito's, children's, waitresses'
Pronoun	takes the place of a noun or another pronoun	
Personal	refers to the person making a statement, the person(s) being addressed, or the person(s) or thing(s) the statement is about	I, me, my, mine, we, us, our, ours, you, your, yours, she, he, it, her, him, hers, his, its, they, them, their, theirs
Reflexive	follows a verb or preposition and refers to a preceding noun or pronoun	myself, yourself, herself, himself, itself, ourselves, yourselves, themselves

continued

Part of Speech	Function	Examples
Intensive	emphasizes a noun or another pronoun	(same as reflexives)
Demonstrative	points to one or more specific persons or things	this, that, these, those
Interrogative	signals a question	who, whom, whose, which, what
Indefinite	refers to one or more persons or things not specifically mentioned	both, all, most, many, anyone, everybody, several, none, some
Relative	introduces an adjective clause by relating it to a word in the clause	who, whom, whose, which, that
Verb	expresses an action, a condition, or a state of being	
Action	tells what the subject does or did, physically or mentally	run, reaches, listened, consider, decides, dreamed
Linking	connects the subject to something that identifies or describes it	am, is, are, was, were, sound, taste, appear, feel, become, remain, seem
Auxiliary	precedes the main verb in a verb phrase	be, have, do, can, could, will, would, may, might
Transitive	directs the action toward someone or something; always has an object	The storm **sank** the ship.
Intransitive	does not direct the action toward someone or something; does not have an object	The ship **sank.**
Adjective	modifies a noun or pronoun	**strong** women, **two** epics, **enough** time
Adverb	modifies a verb, an adjective, or another adverb	walked **out, really** funny, **far** away
Preposition	relates one word to another word	at, by, for, from, in, of, on, to, with
Conjunction	joins words or word groups	
Coordinating	joins words or word groups used the same way	and, but, or, for, so, yet, nor
Correlative	used as a pair to join words or word groups used the same way	both . . . and, either . . . or, neither . . . nor
Subordinating	introduces a clause that cannot stand by itself as a complete sentence	although, after, as, before, because, when, if, unless
Interjection	expresses emotion	wow, ouch, hurrah

Quick Reference: The Sentence and Its Parts

The diagrams that follow will give you a brief review of the essentials of a sentence and some of its parts.

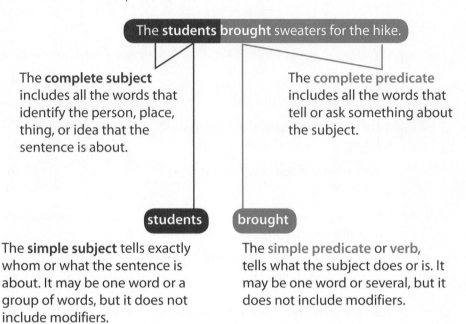

The **students brought** sweaters for the hike.

The **complete subject** includes all the words that identify the person, place, thing, or idea that the sentence is about.

The complete predicate includes all the words that tell or ask something about the subject.

students

The **simple subject** tells exactly whom or what the sentence is about. It may be one word or a group of words, but it does not include modifiers.

brought

The simple predicate or verb, tells what the subject does or is. It may be one word or several, but it does not include modifiers.

Every word in a sentence is part of a complete subject or a complete predicate.

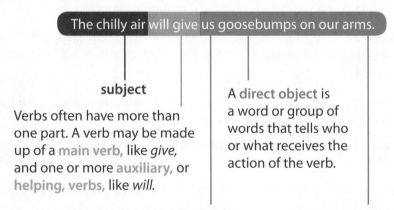

The chilly air will give us goosebumps on our arms.

subject

Verbs often have more than one part. A verb may be made up of a main verb, like *give*, and one or more auxiliary, or helping, verbs, like *will*.

A direct object is a word or group of words that tells who or what receives the action of the verb.

An **indirect object** is a word or group of words that tells to whom or for whom or to what or for what the verb's action is performed. A sentence can have an indirect object only if it has a direct object. The indirect object always comes before the direct object.

A **prepositional phrase** consists of a preposition, its object, and any modifiers of the object. In this phrase, *on* is the preposition, *arms* is the object, and *our* modifies *arms*.

Quick Reference: Punctuation

Mark	Function	Examples

End Marks
  period,
  question mark,
  exclamation
  point
	ends a sentence	We can start now.
		When would you like to leave?
		What a fantastic hit!

period	follows an initial or abbreviation **Exception**: postal abbreviations of states	Mrs. Dorothy Parker, Apple Inc., C. P. Cavafy, P.M., lb., oz., Blvd., Dr., NE (Nebraska), NV (Nevada)

period	follows a number or letter in an outline or a list	I. Volcanoes
		  A. Central-vent
		    1. Shield

Comma	separates parts of a compound sentence	I had never disliked poetry, but now I really love it.
	separates items in a series	She is brave, loyal, and kind.
	separates adjectives of equal rank that modify the same noun	The slow, easy route is best.
	sets off a term of address	Maria, how can I help you? You must do something, soldier.
	sets off a parenthetical expression	Hard workers, as you know, don't quit. I'm not a quitter, believe me.
	sets off an introductory word, phrase, or dependent clause	Yes, I forgot my key. At the beginning of the day, I feel fresh. While she was out, I was here. Having finished my chores, I went out.
	sets off a nonessential phrase or clause	Ed Pawn, the captain of the chess team, won. Ed Pawn, who is the captain, won. The two leading runners, sprinting toward the finish line, finished in a tie.
	sets off parts of dates and addresses	Mail it by May 14, 2010, to the Hauptman Company, 321 Market Street, Memphis, Tennessee.
	separates words to avoid confusion	By noon, time had run out. What the minister does, does matter. While cooking, Jim burned his hand.

continued

Mark	Function	Examples
Semicolon	separates items in a series that contain commas	We spent the first week of summer vacation in Chicago, Illinois; the second week in St. Louis, Missouri; and the third week in Albany, New York.
	separates parts of a compound sentence that are not joined by a coordinating conjunction	The last shall be first; the first shall be last. I read the Bible; however, I have not memorized it.
	separates parts of a compound sentence when the parts contain commas	After I ran out of money, I called my parents; but only my sister was home, unfortunately.
Colon	introduces a list	The names we wrote were the following: Dana, John, and Will.
	introduces a long quotation	Abraham Lincoln wrote: "Four score and seven years ago, our fathers brought forth on this continent a new nation. . . ."
	follows the salutation of a business letter	To Whom It May Concern: Dear Leonard Atole:
	separates certain numbers	1:28 P.M., Genesis 2:5
Dash	indicates an abrupt break in thought	I was thinking of my mother—who is arriving tomorrow— just as you walked in.
Parentheses	enclose less important material	It was so unlike him (John is always on time) that I began to worry. The last World Series game (did you see it?) was fun.
Ellipses	replace material omitted from a quotation	"Early one morning, Mrs. Bunnin wobbled into the classroom lugging a large cardboard box. . . . Robert was at his desk scribbling a ball-point tattoo . . . on the tops of his knuckles."
Italics	indicate the title of a book, a play, a magazine, a long poem, an opera, a film, or a TV series, or the name of a ship	*Colin Powell: Military Leader, The Prince and the Pauper, Time, After the Hurricane, The Marriage of Figaro, Hatchet, American Idol, Titanic*

continued

Mark	Function	Examples
Hyphen	joins parts of a compound adjective before a noun	That's a not-so-happy face.
	joins parts of a compound with *all-, ex-, self-,* or *-elect*	The ex-firefighter helped rescue him. Our president-elect is self-conscious.
	joins parts of a compound number (to ninety-nine)	My bicycle wheel has twenty-six spokes.
	joins parts of a fraction	My cup is one-third full.
	joins a prefix to a word beginning with a capital letter	Were your grandparents born post-World War II? The mid-April snow-storm surprised everyone.
	indicates that a word is divided at the end of a line	How could you have any reason-able expectations of getting a new computer?

Quick Reference: Capitalization

Category	Examples
People and Titles	
Names and initials of people	Maya Angelou, **W.E.B. DuBois**
Titles used before a name	Mrs. Price, Scoutmaster Brenkman
Deities and members of religious groups	Jesus, Allah, Buddha, Zeus, Baptists
Names of ethnic and national groups	Hispanics, Jews, African Americans
Geographical Names	
Cities, states, countries, continents	Philadelphia, Kansas, Japan, Europe
Regions, bodies of water, mountains	the South, Lake Baikal, Mount Everest
Geographic features, parks	Great Basin, Yellowstone National Park
Streets and roads, planets	318 East Sutton Drive, Charles Court, Jupiter, Mars
Organizations, Events, Etc.	
Companies, organizations, teams	Ford Motor Company, Boy Scouts of America, St. Louis Cardinals
Buildings, bridges, monuments	Empire State Building, Eads Bridge, Washington Monument
Documents, awards	Declaration of Independence, Stanley Cup
Special named events	Mardi Gras, World Series
Government bodies, historical periods and events	U.S. Senate, House of Representatives, Middle Ages, Vietnam War
Days and months, holidays	Thursday, March, Thanksgiving, Labor Day
Specific cars, boats, trains, planes	Porsche, *Carpathia*, *Southwest Chief*, Concorde
Proper Adjectives	
Adjectives formed from proper nouns	French cooking, Spanish omelet, Edwardian age

continued

First Words and the Pronoun *I*	
First word in a sentence or quotation	**T**his is it. **H**e said, "**L**et's go." **I** have it.
First word of a sentence in parentheses that is not within another sentence	The spelling rules are covered in another section. (**C**onsult that section for more information.)
First words in the salutation and closing of a letter	**D**ear Madam, **V**ery truly yours,
First word, last word, and all important words in a title	"**A**lone in the **N**ets," *Under the Royal Palms*

Grammar Handbook

1 Nouns

A **noun** is a word used to name a person, a place, a thing, an idea, a quality, or an action. Nouns can be classified in several ways.

For more information on different types of nouns, see **Quick Reference: Parts of Speech,** page R2.

1.1 COMMON NOUNS

Common nouns are general names, common to entire groups.

1.2 PROPER NOUNS

Proper nouns name specific, one-of-a-kind people, places, and things.

Common	Proper
volcano, student, country, president	Mount Vesuvius, June, China, President Cleveland

For more information, see **Quick Reference: Capitalization,** page R8.

1.3 SINGULAR AND PLURAL NOUNS

A noun may take a singular or a plural form, depending on whether it names a single person, place, thing, or idea or more than one. Make sure you use appropriate spellings when forming plurals.

Singular	Plural
walrus, bully, lagoon, goose	walruses, bullies, lagoons, geese

For more information, see **Forming Plural Nouns,** page R68.

1.4 POSSESSIVE NOUNS

A **possessive noun** shows who or what owns something.

For more information, see **Forming Possessives,** page R69.

2 Pronouns

A **pronoun** is a word that is used in place of a noun or another pronoun. The word or word group to which the pronoun refers is called its **antecedent.**

2.1 PERSONAL PRONOUNS

Personal pronouns change their form to express person, number, gender, and case. The forms of these pronouns are shown in the following chart.

	Nominative	Objective	Possessive
Singular			
First Person	I	me	my, mine
Second Person	you	you	your, yours
Third Person	she, he, it	her, him, it	her, hers, his, its
Plural			
First Person	we	us	our, ours
Second Person	you	you	your, yours
Third Person	they	them	their, theirs

2.2 AGREEMENT WITH ANTECEDENT

Pronouns should agree with their antecedents in number, gender, and person.

If an antecedent is singular, use a singular pronoun.

> EXAMPLE: *That **poem** was fun to read. **It** rhymed.*

If an antecedent is plural, use a plural pronoun.

> EXAMPLES: ***Poets** choose **their** words carefully. I like **poems**, but Mischa doesn't care for **them**.*

The gender of a pronoun must be the same as the gender of its antecedent.

> EXAMPLE: ***Eve Merriam's** creativity makes **her** poems easy to remember.*

The person of the pronoun must be the same as the person of its antecedent. As the chart in Section 2.1 shows, a pronoun can be in first-person, second-person, or third-person form.

> EXAMPLES: ***We** each have **our** favorite poets.*

Grammar Practice

Rewrite each sentence so that the underlined pronoun agrees with its antecedent.

1. The speaker in Maya Angelou's poem "Life Doesn't Frighten Me" talks about <u>their</u> fears.
2. When I read this poem, <u>we</u> felt braver already.
3. Scary things lose <u>its</u> power.
4. Even frogs and snakes don't seem as bad as <u>you</u> usually do.
5. I want to know how to be unafraid in <u>her</u> life.

2.3 PRONOUN FORMS

Personal pronouns change form to show how they function in sentences. The three forms are the subject form, the object form, and the possessive form. For examples of these pronouns, see the chart in Section 2.1.

A **subject pronoun** is used as a subject in a sentence.

> EXAMPLES: *Steven is my brother. **He** is the best player on the team.*

Also use the subject form when the pronoun follows a linking verb.

> EXAMPLE: *The girl in the closet was **she**.*

An **object pronoun** is used as a direct object, an indirect object, or the object of a preposition.

SUBJECT   OBJECT
They locked her in it.
OBJECT OF PREPOSITION

A **possessive pronoun** shows ownership. The pronouns *mine, yours, hers, his, its, ours,* and *theirs* can be used in place of nouns.

> EXAMPLE: *The cat is **mine**.*

The pronouns *my, your, her, his, its, our,* and *their* are used before nouns.

> EXAMPLE: *I found **her** keys on the floor.*

WATCH OUT! Many spelling errors can be avoided if you watch out for *its* and *their*. Don't confuse the possessive pronoun *its* with the contraction *it's*, meaning "it is" or "it has." The homonyms *they're* (a contraction of *they are*) and *there* ("in that place") are often mistakenly used for *their*.

TIP To decide which pronoun to use in a comparison, such as "He tells better tales than (*I* or *me*)," fill in the missing word(s): *He tells better tales than I tell.*

Grammar Practice

Write the correct pronoun form to complete each sentence.

1. When (he, him) is done with the book, I will give it to you.
2. Mary is going to invite (her, she) to go rollerskating.
3. My friends have lost (their, they) tickets.
4. (We, Us) can cook vegetables on the grill tonight, or we can make a salad.
5. (I, Me) sent an e-mail earlier today to my aunt.

2.4 REFLEXIVE AND INTENSIVE PRONOUNS

These pronouns are formed by adding *-self* or *-selves* to certain personal pronouns. Their forms are the same, and they differ only in how they are used.

A **reflexive pronoun** follows a verb or preposition and reflects back on an earlier noun or pronoun.

> EXAMPLES: *He likes himself too much. She is now herself again.*

Intensive pronouns intensify or emphasize the nouns or pronouns to which they refer.

> EXAMPLES: *They themselves will educate their children.*
> *You yourself did it.*

WATCH OUT! Avoid using *hisself* or *theirselves.* Standard English does not include these forms.

> NONSTANDARD: *The children congratulated theirselves.*

> STANDARD: *The children congratulated themselves.*

2.5 DEMONSTRATIVE PRONOUNS

Demonstrative pronouns point out things and persons near and far.

	Singular	Plural
Near	this	these
Far	that	those

2.6 INDEFINITE PRONOUNS

Indefinite pronouns do not refer to specific persons or things and usually have no antecedents. The chart shows some commonly used indefinite pronouns.

Singular	Plural	Singular or Plural	
another	both	all	none
anybody	few	any	some
no one	many	more	most
neither			

TIP Indefinite pronouns that end in *one, body,* or *thing* are always singular.

> INCORRECT: *Did everybody play their part well?*

If the indefinite pronoun might refer to either a male or a female, **his or her** may be used to refer to it, or the sentence may be rewritten.

> CORRECT: *Did everybody play his or her part well? Did all the students play their parts well?*

2.7 INTERROGATIVE PRONOUNS

An **interrogative pronoun** tells a reader or listener that a question is coming. The interrogative pronouns are **who, whom, whose, which,** and **what.**

> EXAMPLES: *Who is going to rehearse with you? From whom did you receive the script?*

TIP *Who* is used as a subject; **whom** is used as an object. To find out which pronoun you need to use in a question, change the question to a statement.

> QUESTION: *(Who/Whom) did you meet there?*

> STATEMENT: *You met (?) there.*

Since the verb has a subject (**you**), the needed word must be the object form, **whom.**

> EXAMPLE: *Whom did you meet there?*

WATCH OUT! A special problem arises when you use an interrupter, such as **do you think,** within a question.

> EXAMPLE: *(Who/Whom) do you think will win?*

If you eliminate the interrupter, it is clear that the word you need is **who.**

2.8 RELATIVE PRONOUNS

Relative pronouns relate, or connect, adjective clauses to the words they modify in sentences. The noun or pronoun that a relative clause modifies is the antecedent of the relative pronoun. Here are the relative pronouns and their uses.

	Subject	Object	Possessive
Person	who	whom	whose
Thing	which	which	whose
Thing/Person	that	that	whose

Often, short sentences with related ideas can be combined by using a relative pronoun to create a more effective sentence.

SHORT SENTENCE: *Lucy is an accountant.*

RELATED SENTENCE: *She helped us do our taxes.*

COMBINED SENTENCE: *Lucy is an accountant who helped us do our taxes.*

Grammar Practice

Write the correct form of each incorrect pronoun.

1. John is a car salesman whom helped me buy a new automobile.
2. The pitcher threw the ball to I.
3. To who should I address this letter?
4. Us love the sea.
5. Betty is as smart as her is.

2.9 PRONOUN REFERENCE PROBLEMS

You should always be able to identify the word a pronoun refers to. Avoid problems by rewriting sentences.

An **indefinite reference** occurs when the pronoun *it, you,* or *they* does not clearly refer to a specific antecedent.

UNCLEAR: *They told me how the story ended, and it was annoying.*

CLEAR: *They told me how the story ended, and I was annoyed.*

A **general reference** occurs when the pronoun *it, this, that, which,* or *such* is used to refer to a general idea rather than a specific antecedent.

UNCLEAR: *I'd rather not know what happens. That keeps me interested.*

CLEAR: *I'd rather not know what happens. Not knowing keeps me interested.*

Ambiguous means "having more than one possible meaning." An **ambiguous reference** occurs when a pronoun could refer to two or more antecedents.

UNCLEAR: *Jan told Danielle that she would read her story aloud.*

CLEAR: *Jan told Danielle that she would read Danielle's story aloud.*

Grammar Practice

Rewrite the following sentences to correct indefinite, ambiguous, and general pronoun references.

1. The teacher was speaking to Maggie, and she looked unhappy.
2. High winds developed. This trapped mountain climbers in their tents.
3. Although Matt likes working at a donut shop, he doesn't eat them.
4. The pitcher was set on the glass-topped table and it broke.
5. They unloaded the clothes from the boxes and then threw them away.

3 Verbs

A **verb** is a word that expresses an action, a condition, or a state of being.

For more information, see **Quick Reference: Parts of Speech,** page R2.

3.1 ACTION VERBS

Action verbs express mental or physical activity.

> EXAMPLE: *Lucy ran several miles every day.*

3.2 LINKING VERBS

Linking verbs join subjects with words or phrases that rename or describe them.

> EXAMPLE: *After a few months, her shoes were worn out.*

3.3 PRINCIPAL PARTS

Action and linking verbs typically have four principal parts, which are used to form verb tenses. The principal parts are the **present,** the **present participle,** the **past,** and the **past participle.**

Action verbs and some linking verbs also fall into two categories: regular and irregular.

A **regular verb** is a verb that forms its past and past participle by adding *-ed* or *-d* to the present form.

Present	Present Participle	Past	Past Participle
jump	(is) jumping	jumped	(has) jumped
solve	(is) solving	solved	(has) solved
grab	(is) grabbing	grabbed	(has) grabbed
carry	(is) carrying	carried	(has) carried

An **irregular verb** is a verb that forms its past and past participle in some other way than by adding *–ed* or *–d* to the present form.

Present	Present Participle	Past	Past Participle
begin	(is) beginning	began	(has) begun
break	(is) breaking	broke	(has) broken
go	(is) going	went	(has) gone

3.4 VERB TENSE

The **tense** of a verb indicates the time of the action or the state of being. An action or state of being can occur in the present, the past, or the future. There are six tenses, each expressing a different range of time.

The **present tense** expresses an action or state that is happening at the present time, occurs regularly, or is constant or generally true. Use the present part.

> NOW: *This apple is rotten.*
> REGULAR: *I eat an apple every day.*
> GENERAL: *Apples are round.*

The **past tense** expresses an action that began and ended in the past. Use the past part.

> EXAMPLE: *They settled the argument.*

The **future tense** expresses an action or state that will occur. Use *shall* or *will* with the present part.

> EXAMPLE: *You will understand someday.*

The **present perfect tense** expresses an action or state that (1) was completed at an indefinite time in the past or (2) began in the past and continues into the present. Use *have* or *has* with the past participle.

> EXAMPLE: *These buildings have existed for centuries.*

The **past perfect tense** expresses an action in the past that came before another action in the past. Use *had* with the past participle.

> EXAMPLE: *I had told you, but you forgot.*

The **future perfect tense** expresses an action in the future that will be completed before another action in the future. Use **shall have** or **will have** with the past participle.

> EXAMPLE: *She will have found the note by the time I get home.*

TIP A past-tense form of an irregular verb is not used with an auxiliary, or helping, verb, but a past-participle main irregular verb is always used with an auxiliary verb.

> INCORRECT: *He has did that too many times.* (*Did* is the past-tense form of an irregular verb and shouldn't be used with *has*.)

> INCORRECT: *He done that too many times.* (*Done* is the past participle of an irregular verb and shouldn't be used without an auxiliary verb.)

> CORRECT: *He has done that too many times.*

3.5 PROGRESSIVE FORMS

The progressive forms of the six tenses show ongoing actions. Use forms of **be** with the present participles of verbs.

> PRESENT PROGRESSIVE: *Angelo is taking the test.*
>
> PAST PROGRESSIVE: *Angelo was taking the test.*
>
> FUTURE PROGRESSIVE: *Angelo will be taking the test.*
>
> PRESENT PERFECT PROGRESSIVE: *Angelo has been taking the test.*
>
> PAST PERFECT PROGRESSIVE: *Angelo had been taking the test.*
>
> FUTURE PERFECT PROGRESSIVE: *Angelo will have been taking the test.*

WATCH OUT! Do not shift from tense to tense needlessly. Watch out for these special cases:

- In most compound sentences and in sentences with compound predicates, keep the tenses the same.

> INCORRECT: *She smiled and shake his hand.*
>
> CORRECT: *She smiled and shook his hand.*

- If one past action happens before another, do shift tenses.

INCORRECT: *He remembered what he studied.*

CORRECT: *He remembered what he had studied.*

Grammar Practice

Rewrite each sentence using a form of the verb(s) in parentheses. Identify each form that you use.

1. Helen Keller (become) blind and deaf before she (be) two.
2. A wonderful teacher (change) her life.
3. Anne Sullivan (be) almost blind before she (have) an operation.
4. Even now, Keller (be) an inspiration to everyone with a disability.
5. People (remember) both Helen and her teacher for years to come.

Rewrite each sentence to correct an error in tense.

1. Helen Keller writes a book about her life.
2. She described how she learns to understand language.
3. She felt like she knew it once and forgotten it.
4. Anne Sullivan was a determined teacher and does not give up.
5. Helen had began a life of learning.

3.6 ACTIVE AND PASSIVE VOICE

The voice of a verb tells whether its subject performs or receives the action expressed by the verb. When the subject performs the action, the verb is in the **active voice.** When the subject is the receiver of the action, the verb is in the **passive voice.**

Compare these two sentences:

> ACTIVE: *Nancy Wood wrote "Animal Wisdom."*
>
> PASSIVE: *"Animal Wisdom" was written by Nancy Wood.*

To form the passive voice, use a form of **be** with the past participle of the verb.

WATCH OUT! Use the passive voice sparingly. It can make writing awkward and less direct.

AWKWARD: *"Animal Wisdom" is a poem that was written by Nancy Wood.*

BETTER: *Nancy Wood wrote the poem "Animal Wisdom."*

There are occasions when you will choose to use the passive voice because:

- you want to emphasize the receiver: *The king was shot.*
- the doer is unknown: *My books were stolen.*
- the doer is unimportant: *French is spoken here.*

4 Modifiers

Modifiers are words or groups of words that change or limit the meanings of other words. Adjectives and adverbs are common modifiers.

4.1 ADJECTIVES

Adjectives modify nouns and pronouns by telling which one, what kind, how many, or how much.

WHICH ONE: *this, that, these, those*
EXAMPLE: *This poem moves along quickly.*
WHAT KIND: *square, dirty, fast, regular*
EXAMPLE: *Fast runners make baseball exciting.*
HOW MANY: *some, few, both, thousands*
EXAMPLE: *Thousands of fans cheer in the stands.*
HOW MUCH: *more, less, enough, as much*
EXAMPLE: *I had more fun watching the game than I expected.*

4.2 PREDICATE ADJECTIVES

Most adjectives come before the nouns they modify, as in the examples above. A **predicate adjective,** however, follows a linking verb and describes the subject.

EXAMPLE: *Baseball players are strong.*

Be especially careful to use adjectives (not adverbs) after such linking verbs as *look, feel, grow, taste,* and *smell.*

EXAMPLE: *Exercising feels good.*

4.3 ADVERBS

Adverbs modify verbs, adjectives, and other adverbs by telling where, when, how, or to what extent.

WHERE: *The children played outside.*
WHEN: *The author spoke yesterday.*
HOW: *We walked slowly behind the leader.*
TO WHAT EXTENT: *He worked very hard.*

Adverbs may occur in many places in sentences, both before and after the words they modify.

EXAMPLE: *Suddenly the wind shifted.*
The wind suddenly shifted.
The wind shifted suddenly.

4.4 ADJECTIVE OR ADVERB?

Many adverbs are formed by adding *–ly* to adjectives.

EXAMPLES: *sweet, sweetly; gentle, gently*

However, *–ly* added to a noun will usually yield an adjective.

EXAMPLES: *friend, friendly; woman, womanly*

4.5 COMPARISON OF MODIFIERS

Modifiers can be used to compare two or more things. The form of a modifier shows the degree of comparison. Both adjectives and adverbs have **comparative** and **superlative forms.**

The **comparative form** is used to compare two things, groups, or actions.

EXAMPLES: *Today's weather is hotter than yesterday's.*
The boy got tired more quickly than his sister did.

The **superlative form** is used to compare more than two things, groups, or actions.

> EXAMPLES: *This has been the hottest month ever recorded.*
>
> *Older people were most affected by the heat.*

4.6 REGULAR COMPARISONS

Most one-syllable and some two-syllable adjectives and adverbs have comparatives and superlatives formed by adding *-er* and *-est.* All three-syllable and most two-syllable modifiers have comparatives and superlatives formed with *more* or *most.*

Modifier	Comparative	Superlative
messy	messier	messiest
quick	quicker	quickest
wild	wilder	wildest
tired	more tired	most tired
often	more often	most often

WATCH OUT! Note that spelling changes must sometimes be made to form the comparatives and superlatives of modifiers.

> AWKWARD: *friendly, friendlier* (Change *y* to *i* and add the ending.)
>
> *sad, sadder* (Double the final consonant and add the ending.)

4.7 IRREGULAR COMPARISONS

Some commonly used modifiers have irregular comparative and superlative forms. They are listed in the following chart. You may wish to memorize them.

Modifier	Comparative	Superlative
good	better	best
bad	worse	more
far	farther *or* further	farthest *or* furthest
little	less *or* lesser	least
many	more	most
well	better	best
much	more	most

4.8 PROBLEMS WITH MODIFIERS

Study the tips that follow to avoid common mistakes.

Farther* and *Further Use *farther* for distances; use *further* for everything else.

Double Comparisons Make a comparison by using *-er/-est* or by using *more/most.* Using *-er* with *more* or using *-est* with *most* is incorrect.

> INCORRECT: *I like her more better than she likes me.*
>
> CORRECT: *I like her better than she likes me.*

Illogical Comparisons An illogical or confusing comparison occurs when two unrelated things are compared or when something is compared with itself. The word *other* or the word *else* should be used when comparing an individual member to the rest of a group.

> ILLOGICAL: *I like "A Voice" more than any poem.* (implies that "A Voice" isn't a poem)
>
> LOGICAL: *I like "A Voice" more than any other poem.* (identifies that "A Voice" is a poem)

Bad* vs. *Badly *Bad,* always an adjective, is used before a noun or after a linking verb. *Badly,* always an adverb, never modifies a noun. Be sure to use the right form after a linking verb.

INCORRECT: *I felt badly that I missed the game.*

CORRECT: *I felt bad that I missed the game.*

Good vs. Well *Good* is always an adjective. It is used before a noun or after a linking verb. *Well* is often an adverb meaning "expertly" or "properly." *Well* can also be used as an adjective after a linking verb when it means "in good health."

INCORRECT: *I wrote my essay good.*

CORRECT: *I wrote my essay well.*

CORRECT: *I didn't feel well when I wrote it, though.*

Double Negatives If you add a negative word to a sentence that is already negative, the result will be an error known as a double negative. When using *not* or *-n't* with a verb, use *any-* words, such as *anybody* or *anything,* rather than *no-* words, such as *nobody* or *nothing,* later in the sentence.

INCORRECT: *The teacher didn't like nobody's paper.*

CORRECT: *The teacher didn't like anybody's paper.*

Using *hardly, barely,* or *scarcely* after a negative word is also incorrect.

INCORRECT: *My friends couldn't hardly catch up.*

CORRECT: *My friends could hardly catch up.*

Misplaced Modifiers Sometimes a modifier is placed so far away from the word it modifies that the intended meaning of the sentence is unclear. Prepositional phrases and participial phrases are often misplaced. Place modifiers as close as possible to the words they modify.

MISPLACED: *We found the child in the park who was missing.*

CLEARER: *We found the child who was missing in the park.* (The child was missing, not the park.)

Dangling Modifiers Sometimes a modifier doesn't appear to modify any word in a sentence. Most dangling modifiers are participial phrases or infinitive phrases.

DANGLING: *Looking out the window, his brother was seen driving by.*

CLEARER: *Looking out the window, Josh saw his brother driving by.*

Grammar Practice

Choose the correct word from each pair in parentheses.

1. According to my neighbor, squirrels are a (bad, badly) problem in the area.
2. The (worst, worse) time of the year to go to India is in the summer.
3. The boy didn't have (any, no) interest in playing baseball.
4. Molly sings really (good, well), though.
5. Tom was (more, most) daring than any other boy scout on the trip.

Grammar Practice

Rewrite each sentence that contains a misplaced or dangling modifier. Write "correct" if the sentence is written correctly.

1. Coyotes know how to survive in the wild.
2. Hunting their prey, we have seen them in the forest.
3. Looking out the window, a coyote was seen in the yard.
4. My brother and I found books about coyotes at the library.
5. We learned that wolves are their natural enemies reading about them.

5 The Sentence and Its Parts

A **sentence** is a group of words used to express a complete thought. A complete sentence has a subject and a predicate.

For more information, see **Quick Reference: The Sentence and Its Parts,** page R4.

5.1 KINDS OF SENTENCES

There are four basic types of sentences.

Type	Definition	Example
Declarative	states a fact, a wish, an intent, or a feeling	Salisbury writes about young people.
Interrogative	asks a question	Have you read "The Ravine"?
Imperative	gives a command or direction	Find a copy.
Exclamatory	expresses strong feeling or excitement	It's really suspenseful!

5.2 COMPOUND SUBJECTS AND PREDICATES

A compound subject consists of two or more subjects that share the same verb. They are typically joined by the coordinating conjunction *and* or *or.*

EXAMPLE: *A short story or novel will keep you interested.*

A compound predicate consists of two or more predicates that share the same subject. They too are usually joined by a coordinating conjunction such as *and, but,* or *or.*

EXAMPLE: *The class finished all the poetry but did not read the short stories.*

5.3 COMPLEMENTS

A **complement** is a word or group of words that completes the meaning of a sentence. Some sentences contain only a subject and a verb. Most sentences, however, require additional words placed after the verb to complete the meaning of the sentence. There are three kinds of complements: direct objects, indirect objects, and subject complements.

Direct objects are words or word groups that receive the action of action verbs. A direct object answers the question *what* or *who.*

EXAMPLES: *Daria caught the ball.* (Caught what?)
She tagged the runner. (Tagged who?)

Indirect objects tell to whom or what or for whom or what the actions of verbs are performed. Indirect objects come before direct objects. In the examples that follow, the indirect objects are highlighted.

EXAMPLES: *The audience gave us a standing ovation.* (Gave to whom?)
We offered the newspaper an interview.
(Offered to what?)

Subject complements come after linking verbs and identify or describe the subjects. A subject complement that names or identifies a subject is called a **predicate nominative.** Predicate nominatives include **predicate nouns** and **predicate pronouns.**

EXAMPLES: *The students were happy campers.*
The best actor in the play is he.

A subject complement that describes a subject is called a **predicate adjective.**

EXAMPLE: *The coach seemed thrilled.*

6 Phrases

A **phrase** is a group of related words that does not contain a subject and a predicate but functions in a sentence as a single part of speech.

6.1 PREPOSITIONAL PHRASES

A **prepositional phrase** is a phrase that consists of a preposition, its object, and any modifiers of the object. Prepositional phrases that modify nouns or pronouns are called **adjective phrases.** Prepositional phrases that modify verbs, adjectives, or adverbs are **adverb phrases.**

ADJECTIVE PHRASE: *The central character of the story is a villain.*

ADVERB PHRASE: *He reveals his nature in the first scene.*

6.2 APPOSITIVES AND APPOSITIVE PHRASES

An **appositive** is a noun or pronoun that identifies or renames another noun or pronoun. An **appositive phrase** includes an appositive and modifiers of it. An appositive usually follows the noun or pronoun it identifies.

An appositive can be either **essential** or **nonessential.** An **essential appositive** provides information that is needed to identify what is referred to by the preceding noun or pronoun.

> EXAMPLE: *Longfellow's poem is about the American patriot Paul Revere.*

A **nonessential appositive** adds extra information about a noun or pronoun whose meaning is already clear. Nonessential appositives and appositive phrases are set off with commas.

> EXAMPLE: *The story, a poem, has historical inaccuracies.*

7 Verbals and Verbal Phrases

A **verbal** is a verb form that is used as a noun, an adjective, or an adverb. A **verbal phrase** consists of a verbal along with its modifiers and complements. There are three kinds of verbals: infinitives, participles, and gerunds.

7.1 INFINITIVES AND INFINITIVE PHRASES

An **infinitive** is a verb form that usually begins with *to* and functions as a noun, an adjective, or an adverb. An **infinitive phrase** consists of an infinitive plus its modifiers and complements.

> NOUN: *To be happy is not easy.* (subject) *I want to have fun.* (direct object)

My hope is to enjoy every day. (predicate nominative)

ADJECTIVE: *That's a goal to be proud of.* (adjective modifying goal)

ADVERB: *I'll work to achieve it.* (adverb modifying work)

Because *to,* the sign of the infinitive, precedes infinitives, it is usually easy to recognize them. However, sometimes *to* may be omitted.

> EXAMPLE: *No one can help me [to] achieve my goal.*

7.2 PARTICIPLES AND PARTICIPIAL PHRASES

A **participle** is a verb form that functions as an adjective. Like adjectives, participles modify nouns and pronouns. Most participles are present-participle forms ending in *-ing,* or past-participle forms ending in *-ed* or *-en.* In the examples below, the participles are highlighted.

> MODIFYING A NOUN: *The waxed floor was sticky.*
>
> MODIFYING A PRONOUN: *Sighing, she mopped up the mess.*

Participial phrases are participles with all their modifiers and complements.

> MODIFYING A NOUN: *The girls working on the project are very energetic.*
>
> MODIFYING A PRONOUN: *Having finished his work, he took a nap.*

7.3 DANGLING AND MISPLACED PARTICIPLES

A participle or participial phrase should be placed as close as possible to the word that it modifies. Otherwise the meaning of the sentence may not be clear.

> MISPLACED: *The boys were looking for squirrels searching the trees.*
>
> CLEARER: *The boys searching the trees were looking for squirrels.*

A participle or participial phrase that does not clearly modify anything in a sentence is called a **dangling participle.** A dangling participle causes confusion because it appears to modify a word that it cannot sensibly modify. Correct a dangling participle by providing a word for the participle to modify.

> DANGLING: *Waiting for the show to start, the phone rang.* (The phone wasn't waiting.)
>
> CLEARER: *Waiting for the show to start, I heard the phone ring.*

7.4 GERUNDS AND GERUND PHRASES

A **gerund** is a verb form ending in *-ing* that functions as a noun. Gerunds may perform any function nouns perform.

> SUBJECT: *Cooking is a good way to relax.*
>
> DIRECT OBJECT: *I enjoy cooking.*
>
> INDIRECT OBJECT: *They should give cooking a chance.*
>
> SUBJECT COMPLEMENT: *My favorite pastime is cooking.*
>
> OBJECT OF PREPOSITION: *A love of cooking runs in the family.*

Gerund phrases are gerunds with all their modifiers and complements.

> SUBJECT: *Depending on luck never got me far.*
>
> OBJECT OF PREPOSITION: *I will finish before leaving the office.*
>
> APPOSITIVE: *Her hobby, training horses, finally led to a career.*

Grammar Practice

Rewrite each sentence, adding the type of phrase shown in parentheses.

1. "Fine?" is by Margaret Peterson Haddix. (appositive phrase)
2. Bailey suffered from a migraine head-ache. (infinitive phrase)
3. Bailey had an MRI. (prepositional phrase)
4. The pediatric wing is full. (gerund phrase)
5. Bailey's mom leaves the hospital. (participial phrase)

8 Clauses

A **clause** is a group of words that contains a subject and a predicate. A sentence may contain one clause or more than one. The sentence in the following example contains two clauses. The subject and verb in each clause are highlighted.

> EXAMPLE: *Some students like to play sports, but others prefer to play music.*

There are two kinds of clauses: independent clauses and subordinate clauses.

8.1 INDEPENDENT AND SUBORDINATE CLAUSES

An independent clause expresses a complete thought and can stand alone as a sentence.

> INDEPENDENT CLAUSE: *I read "The Banana Tree."*

A sentence may contain more than one independent clause.

> EXAMPLE: *I read it once, and I liked it.*

In the preceding example, the coordinating conjunction *and* joins two independent clauses.

For more information, see **Coordinating Conjunctions,** page R3.

A **subordinate (dependent) clause** cannot stand alone as a sentence because it does not express a complete thought. By itself, a subordinate clause is a sentence fragment. It needs an independent clause to complete its meaning. Most subordinate clauses are introduced by words such as *after, although, because, if, that, when,* and *while.*

> SUBORDINATE CLAUSE: *Because they worked hard.*

A subordinate clause can be joined to an independent clause to make a sentence that expresses a complete thought. In the following example, the subordinate clause explains why the students did well on the test.

> EXAMPLE: *The students did well on the test because they worked hard.*

9 The Structure of Sentences

When classified by their structure, there are four kinds of sentences: simple, compound, complex, and compound-complex.

9.1 SIMPLE SENTENCES

A **simple sentence** is a sentence that has one independent clause and no subordinate clauses. Even a simple sentence can include many details.

> EXAMPLES: *Chloe looked for the train.*
> *Seth drove to the station in an old red pickup truck.*

A simple sentence may contain a compound subject or a compound verb. A compound subject is made up of two or more subjects that share the same verb. A compound verb is made up of two or more verbs that have the same subject.

> EXAMPLES: *Seth and Chloe drove to the station.*
> (compound subject)
> *They waved and shouted as the train pulled in.*
> (compound verb)

9.2 COMPOUND SENTENCES

A **compound sentence** consists of two or more independent clauses. The clauses in compound sentences are joined with commas and coordinating conjunctions (*and, but, or, nor, yet, for, so*) or with semicolons. Like simple sentences, compound sentences do not contain any subordinate clauses.

> EXAMPLES: *We all get older, but not everyone gets wiser.*
> *Some young people don't want to grow up; others grow up too quickly.*

WATCH OUT! Do not confuse compound sentences with simple sentences that have compound parts.

> EXAMPLE: *Books and clothes were scattered all over her room.*

Here, the conjunction *and* is used to join the parts of a compound subject, not the clauses in a compound sentence.

9.3 COMPLEX SENTENCES

A **complex sentence** consists of one independent clause and one or more subordinate clauses. Most subordinate clauses start with words such as *when, until, who, where, because,* and *so that.*

EXAMPLES: *While I eat my breakfast, I often wonder what I'll be like in ten years. When I think about the future, I see a canvas that has nothing on it.*

Write these sentences on a sheet of paper. Underline each independent clause once and each subordinate clause twice.

1. Although the Foster Grandparent Program is more than 40 years old, many people do not know about it.

2. This program was established so that children with special needs could get extra attention.

3. Anyone can volunteer who is at least 60 years old and meets other requirements.

4. After a volunteer is trained, he or she works 15 to 40 hours a week.

5. Foster grandparents often help with homework so that the children can improve in school.

6. Since this program was founded in 1965, there have been foster grandparent projects in all 50 states.

9.4 COMPOUND-COMPLEX SENTENCES

A **compound-complex** sentence contains two or more independent clauses and one or more subordinate clauses. Compound-complex sentences are both compound and complex. If you start with a compound sentence, all you need to do to form a compound-complex sentence is add a subordinate clause.

COMPOUND: *All the students knew the answer, yet they were too shy to volunteer.*

COMPOUND–COMPLEX: *All the students knew the answer that their teacher expected, yet they were too shy to volunteer.*

Identify each sentence as compound (*CD*), complex (*C*), or compound-complex (*CC*).

1. In 1998, a hurricane swept through Central America, where it hit Honduras and Nicaragua especially hard.

2. Hurricane Mitch was one of the strongest storms ever in this region; it caused great destruction.

3. People on the coast tried to flee to higher ground, but flooding and mudslides made escape difficult.

4. More than 9,000 people were killed, and crops and roads were wiped out.

5. TV images of homeless and hungry people touched many Americans, who responded generously.

6. They donated money and supplies, which were flown to the region.

7. Volunteers helped clear roads so that supplies could get to villages that needed them.

8. Charity groups distributed food and safe drinking water, and they handed out sleeping bags and mosquito nets, which were needed in the tropical climate.

9. Medical volunteers treated people who desperately needed care.

10. Other volunteers rebuilt homes, and they helped restore the farm economy so that people could earn a living again.

10 Writing Complete Sentences

Remember, a sentence is a group of words that expresses a complete thought. In writing that you wish to share with a reader, try to avoid both sentence fragments and run-on sentences.

10.1 CORRECTING FRAGMENTS

A **sentence fragment** is a group of words that is only part of a sentence. It does not express a complete thought and may be confusing to a reader or listener. A sentence fragment may be lacking a subject, a predicate, or both.

FRAGMENT: *Didn't care about sports.* (no subject)

CORRECTED: *The lawyer didn't care about sports.*

FRAGMENT: *Her middle-school son.* (no predicate)

CORRECTED: *Her middle-school son played on the soccer team.*

FRAGMENT: *Before every game.* (neither subject nor predicate)

CORRECTED: *Before every game, he tried to teach his mom the rules.*

In your writing, fragments may be a result of haste or incorrect punctuation. Sometimes fixing a fragment will be a matter of attaching it to a preceding or following sentence.

FRAGMENT: *She made an effort. But just couldn't make sense of the game.*

CORRECTED: *She made an effort but just couldn't make sense of the game.*

10.2 CORRECTING RUN-ON SENTENCES

A **run-on sentence** is made up of two or more sentences written as though they were one. Some run-ons have no punctuation within them. Others may have only commas where conjunctions or stronger punctuation marks are necessary. Use your judgment in correcting run-on sentences, as you have choices. You can change a run-on to two sentences if the thoughts are not closely connected. If the thoughts are closely related, you can keep the run-on as one sentence by adding a semicolon or a conjunction.

RUN–ON: *Most parents watched the game his mother read a book instead.*

MAKE TWO SENTENCES: *Most parents watched the game. His mother read a book instead.*

RUN–ON: *Most parents watched the game they played sports themselves.*

USE A SEMICOLON: *Most parents watched the game; they played sports themselves.*

ADD A CONJUNCTION: *Most parents watched the game since they played sports themselves.*

WATCH OUT! When you form compound sentences, make sure you use appropriate punctuation: a comma before a coordinating conjunction, a semicolon when there is no coordinating conjunction. A very common mistake is to use a comma without a conjunction or instead of a semicolon. This error is called a **comma splice.**

INCORRECT: *He finished the job, he left the village.*

CORRECT: *He finished the job, and he left the village.*

11 Subject-Verb Agreement

The subject and verb in a clause must agree in number. Agreement means that if the subject is singular, the verb is also singular, and if the subject is plural, the verb is also plural.

11.1 BASIC AGREEMENT

Fortunately, agreement between subjects and verbs in English is simple. Most verbs show the difference between singular and plural only in the third person of the present tense. In the present tense, the third-person singular form ends in **-s.**

Present-Tense Verb Forms	
Singular	**Plural**
I sleep	we sleep
you sleep	you sleep
she, he, it sleeps	they sleep

11.2 AGREEMENT WITH *BE*

The verb *be* presents special problems in agreement, because this verb does not follow the usual verb patterns.

Forms of *Be*			
Present Tense		**Past Tense**	
Singular	**Plural**	**Singular**	**Plural**
I am	we are	I was	we were
you are	you are	you were	you were
she, he, it is	they are	she, he, it was	they were

11.3 WORDS BETWEEN SUBJECT AND VERB

A verb agrees only with its subject. When words come between a subject and a verb, ignore them when considering proper agreement. Identify the subject and make sure the verb agrees with it.

EXAMPLES: *The poem I read describes a moose. The moose in the poem searches for a place where he belongs.*

11.4 AGREEMENT WITH COMPOUND SUBJECTS

Use plural verbs with most compound subjects joined by the word *and.*

EXAMPLE: *My father and his friends play chess every day.*

To confirm that you need a plural verb, you could substitute the plural pronoun *they* for *my father and his friends.*

If a compound subject is thought of as a unit, use a singular verb. Test this by substituting the singular pronoun *it.*

EXAMPLE: *A bagel and cream cheese [it] is my usual breakfast.*

Use a singular verb with a compound subject that is preceded by *each, every,* or *many a.*

EXAMPLES: *Each novel and short story seems grounded in personal experience.*

When the parts of a compound subject are joined by *or, nor,* or the correlative conjunctions *either . . . or* or *neither . . . nor,* make the verb agree with the noun or pronoun nearest the verb.

EXAMPLES: *Cookies or ice cream is my favorite dessert.*
Either Cheryl or her parents are being invited.
Neither ice storms nor snow is predicted today.

11.5 PERSONAL PRONOUNS AS SUBJECTS

When using a personal pronoun as a subject, make sure to match it with the correct form of the verb *be.* (See the chart in Section 11.2.) Note especially that the pronoun *you* takes the forms *are* and *were,* regardless of whether it is singular or plural.

WATCH OUT! *You is* and *you was* are nonstandard forms and should be avoided in writing and speaking. *We was* and *they was* are also forms to be avoided.

INCORRECT: *You was a good student.*
CORRECT: *You were a good student.*
INCORRECT: *They was starting a new school.*
CORRECT: *They were starting a new school.*

11.6 INDEFINITE PRONOUNS AS SUBJECTS

Some indefinite pronouns are always singular; some are always plural.

Singular Indefinite Pronouns			
another	either	neither	one
anybody	every-body	nobody	somebody
anyone	everyone	no one	someone
anything	every-thing	nothing	something
each	much		

EXAMPLES: *Each of the writers was given an award.*
Somebody in the room upstairs is sleeping.

Plural Indefinite Pronouns			
both	few	many	several

EXAMPLES: *Many of the books in our library are not in circulation.*
Few have been returned recently.

Still other indefinite pronouns may be either singular or plural.

Singular or Plural Indefinite Pronouns		
all	more	none
any	most	some

The number of the indefinite pronoun *any* or *none* often depends on the intended meaning.

EXAMPLES: *Any of these stories has an important message.* (any one story)
Any of these stories have important messages. (all of the many stories)

The indefinite pronouns *all, some, more, most,* and *none* are singular when they refer to quantities or parts of things. They are plural when they refer to numbers of individual things. Context will usually give a clue.

EXAMPLES: *All of the flour is gone.* (referring to a quantity)
All of the flowers are gone. (referring to individual items)

11.7 INVERTED SENTENCES

A sentence in which the subject follows the verb is called an **inverted sentence.** A subject can follow a verb or part of a verb phrase in a question; a sentence beginning with *here* or *there*; or a sentence in which an adjective, an adverb, or a phrase is placed first.

EXAMPLES: *Here comes the scariest part. There goes the hero with a flashlight.*
Then, into the room rushes a big black cat!

TIP To check subject-verb agreement in some inverted sentences, place the subject before the verb. For example, change **There are many people** to **Many people are there.**

11.8 SENTENCES WITH PREDICATE NOMINATIVES

In a sentence containing a predicate noun (nominative), the verb should agree with the subject, not the predicate noun.

EXAMPLES: *Josh's jokes are a source of laughter.* (*Jokes* is the subject—not *source*—and it takes the plural verb *are.*)
One source of laughter is Josh's jokes. (The subject is *source*—not *jokes*—and it takes the singular verb *is.*)

11.9 *DON'T* AND *DOESN'T* AS AUXILIARY VERBS

The auxiliary verb **doesn't** is used with singular subjects and with the personal pronouns **she, he,** and **it.** The auxiliary verb **don't** is used with plural subjects and with the personal pronouns **I, we, you,** and **they.**

SINGULAR: *The humor doesn't escape us. Doesn't the limerick about Dougal MacDougal make you laugh?*

PLURAL: *We don't usually forget such funny images.*
Don't people like to recite limericks?

11.10 COLLECTIVE NOUNS AS SUBJECTS

Collective nouns are singular nouns that name groups of persons or things. *Team,* for example, is a collective name of a group of individuals. A collective noun takes a singular verb when the group acts as a single unit. It takes a plural verb when the members of the group act separately.

EXAMPLES: *The class creates a bulletin board of limericks.* (The class as a whole creates the board.)
The faculty enjoy teaching poetry. (The individual members enjoy teaching poetry.)

11.11 RELATIVE PRONOUNS AS SUBJECTS

When the relative pronoun *who, which,* or *that* is used as a subject in an adjective clause, the verb in the clause must agree in number with the antecedent of the pronoun.

> SINGULAR: *The **myth** from ancient Greece that interests me most is "The Apple of Discord I."*

The antecedent of the relative pronoun *that* is the singular *myth*; therefore, *that* is singular and must take the singular verb *interests.*

> PLURAL: *James Berry and Sandra Cisneros are writers who publish short stories.*

The antecedent of the relative pronoun *who* is the plural subject *writers.* Therefore *who* is plural, and it takes the plural verb *publish.*

Grammar Practice

Locate the subject of each verb in parentheses in the sentences below. Then choose the correct verb form.

1. George Graham Vest's "Tribute to a Dog" (describes, describe) the friendship and loyalty canines show humans.

2. Stories about a dog (is, are) touching.

3. Besides dogs, few animals (has, have) an innate desire to please humans.

4. Many traits specific to dogs (bring, brings) their owners happiness.

5. No matter if the owner is rich or poor, a dog, and all canines for that matter, (acts, act) with love and devotion.

6. There (is, are) countless reasons to own a dog.

7. A dog's unselfishness (endears, endear) it to its owner.

8. (Doesn't, Don't) a dog offer its owner constant affection and guardianship?

9. A man's dog (stands, stand) by him in prosperity and in poverty.

10. A dog (guards, guard) his master as if the owner was a prince.

Vocabulary and Spelling

The key to becoming an independent reader is to develop a tool kit of vocabulary strategies. By learning and practicing the strategies, you'll know what to do when you encounter unfamiliar words while reading. You'll also know how to refine the words you use for different situations—personal, school, and work.

Being a good speller is important when communicating your ideas in writing. Learning basic spelling rules and checking your spelling in a dictionary will help you spell words that you may not use frequently.

1 Using Context Clues

The context of a word is made up of the punctuation marks, words, sentences, and paragraphs that surround the word. A word's context can give you important clues about its meaning.

1.1 GENERAL CONTEXT

Sometimes you need to determine the meaning of an unfamiliar word by reading all the information in a passage.

> *Kevin set out the broom, a dustpan, and three trash bags before beginning the* monumental *task of cleaning his room.*

You can figure out from the context that *monumental* means "huge."

1.2 SPECIFIC CONTEXT CLUES

Sometimes writers help you understand the meanings of words by providing specific clues such as those shown in the chart. When reading content area materials, use word, sentence, and paragraph clues to help you figure out meanings.

1.3 IDIOMS, SLANG, AND FIGURATIVE LANGUAGE

Use context clues to figure out the meanings of idioms, slang, and figurative language.

An **idiom** is an expression whose overall meaning differs from the meaning of the individual words.

> *The mosquitos drove us crazy on our hike. (Drove us crazy means "irritated.")*

Slang is informal language that features made-up words and ordinary words that are used to mean something different from their meanings in formal English.

> *That's a really cool backpack you're wearing. (Cool means "excellent.")*

Figurative language is language that communicates meaning beyond the literal meaning of the words.

> *Like a plunging horse, my car kicked up dirt, moved ahead quickly, and made a loud noise when I hit the gas. (Kicked up dirt, moved ahead, and made a loud noise describe a plunging horse.)*

Specific Context Clues		
Type of Clue	**Key Words/ Phrases**	**Example**
Definition or restatement of the meaning of the word	or, which is, that is, in other words, also known as, also called	In 1909, a French inventor flew a *monoplane*, or a **single-winged plane.**

continued

Type of Clue	Key Words/ Phrases	Example
Example following an unfamiliar word	such as, like, as if, for example, especially, including	The stunt pilot performed *acrobatics,* such as **dives and wingwalking.**
Comparison with a more familiar word or concept	as, like, also, similar to, in the same way, likewise	The doctor prescribed a *bland* diet, similar to the **rice and potatoes** he was already eating.
Contrast with a familiar word or experience	unlike, but, however, although, on the other hand, on the contrary	The moon will *diminish* at the end of the month; however it will **grow** during the first part of the month.
Cause-and-effect relationship in which one term is familiar	because, since, when, conse-quently, as a result, therefore	Because their general was *valiant,* the soldiers **showed courage** in battle.

2 Analyzing Word Structure

Many words can be broken into smaller parts. These word parts include base words, roots, prefixes, and suffixes.

2.1 BASE WORDS

A **base word** is a word part that by itself is also a word. Other words or word parts can be added to base words to form new words.

2.2 ROOTS

A **root** is a word part that contains the core meaning of the word. Many English words contain roots that come from older languages such as Greek and Latin. Knowing the meanings of a word's root can help you determine the word's meaning.

Root	Meaning	Example
auto (Greek)	self, same	**auto**mobile
hydr (Greek)	water	**hydr**ant
cent (Latin)	hundred	**cent**ury
circ (Latin)	ring	**circ**le
port (Latin)	carry	**port**able

2.3 PREFIXES

A **prefix** is a word part attached to the beginning of a word. Most prefixes come from Greek, Latin, or Old English (OE).

Prefix	Meaning	Example
dis- (Latin)	not	**dis**honest
auto- (Greek)	self, same	**auto**biography
un- (OE)	the opposite of, not	**un**happy
re- (Latin)	carry, back	**re**pay

2.4 SUFFIXES

A **suffix** is a word part that appears at the end of a root or base word to form a new word.

Some suffixes do not change word meaning. These suffixes are:

- added to nouns to change the number of persons or objects
- added to verbs to change the tense
- added to modifiers to change the degree of comparison

Suffix	Meaning	Example
-s, -es	to change the number of a noun	lock + s = locks
-d, -ed, -ing	to change verb tense	stew + ed = stewed
-er, -est	to indicate comparison in modifiers	mild + er = milder soft + est = softest

Other suffixes can be added to the root or base to change the word's meaning. These suffixes can also determine a word's part of speech.

Suffix	Meaning	Example
-ion (Latin)	process of	operation
-able (Latin)	capable of	readable
-ize (Greek)	to cause or become	legalize

Strategies for Understanding New Words

- If you recognize elements—prefix, suffix, root, or base—of a word, you may be able to guess its meaning by analyzing one or two elements.
- Think about the way the word is used in the sentence. Use the context and the word parts to make a logical guess about the word's meaning.
- Look in a dictionary to see if you are correct.

3 Understanding Word Origins

3.1 ETYMOLOGIES

Etymologies show the origin and historical development of a word. When you study a word's history and origin, you can find out when, where, and how the word came to be.

em·per·or (ĕm´pər-ər) *n.* **1.** The male ruler of an empire. **2a.** The emperor butterfly. **b.** The emperor moth. [Middle English emperour, from Old French *empereor*, from Latin imperātor, from *imperāre*, to command: *in-*, *in*; see EN–[1] + *parāre*, to prepare.]

3.2 WORD FAMILIES

Words that have the same root make up a word family and have related meanings. The following chart shows a common Greek root and a common Latin root. Notice how the meanings of the example words are related to the meanings of their roots.

Latin Root	*man:* "hand"	
English	**manual** by hand **manage** handle **manuscript** document written by hand	
Greek Root	*phon:* "sound"	
English	**telephone** an instrument that transmits sound **phonograph** machine that reproduces sound **phonetic** representing sounds of speech	

3.3 FOREIGN WORDS IN ENGLISH

The English language includes words from other languages, such as French, Dutch, Spanish, Italian, and Chinese. Many words have stayed the way they were in their original language.

French	Dutch	Spanish	Italian
ballet	boss	canyon	diva
vague	caboose	rodeo	cupola
mirage	dock	bronco	spaghetti

Practice and Apply

Look up the origin and meaning of each word listed in the preceding chart. Then use each word in a sentence.

4 Synonyms and Antonyms

4.1 SYNONYMS

A **synonym** is a word with a meaning similar to that of another word. You can find synonyms in a thesaurus or a dictionary. In a dictionary, synonyms are often given as part of the definition of a word. The following word pairs are synonyms:

satisfy/please   occasionally/sometimes
rob/steal   schedule/agenda

4.2 ANTONYMS

An **antonym** is a word with a meaning opposite that of another word. The following word pairs are antonyms.

accurate/incorrect   similar/different
fresh/stale   unusual/ordinary

5 Denotation and Connotation

5.1 DENOTATION

A word's dictionary meaning is called its **denotation.** For example, the denotation of the word *thin* is "having little flesh; spare; lean."

5.2 CONNOTATION

The images or feelings you connect to a word add a finer shade of meaning, called **connotation.** The connation of a word goes beyond its basic dictionary definition. Writers use connotations of words to communicate positive or negative feelings.

Positive	Negative
slender	scrawny
thrifty	cheap
young	immature

Make sure you understand the denotation and connotation of a word when you read it or use it in your writing.

6 Analogies

An **analogy** is a comparison between two things that are similar in some way but are otherwise not alike. Analogies are sometimes used in writing when unfamiliar subjects or ideas are explained in terms of familiar ones. Analogies often appear on tests as well. In an analogy problem, the analogy is expressed using two groups of words. The relationship between the first pair of words is the same as the relationship between the second pair of words. Some analogy problems are expressed like this:

in love **:** hate **::** war **:** _____

a. soldier **b.** peace **c.** battle **d.** argument

Follow these steps to determine the correct answer:

- Read the problem as "*Love* is to *hate* as *war* is to . . . ."
- Ask yourself how the words *love* and *hate* are related. (*Love* and *hate* are antonyms.)
- Ask yourself which answer choice is an antonym of *war.* (*Peace* is an antonym of *war,* therefore *peace* is the best answer.)

7 Homonyms, Homographs, and Homophones

7.1 HOMONYMS

Homonyms are words that have the same spelling and sound but have different meanings.

> The snake *shed* its skin in the *shed* behind the house.

Shed can mean "to lose by natural process," but an identically spelled word means "a small structure."

Sometimes only one of the meanings of a homonym may be familiar to you. Use context clues to help you figure out the meaning of an unfamiliar word.

7.2 HOMOGRAPHS

Homographs are words that are spelled the same but have different meanings and origins. Some are also pronounced differently, as in these examples:

> Please *close* the door. (klōz)
> That was a *close* call. (klōs)

If you see a word used in a way that is unfamiliar to you, check a dictionary to see if it is a homograph.

7.3 HOMOPHONES

Homophones are words that sound alike but have different meanings and spellings. The following homophones are frequently misused:

it's/its   they're/their/there
to/too/two   stationary/stationery

Many misused homophones are pronouns and contractions. Whenever you are unsure whether to write **your** or **you're** and **who's** or **whose,** ask yourself if you mean **you are** and **who is/has.** If you do, write the contraction. For other homophones, such as **fair** and **fare,** use the meaning of the word to help you decide which one to use.

8 Words with Multiple Meanings

Over time, some words have acquired additional meanings that are based on the original meaning.

> I had to be replaced in the cast of the play because of the cast on my arm.

These two uses of cast have different meanings, but both of them have the same origin. You will find all the meanings of cast listed in one entry in the dictionary. Context can also help you figure out the meaning of the word.

9 Specialized Vocabulary

Specialized vocabulary is a group of terms suited to a particular field of study or work. For example, science, mathematics, and history all have their own technical or specialized vocabularies. To figure out specialized terms, you can use context clues and reference sources, such as dictionaries on specific subjects, atlases, or manuals.

10 Using Reference Sources

10.1 DICTIONARIES

A **general dictionary** will tell you not only a word's definitions but also its pronunciation, syllabication, parts of speech, history, and origin.

tan·gi·ble (tăn´jə-bəl) *adj.*
1a. Discernible by the touch; palpable. **b.** Possible to touch. **c.** Possible to be treated as fact; real or concrete. **2.** Possible to understand or realize. **3.** *Law* That can be valued monetarily. [Late Latin *tangibilis*, from Latin *tangere*, to touch.]

1. Entry word syllabication
2. Pronunciation
3. Part of speech
4. Definitions
5. Etymology

A **specialized dictionary** focuses on terms related to a particular field of study or work. Use a dictionary to check the spelling of any word you are unsure of in your reading.

10.2 THESAURI

A **thesaurus** (plural, *thesauri*) is a dictionary of synonyms. A thesaurus can be especially helpful when you find yourself using the same modifiers over and over again.

10.3 SYNONYM FINDERS

A **synonym finder** is often included in wordprocessing software. It enables you to highlight a word and be shown a display of its synonyms.

10.4 GLOSSARIES

A **glossary** is a list of specialized terms and their definitions. It is often found in the back of a book and sometimes includes pronunciations. Many textbooks contain glossaries. In fact, this textbook has three glossaries: the **Glossary of Literary and Informational Terms,** the **Glossary of Academic Vocabulary,** and the **Glossary of Critical Vocabulary.** Use these glossaries to help you understand how terms are used in this textbook.

11 Spelling Rules

11.1 WORDS ENDING IN A SILENT *E*

Before adding a suffix beginning with a vowel or *y* to a word ending in a silent *e,* drop the *e* (with some exceptions).

> amaze + -ing = amazing
> love + -able = lovable
> create + -ed = created
> nerve + -ous = nervous

Exceptions: *change + -able = changeable; courage + -ous = courageous*

When adding a suffix beginning with a consonant to a word ending in a silent *e,* keep the *e* (with some exceptions).

> late + -ly = lately
> spite + -ful = spiteful
> noise + -less = noiseless
> state + -ment = statement

Exceptions: *truly, argument, ninth, wholly, awful,* and *others*

When a suffix beginning with *a* or *o* is added to a word with a final silent *e,* the final *e* is usually retained if it is preceded by a soft *c* or a soft *g.*

> bridge + -able = bridgeable
> peace + -able = peaceable
> outrage + -ous = outrageous
> advantage + -ous = advantageous

When a suffix beginning with a vowel is added to words ending in *ee* or *oe,* the final, silent *e* is retained.

> agree + -ing = agreeing
> free + -ing = freeing
> hoe + -ing = hoeing
> see + -ing = seeing

11.2 WORDS ENDING IN *Y*

Before adding most suffixes to a word that ends in *y* preceded by a consonant, change the *y* to *i.*

> easy + -est = easiest

crazy + -est = craziest

silly + -ness = silliness

marry + -age = marriage

Exceptions: *dryness, shyness,* and *slyness*

However, when you add **-ing,** the **y** does not change.

empty + -ed = emptied   but

empty + -ing = emptying

When adding a suffix to a word that ends in **y** preceded by a vowel, the **y** usually does not change.

play + -er = player

employ + -ed = employed

coy + -ness = coyness

pay + -able = payable

11.3 WORDS ENDING IN A CONSONANT

In one-syllable words that end in one consonant preceded by one short vowel, double the final consonant before adding a suffix beginning with a vowel, such as **-ed** or **-ing.** These are sometimes called 1+1+1 words.

dip + -ed = dipped

set + -ing = setting

slim + -est = slimmest

fit + -er = fitter

The rule does not apply to words of one syllable that end in a consonant preceded by two vowels.

feel + -ing = feeling

peel + -ed = peeled

reap + -ed = reaped

loot + -ed = looted

In words of more than one syllable, double the final consonant when (1) the word ends with one consonant preceded by one vowel and (2) when the word is accented on the last syllable.

be·gin´   per·mit´   re·fer´

In the following examples, note that in the new words formed with suffixes, the accent remains on the same syllable.

be·gin´ + -ing = be·gin´ning = beginning

per·mit´ + -ed = per·mit´ted = permitted

Exceptions: In some words with more than one syllable, though the accent remains on the same syllable when a suffix is added, the final consonant is nevertheless not doubled, as in the following examples.

tra´vel + er = tra´vel·er = traveler

mar´ket + er = mar´ket·er = marketer

In the following examples, the accent does not remain on the same syllable; thus, the final consonant is not doubled:

re·fer´ + -ence = ref´er·ence = reference

con·fer´ + -ence = con´fer·ence = conference

11.4 PREFIXES AND SUFFIXES

When adding a prefix to a word, do not change the spelling of the base word. When a prefix creates a double letter, keep both letters.

dis- + approve = disapprove

re- + build = rebuild

ir- + regular = irregular

mis- + spell = misspell

anti- + trust = antitrust

il- + logical = illogical

When adding **-ly** to a word ending in **l,** keep both **l's.** When adding **-ness** to a word ending in **n,** keep both **n's.**

careful + -ly = carefully

sudden + -ness = suddenness

final + -ly = finally

thin + -ness = thinness

11.5 FORMING PLURAL NOUNS

To form the plural of most nouns, just add **-s.**

prizes   dreams   circles   stations

For most singular nouns ending in **o,** add **-s.**

solos   halos   studios   photos   pianos

For a few nouns ending in **o,** add **-es.**

heroes   tomatoes   potatoes   echoes

When a singular noun ends in **s, sh, ch, x,** or **z,** add **-es.**

waitresses   brushes   ditches

axes   buzzes

When a singular noun ends in **y** with a consonant before it, change the **y** to **i** and add **-es.**

army—armies   candy—candies
baby—babies   diary—diaries
ferry—ferries   conspiracy—conspiracies

When a vowel (**a, e, i, o, u**) comes before the **y,** just add **-s.**

boy—boys   way—ways
array—arrays   alloy—alloys
weekday—weekdays jockey—jockeys

For most nouns ending in **f** or **fe,** change the **f** to **v** and add **-es** or **-s.**

life—lives   loaf—loaves
calf—calves   knife—knives
thief—thieves   shelf—shelves

For some nouns ending in **f,** add **-s** to make the plural.

roofs   chiefs   reefs   beliefs

Some nouns have the same form for both singular and plural.

deer   sheep   moose   salmon   trout

For some nouns, the plural is formed in a special way.

man—men   goose—geese
ox—oxen   woman—women
mouse—mice   child—children

For a compound noun written as one word, form the plural by changing the last word in the compound to its plural form.

stepchild—stepchildren   firefly—fireflies

If a compound noun is written as a hyphenated word or as two separate words, change the most important word to the plural form.

brother-in-law—brothers-in-law
life jacket—life jackets

11.6 FORMING POSSESSIVES

If a noun is singular, add **'s.**

mother—my mother's car
Ross—Ross's desk

Exception: An apostrophe alone is used to indicate the possessive case with the names Jesus and Moses and with certain names in classical mythology (such as Zeus).

If a noun is plural and ends with **s,** add an apostrophe.

parents—my parents' car
the Santinis—the Santinis' house

If a noun is plural but does not end in **s,** add **'s.**

people—the people's choice
women—the women's coats

11.7 SPECIAL SPELLING PROBLEMS

Only one English word ends in **-sede:** supersede. Three words end in **-ceed: exceed, proceed,** and **succeed.** All other verbs ending in the sound "seed" are spelled with **-cede.**

concede   precede   recede   secede

In words with **ie** or **ei,** when the sound is long **e** (as in **she**), the word is spelled **ie** except after **c** (with some exceptions).

i before *e*	thief	relieve	field
piece	grieve	pier	
except	conceit	perceive	ceiling
after *c*	receive	receipt	
Exceptions:	either	neither	weird
leisure	seize		

11.8 USING A SPELL CHECKER

Most computer word processing programs have spell checkers to catch misspellings. Most computer spell checkers do not correct errors automatically. Instead, they stop at a word and highlight it. Sometimes the highlighted word may not be misspelled; it may be that the program's dictionary does not include the word. Keep in mind that spell checkers will identify only misspelled words, not misused words. For example, if you used *their* when you meant to use *there,* a spelling checker will not catch the error.

12 Commonly Confused Words

Words	Definitions	Examples
accept/ except	The verb *accept* means "to receive" or "to believe." *Except* is usually a preposition meaning "excluding."	Did the teacher **accept** your report? Everyone smiled for the photographer **except** Jody.
advice/advise	*Advise* is a verb. *Advice* is a noun naming that which an *adviser* gives.	I **advise** you to take that job. Whom should I ask for **advice**?
affect/effect	As a verb, *affect* means "to influence." *Effect* as a verb means "to cause." If you want a noun, you will almost always want *effect*.	How deeply did the news **affect** him? The students tried to **effect** a change in school policy. What **effect** did the acidic soil produce in the plants?
all ready/ already	*All ready* is an adjective meaning "fully ready." *Already* is an adverb meaning "before" or "by this time."	He was **all ready** to go at noon. I have **already** seen that movie.
desert/ dessert	*Desert* (dĕz´ərt) means "a dry, sandy, barren region." *Desert* (dĭ-zûrt´) means "to abandon." *Dessert* (dĭ-zûrt´) is a sweet, such as cake.	The Sahara, in North Africa, is the world's largest **desert.** The night guard did not **desert** his post. Alison's favorite **dessert** is chocolate cake.
among/ between	*Between* is used when you are speaking of only two things. *Among* is used for three or more.	**Between** ice cream and sherbet, I prefer the latter. Gary Soto is **among** my favorite authors.
bring/take	*Bring* is used to denote motion toward a speaker or place. *Take* is used to denote motion away from such a person or place.	**Bring** the books over here, and I will **take** them to the library.
fewer/less	*Fewer* refers to the number of separate, countable units. *Less* refers to bulk quantity.	We have **less** literature and **fewer** selections in this year's curriculum.

contined

Words	Definitions	Examples
leave/let	*Leave* means "to allow something to remain behind." *Let* means "to permit."	The librarian will **leave** some books on display but will not **let** us borrow any.
lie/lay	To *lie* is "to rest or recline." It does not take an object. *Lay* always takes an object.	Rover loves to **lie** in the sun. We always **lay** some bones next to him.
loose/lose	*Loose* (lo͞os) means "free, not restrained." *Lose* (lo͞oz) means "to misplace" or "to fail to find."	Who turned the horses **loose**? I hope we won't **lose** any of them.
passed/past	*Passed* is the past tense of *pass* and means "went by." *Past* is an adjective that means "of a former time." *Past* is also a noun that means "time gone by."	We **passed** through the Florida Keys during our vacation. My **past** experiences have taught me to set my alarm. Ebenezer Scrooge is a character who relives his **past**.
than/then	Use *than* in making comparisons. Use *then* on all other occasions.	Ramon is stronger **than** Mark. Cut the grass and **then** trim the hedges.
two/too/to	*Two* is the number. *Too* is an adverb meaning "also" or "very." Use *to* before a verb or as a preposition.	Meg had **to** go **to** town, **too**. We had **too** much reading **to** do. **Two** chapters is **too** many.
their/there/they're	*Their* means "belonging to them." *There* means "in that place." *They're* is the contraction for "they are."	**There** is a movie playing at 9 P.M. **They're** going to see it with me. Sakara and Jessica drove away in **their** car after the movie.

Using the Glossary

This glossary is an alphabetical list of vocabulary words found in the selections in this book. Use this glossary just as you would a dictionary—to determine the meanings, parts of speech, pronunciation, and syllabication of words. (Some technical, foreign, and more obscure words in this book are not listed here but are defined for you in the footnotes that accompany many of the selections.)

Many words in the English language have more than one meaning. This glossary gives the meanings that apply to the words as they are used in the selections in this book. Words closely related in form and meaning are listed together in one entry (for instance, *consumption* and *consume*), and the definition is given for the first form.

The following abbreviations are used to identify parts of speech of words:

adj. adjective   *adv.* adverb   *n.* noun   *v.* verb

Each word's pronunciation is given in parentheses. A guide to the pronunciation symbols appears in the Pronunciation Key below. The stress marks in the Pronunciation Key are used to indicate the force given to each syllable in a word. They can also help you determine where words are divided into syllables.

For more information about the words in this glossary or for information about words not listed here, consult a dictionary.

Pronunciation Key

Symbol	Examples	Symbol	Examples	Symbol	Examples	Sounds in Foreign Words	
ă	pat	l	lid, needle* (nēd'l)	sh	ship, dish		
ā	pay			t	tight, stopped	KH	*German* ich, ach; *Scottish* loch
ä	father	m	mum	th	thin		
âr	care	n	no, sudden* (sud'n)	*th*	this	N	*French*, bon (bôn)
b	bib			ŭ	cut	œ	*French* feu, œuf; *German* schön
ch	church	ng	thing	ûr	urge, term, firm, word, heard		
d	deed, milled	ŏ	pot			ü	*French* tu; *German* uber
ě	pet	ō	toe	v	valve		
ē	bee	ô	caught, paw	w	with		
f	fife, phase, rough	oi	noise	y	yes		
g	gag	ŏŏ	took	z	zebra, xylem		
h	hat	ōō	boot	zh	vision, pleasure, garage		
hw	which	ŏŏr	lure	ə	about, item, edible, gallop, circus		
ĭ	pit	ôr	core				
ī	pie, by	ou	out	ər	butter		
îr	pier	p	pop				
j	judge	r	roar				
k	kick, cat, pique	s	sauce				

*In English the consonants *l* and *n* often constitute complete syllables by themselves.

Stress Marks

The relevant emphasis with which the syllables of a word or phrase are spoken, called stress, is indicated in three different ways. The strongest, or primary, stress is marked with a bold mark (´). An intermediate, or secondary, level of stress is marked with a similar but lighter mark (´). The weakest stress is unmarked. Words of one syllable show no stress mark.

Glossary of Literary and Informational Terms

Act   An act is a major division within a play, similar to a chapter in a book. Each act may be further divided into smaller sections, called scenes. Plays can have as many as five acts, or as few as one.

Adventure Story   An adventure story is a literary work in which action is the main element. An **adventure novel** usually focuses on a main character who is on a mission and faces many challenges and choices.

Alliteration   Alliteration is the repetition of consonant sounds at the beginning of words. Note the repetition of the **d** sound in this line: The **d**aring boy **d**ove into the **d**eep sea.

Allusion   An allusion is a reference to a famous person, place, event, or work of literature.

Almanac   *See* Reference Works.

Analogy   An analogy is a comparison between two things that are alike in some way. Often, writers use analogies to explain unfamiliar subjects or ideas in terms of familiar ones.
See also **Metaphor; Simile.**

Anecdote   An anecdote is a short account of an event that is usually intended to entertain or make a point.

Antagonist   The antagonist is a force working against the protagonist, or main character, in a story, play, or novel. The antagonist is usually another character but can be a force of nature, society itself, or an internal force within the main character.
See also Protagonist.

Appeal to Authority   An appeal to authority is an attempt to persuade an audience by making reference to people who are experts on a subject.

Argument   An argument is speaking or writing that expresses a position on a problem and supports it with reasons and evidence. An argument often anticipates and answers objections that opponents might raise.
See also Claim; Counterargument; Evidence.

Assonance   Assonance is the repetition of vowel sounds within nonrhyming words. An example of assonance is the repetition of the o͞o sound in the following line: Do you like blue?

Assumption   An assumption is an opinion or belief that is taken for granted. It can be about a specific situation, a person, or the world in general. Assumptions are often unstated.

Audience   The audience of a piece of writing is the group of readers that the writer is addressing. A writer considers his or her audience when deciding on a subject, a purpose, a tone, and a style in which to write.

Author's Message   An author's message is the main idea or theme of a particular work.
See also Main Idea; Theme.

Author's Perspective   An author's perspective is the combination of ideas, values, feelings, and beliefs that influences the way the writer looks at a topic. **Tone,** or attitude, often reveals an author's perspective.
See also Author's Purpose; Tone.

Author's Position   An author's position is his or her opinion on an issue or topic.
See also Claim.

Author's Purpose   A writer usually writes for one or more of these purposes: to express thoughts or feelings, to inform or explain, to persuade, or to entertain.
See also Author's Perspective.

Autobiography   An autobiography is a writer's account of his or her own life. In almost every case, it is told from the first-person point of view. An autobiography focuses on the most important events and people in the writer's life over a period of time.
See also Memoir; Personal Narrative.

Ballad   A ballad is a type of narrative poem that tells a story and was originally meant to be sung or recited. Because it tells a story, a ballad has a setting, a plot, and characters. **Folk ballads** were composed orally and handed down by word of mouth from generation to generation.

Bias   In a piece of writing, the author's bias is the side of an issue that he or she favors. Words with extremely positive or negative connotations are often a signal of an author's bias.

Bibliography   A bibliography is a list of related books and other materials used to write a text. Bibliographies can be good sources for further study on a subject.
See also Works Consulted.

Biography   A biography is the true account of a person's life, written by another person. As such, biographies are usually told from a third-person point of view. The writer of a biography—a **biographer**—usually researches his or her subject in order to present accurate information. The best biographers strive for honesty and balance in their accounts of their subjects' lives.

Business Correspondence Business correspondence is written business communications such as business letters, e-mails, and memos. In general, business correspondence is brief, to the point, clear, courteous, and professional.

Cast of Characters In the script of a play, a cast of characters is a list of all the characters in the play, usually in order of appearance. It may include a brief description of each character.

Cause and Effect Two events are related by cause and effect when one event brings about, or causes, the other. The event that happens first is the **cause**; the one that follows is the **effect.** Cause and effect is also a way of organizing an entire piece of writing. It helps writers show the relationships between events or ideas.

Character Characters are the people, animals, or imaginary creatures who take part in the action of a work of literature. Like real people, characters display certain qualities, or **character traits,** that develop and change over time, and they usually have **motivations,** or reasons, for their behaviors.

  Main character: Main characters are the most important characters in literary works. Generally, the plot of a short story focuses on one main character, but a novel may have several main characters.

  Minor characters: The less important characters in a literary work are known as minor characters. The story is not centered on them, but they help carry out the action of the story and help the reader learn more about the main character.

  Dynamic character: A dynamic character is one who undergoes important changes as a plot unfolds. The changes occur because of the character's actions and experiences in the story. The changes are usually internal and may be good or bad. Main characters are usually, though not always, dynamic.

  Static character: A static character is one who remains the same throughout a story. The character may experience events and interact with other characters, but he or she is not changed because of them.

See also Characterization; Character Traits.

Character Development Characters that change during a story are said to undergo character development. Any character can change, but main characters usually develop the most.
See also Character: Dynamic Character.

Characterization The way a writer creates and develops characters is known as characterization. There are four basic methods of characterization.
  • The writer may make direct comments about a character through the voice of the narrator.
  • The writer may describe the character's physical appearance.
  • The writer may present the character's own thoughts, speech, and actions.
  • The writer may present the thoughts, speech, and actions of other characters.

See also Character; Character Traits.

Character Traits Character traits are the qualities shown by a character. Traits may be physical (tall) or expressions of personality (confidence). Writers reveal the traits of their characters through methods of characterization. Sometimes writers directly state a character's traits, but more often readers need to infer traits from a character's words, actions, thoughts, appearance, and relationships. Examples of words that describe traits include *__brave, considerate,__* and *__rude.__*

Chronological Order Chronological order is the arrangement of events in their order of occurrence. This type of organization is used in fictional narratives and in historical writing, biography, and autobiography.

Claim In an argument, a claim is the writer's position on an issue or problem. Although an argument focuses on supporting one claim, a writer may make more than one claim in a text.

Clarify Clarifying is a reading strategy that helps readers understand or make clear what they are reading. Readers usually clarify by rereading, reading aloud, or discussing.

Classification Classification is a pattern of organization in which objects, ideas, and/or information are presented in groups, or classes, based on common characteristics.

Cliché A cliché is an overused expression. "Better late than never" and "hard as nails" are common examples. Good writers generally avoid clichés unless they are using them in dialogue to indicate something about a character's personality.

Climax The climax stage is the point of greatest interest in a story or play. The climax usually occurs toward the end of a story, after the reader has understood the **conflict** and become emotionally involved with the characters. At the climax, the conflict is resolved and the outcome of the plot usually becomes clear.

See also Plot.

Comedy A comedy is a dramatic work that is light and often humorous in tone, usually ending happily with a peaceful resolution of the main conflict.

Compare and Contrast To compare and contrast is to identify the similarities and differences of two or more subjects. Compare and contrast is also a pattern of organizing an entire piece of writing.

See also Pattern of Organization.

Conclusion A conclusion is a statement of belief based on evidence, experience, and reasoning. A valid conclusion is one that logically follows from the facts or statements upon which it is based.

Conflict A conflict is a struggle between opposing forces. Almost every story has a main conflict—a conflict that is the story's focus. An **external conflict** involves a character who struggles against a force outside him- or herself, such as nature, a physical obstacle, or another character. An **internal conflict** is one that occurs within a character. For example, a character with an internal conflict might struggle with fear.

See also Plot.

Connect Connecting is a reader's process of relating the content of a text to his or her own knowledge and experience.

Connotation A word's connotations are the ideas and feelings associated with the word, as opposed to its dictionary definition. For example, the word **bread,** in addition to its basic meaning ("a baked food made from flour and other ingredients"), has connotations of life and general nourishment.

See also Denotation.

Consumer Documents Consumer documents are printed materials that accompany products and services. They usually provide information about the use, care, operation, or assembly of the product or service they accompany. Some common consumer documents are applications, contracts, warranties, manuals, instructions, labels, brochures, and schedules.

Context Clues When you encounter an unfamiliar word, you can often use context clues to understand it. Context clues are the words or phrases surrounding the word that provide hints about the word's meaning.

Counterargument A counterargument is an argument made to oppose another argument. A good argument anticipates opposing viewpoints and provides counterarguments to disprove them.

Couplet A couplet is a rhymed pair of lines. A couplet may be written in any rhythmic pattern. For example, Follow your heart's desire/And good things may transpire.

See also Rhyme; Stanza.

Credibility Credibility is the believability or trustworthiness of a source and the information it provides.

Critical Essay *See* Essay.

Critical Review A critical review is an evaluation or critique by a reviewer, or critic. Types of reviews include film reviews, book reviews, music reviews, and art show reviews.

Cultural Values Cultural values are the behaviors that a society expects from its people.

Database A database is a collection of information that can be quickly and easily accessed and searched and from which information can be easily retrieved. It is frequently presented in an electronic format.

Debate A debate is an organized exchange of opinions on an issue. In school settings, debate is usually a formal contest in which two opposing teams defend and attack a proposition.

See also Argument.

Deductive Reasoning Deductive reasoning is a way of thinking that begins with a generalization, presents a specific situation, and then moves forward with facts and evidence toward a logical conclusion. The following passage has a deductive argument embedded in it: "All students in the math class must take the quiz on Friday. Since Lana is in the class, she had better show up." This deductive argument can be broken down as follows: generalization—All students in the math class must take the quiz on Friday; specific situation—Lana is a student in the math class; conclusion—Therefore, Lana must take the math quiz.

Denotation A word's denotation is its dictionary definition.

See also **Connotation.**

Description Description is writing that helps a reader to picture events, objects, and characters. To create descriptions, writers often use **imagery**—words and phrases that appeal to the reader's senses.

Dialect A dialect is a form of a language that is spoken in a particular place or by a particular group of people. Dialects may feature unique pronunciations, vocabulary, and grammar.

Dialogue Dialogue is written conversation between two or more characters. Writers use dialogue to bring characters to life and to give readers insights into the characters' qualities, traits, and reactions to other characters. In fiction, dialogue is usually set off with quotation marks. In drama, stories are told primarily through dialogue.

Diary A diary is a daily record of a writer's thoughts, experiences, and feelings. As such, it is a type of autobiographical writing. A **journal** is another term for a diary.

Dictionary *See* **Reference Works.**

Drama A drama, or play, is a form of literature meant to be performed by actors in front of an audience. In a drama, the characters' dialogue and actions tell the story. The written form of a drama is called a script. A script usually includes dialogue, a cast of characters, and stage directions that give instructions about performing the drama. The person who writes the drama is known as the playwright or dramatist.

Draw Conclusions To draw a conclusion is to make a judgment or arrive at a belief based on evidence, experience, and reasoning.

Editorial An editorial is an opinion piece that usually appears on the editorial page of a newspaper or as part of a news broadcast. The editorial section of the newspaper presents opinions rather than objective news reports.

See also **Op/Ed Piece.**

Either/Or Fallacy An either/or fallacy is a statement that suggests that there are only two choices available in a situation when in fact there are more than two.

Emotional Appeal An emotional appeal is a message that creates strong feelings in order to make a point.

An appeal to fear is a message that taps into people's fear of losing their safety or security. An appeal to pity is a message that taps into people's sympathy and compassion for others to build support for an idea, a cause, or a proposed action. An appeal to vanity is a message that attempts to persuade by tapping into people's desire to feel good about themselves.

Encyclopedia *See* Reference Works.

Epic Poem An epic poem is a long narrative poem about the adventures of a hero whose actions reflect the ideals and values of a nation or a group of people.

Essay An essay is a short work of nonfiction that deals with a single subject. There are many types of essays. An **expository essay** presents or explains information and ideas. A **persuasive essay** attempts to convince the reader to adopt a certain viewpoint. A **critical essay** evaluates a situation or a work of art. A **personal essay** usually reflects the writer's experiences, feelings, and personality.

Ethical Appeal In an ethical appeal, a writer links a claim to a widely accepted value in order to gain moral support for the claim. The appeal also creates an image of the writer as a trustworthy, moral person.

Evaluate To evaluate is to examine something carefully and to judge its value or worth. A reader can evaluate the actions of a particular character, for example. A reader can also form opinions about the value of an entire work.

Evidence Evidence is a specific piece of information that supports a claim. Evidence can take the form of a fact, a quotation, an example, a statistic, or a personal experience, among other things.

Exaggeration An extreme overstatement of an idea is called an exaggeration. It is often used for purposes of emphasis or humor.

Exposition Exposition is the first stage of a typical story plot. The exposition provides important background information and introduces the setting and the important characters. The conflict the characters face may also be introduced in the exposition, or it may be introduced later, in the rising action.

See also Plot.

Expository Essay *See* Essay.

External Conflict *See* Conflict.

Fable A fable is a brief tale told to illustrate a moral or teach a lesson. Often the moral of a fable appears in a distinct and memorable statement near the tale's beginning or end.

See also Moral.

Fact Versus Opinion A **fact** is a statement that can be proved, or verified. An opinion, on the other hand, is a statement that cannot be proved because it expresses a person's beliefs, feelings, or thoughts.

See also Generalization; Inference.

Fallacious Reasoning Reasoning that includes errors in logic or fallacies.

Fallacy A fallacy is an error of reasoning. Typically, a fallacy is based on an incorrect inference or a misuse of evidence.

See also Either/Or Fallacy; Logical Appeal; Overgeneralization.

Falling Action The falling action is the stage of the plot in which the story begins to draw to a close. The falling action comes after the **climax** and before the **resolution,** also called denouement. Events in the falling action show the results of the important decision or action that happened at the climax. Tension eases as the falling action begins; however, the final outcome of the story is not yet fully worked out at this stage.

See also Climax; Plot.

Fantasy Fantasy is a type of fiction that is highly imaginative and portrays events, settings, or characters that are unrealistic. The setting might be a nonexistent world, the plot might involve magic or the supernatural, and the characters might have superhuman powers.

Faulty Reasoning *See* Fallacy.

Feature Article A feature article is an article in a newspaper or magazine about a topic of human interest or lifestyles.

Fiction Fiction is prose writing that tells an imaginary story. The writer of a short story or novel might invent all the events and characters or might base parts of the story on real people and events. The basic elements of fiction are plot, character, setting, and theme. Different types of fiction include realistic fiction, historical fiction, science fiction, and fantasy.

See also Novel; Novella; Short Story.

Figurative Language In figurative language, words are used in an imaginative way to express ideas that are not literally true. "Megan has a bee in her bonnet" is an example of figurative language. The sentence does not mean that Megan is wearing a bonnet, nor that there is an actual bee in it. Instead, it means that Megan is angry or upset about something. Figurative language is used for comparison, emphasis, and emotional effect.

See also Metaphor; Onomatopoeia; Personification; Simile.

First-Person Point of View *See* **Point of View.**

Flashback In a literary work, a flashback is an interruption of the action to present events that took place at an earlier time. A flashback provides information that can help a reader better understand a character's current situation.

Folklore The traditions, customs, and stories that are passed down within a culture are known as its folklore. Folklore includes various types of literature, such as legends, folk tales, myths, trickster tales, and fables.

See also Fable; Folk Tale; Myth.

Folk Tale A folk tale is a story that has been passed down from generation to generation by word of mouth. Folk tales may be set in the distant past and involve supernatural events. The characters in them may be animals, people, or superhuman beings.

Foreshadowing Foreshadowing occurs when a writer provides hints that suggest future events in a story. Foreshadowing creates suspense and makes readers eager to find out what will happen.

Form The structure or organization of a written work is often called its form. The form of a poem includes the arrangement of its words and lines on the page.

Free Verse Poetry without regular patterns of rhyme and rhythm is called free verse. Some poets use free verse to capture the sounds and rhythms of ordinary speech.

See also Rhyme, Rhythm.

Generalization A generalization is a broad statement about a class or category of people, ideas, or things based on a study of, or a belief about, only some of its members.

See also Overgeneralization; Stereotyping.

Genre The term *genre* refers to a category in which a work of literature is classified. The major genres in literature are fiction, nonfiction, poetry, and drama.

Government Publications Government publications are documents produced by government organizations. Pamphlets, brochures, and reports are just some of the many forms these publications take. Government publications can be good resources for a wide variety of topics.

Graphic Aid A graphic aid is a visual tool that is printed, handwritten, or drawn. Charts, diagrams, graphs, photographs, and maps are examples of graphic aids.

Graphic Organizer A graphic organizer is a "word picture"—a visual illustration of a verbal statement—that helps a reader understand a text. Charts, tables, webs, and diagrams can all be graphic organizers. Graphic organizers and graphic aids can look the same. However, graphic organizers and graphic aids do differ in how they are used. Graphic aids help deliver important information to students using a text. Graphic organizers are actually created by students themselves. They help students understand the text or organize information.

Haiku Haiku is a form of Japanese poetry in which 17 syllables are arranged in three lines of 5, 7, and 5 syllables. The rules of haiku are strict. In addition to following the syllabic count, the poet must create a clear picture that will evoke a strong emotional response in the reader. Nature is a particularly important source of inspiration for Japanese haiku poets, and details from nature are often the subjects of their poems.

Hero A hero is a main character or protagonist in a story. They are typically courageous, strong, honorable, and intelligent. They are protectors of society who hold back the forces of evil and fight to make the world a better place. In modern literature, a hero may simply be the most important character in a story. Such a hero is often an ordinary person with ordinary problems.

Historical Document Historical documents are writings that have played a significant role in human events. The Declaration of Independence, for example, is a historical document.

Historical Fiction A short story or a novel can be called historical fiction when it is set in the past and includes real places and real events of historical importance.

How-To Book A how-to book explains how to do something—usually an activity, a sport, or a household project.

Humor Humor is a quality that provokes laughter or amusement. Writers create humor through exaggeration, amusing descriptions, irony, and witty and insightful dialogue.

Idiom An idiom is an expression that has a meaning different from the meaning of its individual words.

For example, "to let the cat out of the bag" is an idiom meaning "to reveal a secret or surprise."

Imagery Imagery consists of words and phrases that appeal to a reader's five senses. Writers use sensory details to help the reader imagine how things look, feel, smell, sound, and taste.

Implied Main Idea *See* Main Idea.

Index The index of a book is an alphabetized list of important topics covered in the book and the page numbers on which they can be found. An index can be used to quickly find specific information about a topic.

Inductive Reasoning Inductive reasoning is the process of logical reasoning that starts with observations, examples, and facts and moves on to a general conclusion or principle.

Inference An inference is a logical guess that is made based on facts and one's own knowledge and experience.

Informational Text Informational text is writing that provides factual information. Examples include news reports, a science textbook, and lab reports. Informational text also includes literary nonfiction, such as personal essays, opinion pieces, speeches, biographies, and historical accounts.

Internal Conflict *See* Conflict.

Internet The Internet is a global, interconnected system of computer networks that allows for communication through e-mail, listservs, and the World Wide Web. The Internet connects computers and computer users throughout the world.

Interview An interview is a conversation conducted by a writer or reporter in which facts or statements are elicited from another person, recorded, and then broadcast or published.

Irony Irony is a contrast between what is expected and what actually exists or happens. Exaggeration and sarcasm are techniques writers use to express irony.

Journal A journal is a periodical publication used by legal, medical, and other professional organizations. The term may also be used to refer to a diary or daily record. *See* **Diary.**

Legend A legend is a story handed down from the past about a specific person, usually someone of heroic accomplishments. Legends usually have some basis in historical fact.

Limerick A limerick is a short, humorous poem made up of five lines. It usually has the rhyme scheme ***aabba,*** created by two rhyming couplets followed by a fifth line that rhymes with the first couplet. A limerick typically has a sing-song rhythm.

Literary Nonfiction *See* Narrative Nonfiction.

Loaded Language Loaded language consists of words with strongly positive or negative connotations intended to influence a reader's or listener's attitude.

Logical Appeal A logical appeal is a way of writing or speaking that relies on logic and facts. It appeals to people's reasoning or intellect rather than to their values or emotions. Flawed logical appeals—that is, errors in reasoning—are called logical fallacies.

See also **Fallacy.**

Logical Argument A logical argument is an argument in which the logical relationship between the support and claim is sound.

Lyric Poetry Lyric poetry is poetry that presents the personal thoughts and feelings of a single speaker. Most poems, other than narrative poems, are lyric poems. Lyric poetry can be in a variety of forms and cover many subjects, from love and death to everyday experiences.

Main Character *See* Character.

Main Idea The main idea, or central idea, is the most important idea about a topic that a writer or speaker conveys. It can be the central idea of an entire work or of just a paragraph. Often, the main idea of a paragraph is expressed in a topic sentence. However, a main idea may just be implied, or suggested, by details. A main idea is typically supported by details.

Make Inferences *See* **Inference.**

Memoir A memoir is a form of autobiographical writing in which a writer shares his or her personal experiences and observations of important events or people. Often informal in tone, memoirs usually give readers information about a particular person or period of time in the writer's life. In contrast, autobiographies focus on many important people and events in the writer's life over a long period of time.

See also Autobiography; Personal Narrative.

Metaphor A metaphor is a comparison of two things that are basically unlike but have some qualities in common. Unlike a simile, a metaphor does not contain the words ***like*** or ***as.***

See also Figurative Language; Simile.

Meter In poetry, meter is the regular pattern of stressed (ˊ) and unstressed (˘) syllables. Although poems have rhythm, not all poems have regular meter. Each unit of meter is known as a **foot** and is made up of one stressed syllable and one or two unstressed syllables.

See also Rhythm.

Minor Character *See* **Character.**

Monitor Monitoring is the strategy of checking your comprehension as you read and modifying the strategies you are using to suit your needs. Monitoring often includes the following strategies: questioning, clarifying, visualizing, predicting, connecting, and rereading.

Mood Mood is the feeling or atmosphere that a writer creates for the reader. Descriptive words, imagery, and figurative language all influence the mood of a work.

Moral A moral is a lesson that a story teaches. A moral is often stated at the end of a fable.

See also Fable.

Motivation Motivation is the reason why a character acts, feels, or thinks in a certain way. A character may have more than one motivation for his or her actions. Understanding these motivations helps readers get to know the character.

Myth A myth is a traditional story that attempts to answer basic questions about human nature, origins of the world, mysteries of nature, and social customs.

Narrative Writing that tells a story is called a narrative. The events in a narrative may be real or imagined. Autobiographies and biographies are narratives that deal with real people or events. Fictional narratives include short stories, fables, myths, and novels. A narrative may also be in the form of a poem.

See also Autobiography; Biography; Personal Narrative.

Narrative Nonfiction Narrative nonfiction is writing that reads much like fiction, except that the characters, setting, and plot are real rather than imaginary. Narrative nonfiction includes autobiographies, biographies, and memoirs.

Narrative Poetry Poetry that tells a story is called narrative poetry. Like fiction, a narrative poem contains characters, a setting, and a plot. It might also contain such elements of poetry as rhyme, rhythm, imagery, and figurative language.

Narrator The narrator is the voice that tells a story. Sometimes the narrator is a character in the story. At other times, the narrator is an outside voice created by the writer. The narrator is not the same as the writer.

See also Point of View.

News Article A news article is writing that reports on a recent event. In newspapers, news articles are usually brief and to the point, presenting the most important facts first, followed by more detailed information.

Nonfiction Nonfiction is writing that tells about real people, places, and events. Unlike fiction, nonfiction is mainly written to convey factual information. Nonfiction includes a wide range of writing—newspaper articles, letters, essays, biographies, movie reviews, speeches, true-life adventure stories, advertising, and more.

Novel A novel is a long work of fiction. Like a short story, a novel is the product of a writer's imagination. Because a novel is considerably longer than a short story, a novelist can develop the characters and story line more thoroughly.

See also Fiction.

Novella A novella is a work of fiction that is longer than a short story but shorter than a novel. Due to its shorter length, a novella generally includes fewer characters and a less complex plot than a novel.

See also Fiction; Novel; Short Story.

Ode An ode is a type of lyric poem that deals with serious themes, such as justice, truth, or beauty.

Onomatopoeia Onomatopoeia is the use of words whose sounds echo their meanings, such as ***buzz, whisper, gargle,*** and ***murmur.***

Op/Ed Piece An op/ed piece is an opinion piece that typically appears opposite ("op") the editorial page of a newspaper. Unlike editorials, op/ed pieces are written and submitted by readers.

Oral Literature Oral literature, or the oral tradition, consists of stories that have been passed down by word of mouth from generation to generation. Oral literature includes folk tales, legends, and myths. In more recent times, some examples of oral literature have been written down or recorded so that the stories can be preserved.

Organization *See* Pattern of Organization.

Overgeneralization An overgeneralization is a statement that is too broad to be accurate. You can often recognize overgeneralizations by the appearance of words and phrases such as ***all, everyone, every time, any, anything, no one,*** or ***none.*** An example is

"None of the city's workers really cares about keeping the environment clean." In all probability, there are many exceptions. The writer can't possibly know the feelings of every city worker.

Overview An overview is a short summary of a story, a speech, or an essay.

Paraphrase Paraphrasing is the restating of information in one's own words.

See also **Summarize.**

Parody A parody is a humorous imitation of another writer's work. Parodies can take the form of fiction, drama, or poetry. Jon Scieszka's "The True Story of the Three Little Pigs" is an example of a parody.

Pattern of Organization The term ***pattern of organization*** refers to the way ideas and information are arranged and organized. Patterns of organization include cause and effect, chronological, compare and contrast, classification, and problem-solution, among others.

See also Cause and Effect; Chronological Order; Classification; Compare and Contrast; Problem-Solution Order; Sequential Order.

Periodical A periodical is a magazine or another type of publication that is issued on a regular basis.

Personal Narrative A short essay told as a story in the first-person point of view. A personal narrative usually reflects the writer's experiences, feelings, and personality.

See also Autobiography; Memoir.

Personification The giving of human qualities to an animal, object, or idea is known as personification.

See also Figurative Language.

Persuasion Persuasion is the art of swaying others' feelings, beliefs, or actions. Persuasion normally appeals to both the mind and the emotions of readers.

See also Appeal to Authority; Emotional Appeal; Ethical Appeal; Loaded Language; Logical Appeal.

Persuasive Essay *See* Essay.

Play *See* Drama.

Playwright *See* Drama.

Plot The series of events in a story is called the plot. The plot usually centers on a **conflict,** or struggle, faced by the main character. The action that the characters take to solve the problem builds toward a **climax** in the story. At this point, or shortly afterward, the problem is solved and the story ends. Most story plots have five stages: exposition, rising action, climax, falling action, and resolution.

See also Climax; Conflict; Exposition; Falling Action; Rising Action.

Poetry Poetry is a type of literature in which words are carefully chosen and arranged to create certain effects. Poets use a variety of sound devices, imagery, and figurative language to express emotions and ideas.

See also Alliteration; Assonance; Ballad; Free Verse; Imagery; Meter; Narrative Poetry; Rhyme; Rhythm; Stanza.

Point of View Point of view refers to how a writer chooses to narrate a story. When a story is told from the **first-person** point of view, the narrator is a character in the story and uses first-person pronouns, such as ***I, me,*** and ***we.*** In a story told from the **third-person** point of view, the narrator is not a character in the story. A writer's choice of narrator affects the information readers receive.

See also Narrator.

Predict Predicting is a reading strategy that involves using text clues to make a reasonable guess about what will happen next in a story.

Primary Source *See* Sources.

Prior Knowledge Prior knowledge is the knowledge a reader already possesses about a topic. This information might come from personal experiences, expert accounts, books, films, or other sources.

Problem-Solution Order Problem-solution order is a pattern of organization in which a problem is stated and analyzed and then one or more solutions are proposed and examined.

Prop The word ***prop,*** originally an abbreviation of the word ***property,*** refers to any physical object that is used in a drama.

Propaganda Propaganda is any form of communication that is so distorted that it conveys false or misleading information to advance a specific belief or cause.

Prose The word ***prose*** refers to all forms of writing that are not in verse form. The term may be used to describe very different forms of writing, such as short stories and essays.

Protagonist A protagonist is the main character in a story, play, or novel. The protagonist is involved in the main conflict of the story. Usually, the protagonist undergoes changes as the plot runs its course.

Public Document Public documents are documents that were written for the public to provide information that is of public interest or concern. They include government documents, speeches, signs, and rules and regulations.

See also Government Publications.

Pun A pun is a play on words based on similar senses of two or more words, or on various meanings of the same word. A pun is usually made for humorous effect. For example, the fisherman was fired for playing hooky.

Radio Play A radio play is a drama that is written specifically to be broadcast over the radio. Because the audience is not meant to see a radio play, sound effects are often used to help listeners imagine the setting and the action. The stage directions in the play's script indicate the sound effects.

Realistic Fiction Realistic fiction is fiction that is set in the real, modern world. The characters behave like real people and use human abilities to cope with modern life's problems and conflicts.

Recurring Theme *See* Theme.

Reference Work Reference works are sources that contain facts and background information on a wide range of subjects. Most reference works are good sources of reliable information because they have been reviewed by experts. The following are some common reference works: encyclopedias, dictionaries, thesauri, almanacs, atlases, and directories.

Refrain A refrain is one or more lines repeated in each stanza of a poem.

Repetition Repetition is a technique in which a sound, word, phrase, or line is repeated for emphasis or unity. Repetition often helps to reinforce meaning and create an appealing rhythm.

See also Alliteration; Refrain; Sound Devices.

Resolution *See* Falling Action.

Review *See* Critical Review.

Rhetorical Question Rhetorical questions are those that have such obvious answers that they do not require a reply. Writers often use them to suggest that their claim is so obvious that everyone should agree with it.

Rhyme Rhyme is the repetition of sounds at the end of words. Words rhyme when their accented vowels and the letters that follow have identical sounds. ***Pig*** and ***dig*** rhyme, as do ***reaching*** and ***teaching.*** The most common type of rhyme in poetry is called **end**

rhyme, in which rhyming words come at the ends of lines. Rhyme that occurs within a line of poetry is called **internal rhyme.**

Rhyme Scheme A rhyme scheme is a pattern of end rhymes in a poem. A rhyme scheme is noted by assigning a letter of the alphabet, beginning with **a,** to each line. Lines that rhyme are given the same letter.

Rhythm Rhythm is the musical quality created by the alternation of stressed and unstressed syllables in a line of poetry. Poets use rhythm to emphasize ideas and to create moods. Devices such as alliteration, rhyme, and assonance often contribute to creating rhythm.

See also Meter.

Rising Action The rising action is the stage of the plot that develops the **conflict,** or struggle. During this stage, events occur that make the conflict more complicated. The events in the rising action build toward a **climax,** or turning point.

See also Plot.

Scanning Scanning is the process used to search through a text for a particular fact or piece of information. When you scan, you sweep your eyes across a page, looking for key words that may lead you to the information you want.

Scene In drama, the action is often divided into acts and scenes. Each scene presents an episode of the play's plot and typically occurs at a single place and time.

See also Act.

Scenery Scenery is a painted backdrop or other structures used to create the setting for a play.

Science Fiction Science fiction is fiction in which a writer explores unexpected possibilities of the past or the future, combining scientific information with his or her creative imagination. Most science fiction writers create believable worlds, although some create fantasy worlds that have familiar elements.

See also Fantasy.

Scope Scope refers to a work's focus. For example, an article about Austin, Texas, that focuses on the city's history, economy, and residents has a broad scope. An article that focuses only on the restaurants in Austin has a narrower scope.

Script The text of a play, film, or broadcast is called a script.

Secondary Source *See* Source.

Sensory Details Sensory details are words and phrases that appeal to the reader's senses of sight, hearing, touch, smell, and taste.

See also Imagery.

Sequential Order Sequential order is a pattern of organization that shows the order of steps or stages in a process.

Setting The setting of a story, poem, or play is the time and place of the action. Sometimes the setting is clear and well-defined. At other times, it is left to the reader's imagination. Elements of setting include geographic location, historical period (past, present, or future), season, time of day, and culture.

Setting a Purpose The process of establishing specific reasons for reading a text is called setting a purpose. Readers can look at a text's title, headings, and illustrations to guess what it might be about. They can then use these guesses to figure out what they want to learn from reading the text.

Short Story A short story is a work of fiction that centers on a single idea and can be read in one sitting. Generally, a short story has one main conflict that involves the characters and keeps the story moving.

See also Fiction.

Sidebar A sidebar is additional information set in a box alongside or within a news or feature article. Popular magazines often make use of sidebars.

Signal Words In a text, signal words are words and phrases that help show how events or ideas are related. Some common examples of signal words are **and, but, however, nevertheless, therefore,** and **in addition.**

Simile A simile is a figure of speech that makes a comparison between two unlike things using the words **like** or **as.**

See also Figurative Language; Metaphor.

Sound Devices Sound devices are ways of using words for the sound qualities they create. Sound devices can help convey meaning and mood in a writer's work. Some common sound devices include **alliteration, assonance, meter, onomatopoeia, repetition, rhyme,** and **rhythm.**

See also Alliteration; Assonance; Meter; Onomatopoeia; Repetition; Rhyme; Rhythm.

Source A source is anything that supplies information. **Primary sources** are materials created by people who witnessed or took part in the event they supply information about. Letters, diaries, autobiographies, and eyewitness accounts are primary sources. **Secondary sources** are those made by people who were not directly involved in the event or even present when it occurred. Encyclopedias, textbooks, biographies, and most news articles are secondary sources.

Speaker In poetry the speaker is the voice that "talks" to the reader, similar to the narrator in fiction. The speaker is not necessarily the poet.

Speech A speech is a talk or public address. The purpose of a speech may be to entertain, to explain, to persuade, to inspire, or any combination of these purposes.

Stage Directions In the script of a play, the instructions to the actors, director, and stage crew are called the stage directions. Stage directions might suggest scenery, lighting, sound effects, and ways for actors to move and speak. Stage directions often appear in parentheses and in italic type.

Stanza A stanza is a group of two or more lines that form a unit in a poem. Each stanza may have the same number of lines, or the number of lines may vary.

See also Couplet; Form; Poetry.

Stereotype In literature, characters who are defined by a single trait are known as stereotypes. Such characters do not usually demonstrate the complexities of real people. Familiar stereotypes in popular literature include the absent-minded professor and the busybody.

Stereotyping Stereotyping is a dangerous type of overgeneralization. It can lead to unfair judgments of people based on their ethnic background, beliefs, practices, or physical appearance.

Structure The structure of a work of literature is the way in which it is put together. In poetry, structure involves the arrangement of words and lines to produce a desired effect. One structural unit in poetry is the stanza. In prose, structure involves the arrangement of such elements as sentences, paragraphs, and events. **Sentence structure** refers to the length and types of sentences used in a work.

Style A style is a manner of writing. It involves how something is said rather than what is said.

Subject The subject of a literary work is its focus or topic. In an autobiography, for example, the subject is the life of the person telling the story. Subject differs from theme in that theme is a deeper meaning, whereas the subject is the main situation or set of facts described by the text.

Summarize To summarize is to briefly retell the main ideas of a piece of writing in one's own words.

See also Paraphrase.

Support Support is any information that helps to prove a claim.

Supporting Detail *See* Main Idea.

Surprise Ending A surprise ending is an unexpected plot twist at the end of a story. The surprise may be a sudden turn in the action or a piece of information that gives a different perspective to the entire story.

Suspense Suspense is a feeling of growing tension and excitement experienced by a reader. Suspense makes a reader curious about the outcome of a story or an event within a story. A writer creates suspense by raising questions in the reader's mind. The use of **foreshadowing** is one way that writers create suspense.

See also Foreshadowing.

Symbol A symbol is a person, a place, an object, an animal, or an activity that stands for something beyond itself. For example, a flag is a colored piece of cloth that stands for a country. A white dove is a bird that represents peace.

Synthesize To synthesize information means to take individual pieces of information and combine them in order to gain a better understanding of a subject.

Tall Tale A tall tale is a humorously exaggerated story about impossible events, often involving the supernatural abilities of the main character. Stories about folk heroes such as Pecos Bill and Paul Bunyan are typical tall tales.

Teleplay A teleplay is a play written for television. In a teleplay, scenes can change quickly and dramatically. The camera can focus the viewer's attention on specific actions. The camera directions in teleplays are much like the stage directions in stage plays.

Text Feature Text features are elements of a text, such as boldface type, headings, and subheadings, that help organize and call attention to important information. Italic type, bulleted or numbered lists, sidebars, and graphic aids such as charts, tables, timelines, illustrations, and photographs are also considered text features.

Theme A theme is a message about life or human nature that the writer shares with the reader. In many cases, readers must infer the writer's message. One way to infer a theme is to note the lessons learned by the main characters.

> **Recurring themes:** Themes found in a variety of works. For example, authors from different backgrounds might express similar themes having to do with the importance of family values.

> **Universal themes:** Themes that are found throughout the literature of all time periods. For example, Cinderella stories contain a universal theme relating to goodness being rewarded.

See also Moral.

Thesaurus *See* Reference Works.

Thesis Statement A thesis statement, or controlling idea, is the main proposition that a writer attempts to support in a piece of writing.

Third-Person Point of View *See* Point of View.

Title The title of a piece of writing is the name that is attached to it. A title often refers to an important aspect of the work.

Tone The tone of a literary work expresses the writer's attitude toward his or her subject. Words such as **angry, sad,** and **humorous** can be used to describe different tones.

See also Author's Perspective.

Topic Sentence The topic sentence of a paragraph states the paragraph's main idea. All other sentences in the paragraph provide supporting details.

Tragedy A tragedy is a dramatic work that presents the downfall of a character or characters. The events in a tragic plot are set in motion by a decision that is often an error in judgment on the part of the hero. Events are linked in a cause-and-effect relationship and lead to a disastrous conclusion, usually death.

Traits *See* Character.

Treatment The way a topic is handled in a work is referred to as its treatment. Treatment includes the form the writing takes as well as the writer's purpose and tone.

Turning Point *See* Climax.

Universal Theme *See* Theme.

Unsupported Inference A guess that may seem logical but that is not supported by facts.

Visualize Visualizing is the process of forming a mental picture based on written or spoken information.

Voice The term **voice** refers to a writer's unique use of language that allows a reader to "hear" a human personality in the writer's work. Elements of style that contribute to a writer's voice can reveal much about the author's personality, beliefs, and attitudes.

Website A website is a collection of "pages" on the World Wide Web that usually covers a specific subject. Linked pages are accessed by clicking hyperlinks or menus, which send the user from page to page within a website. Websites are created by companies, organizations, educational institutions, government agencies, the military, and individuals.

Word Choice The success of any writing depends on the writer's choice of words. Words not only communicate ideas but also help describe events, characters, settings, and so on. Word choice can make a writer's work sound formal or informal, serious or humorous. A writer must choose words carefully depending on the goal of the piece of writing. For example, a writer working on a science article would probably use technical, formal words; a writer trying to establish the setting in a short story would probably use more descriptive words. Word choice is sometimes referred to as diction.

See also Style.

Workplace Document Workplace documents are materials that are produced or used within a work setting, usually to aid in the functioning of the workplace. They include job applications, office memos, training manuals, job descriptions, and sales reports.

Works Cited The term **works cited** refers to a list of all the works a writer has referred to in his or her text. This list often includes not only books and articles but also Internet sources.

Works Consulted The term **works consulted** refers to a list of all the works a writer consulted in order to create his or her text. It is not limited just to those works cited in the text.

See also Bibliography.

Glossary of Academic Vocabulary

achieve (ə-chēv´) *v.* to succeed or reach a goal

appropriate (ə-prō´prē-ĭt) *adj.* right for the situation

authority (ə-thôr´ĭ-tē) *n.* an expert; the power to give orders and make decisions

benefit (bĕn´ə-fĭt) *n.* to help or improve; *n.* a positive result; a fundraiser for a good cause

circumstance (sûr´kəm-stăns´) *n.* a situation; a condition

consequence (kŏn´sĭ-kwĕns´) *n.* result

constrain (kən-strānt´) *n.* to limit

distinct (dĭ-stĭngkt´) *adj.* easy to tell apart from others; clearly different

emphasize (ĕm´fə-sīz´) *v.* to give something special importance

environment (ĕn-vī´rən-mənt) *n.* surroundings; the natural world

evident (ĕv´ĭ-dənt) *adj.* easily seen or understood; obvious

factor (făk´tər) *n.* someone or something that has an effect on an event, a process, or a situation

illustrate (ĭl´ə-strāt´) *v.* to create pictures for books and magazines; to explain by using examples or pictures

impact (ĭm´păkt´) *n.* influence; *v.* to influence

indicate (ĭn´dĭ-kāt´) *tr.v.* to point out; also, to serve as a sign or symbol of something

individual (ĭn´də-vĭj´ōō-əl) *n.* a single person, animal, or plant

injure (ĭn´jər) *tr.v.* to hurt or harm

instance (ĭn´stəns) *n.* an example; a situation or occurrence

justify (jŭs´tə-fī´) *v.* to give a good reason or explain

legal (lē´gəl) *adj.* allowed by law

occur (ə-kûr´) *v.* to happen

outcome (out´kŭm´) *n.* a result

period (pîr´ē-əd) *n.* a portion of time

principle (prĭn´sə-pəl) *n.* a moral rule or strong belief that influences your actions

relevant (rĕl´ə-vənt) *adj.* important or related

respond (rĭ-spŏnd´) *v.* to answer; to react to

significant (sĭg-nĭf´ĭ-kənt) *adj.* meaningful; important

similar (sĭm´ə-lər) *adj.* alike in appearance or nature, though not identical; having features that are the same

specific (spĭ-sĭf´ĭk) *adj.* concerned with a particular thing; also, precise or exact

tradition (trə-dĭsh´ən) *n.* a group's beliefs and customs

Index of Titles and Authors

Acknowledgments

Excerpt from *Blue Jasmine* by Kashmira Sheth. Text copyright © 2004 by Kashmira Sheth. Reprinted by permission of Charlotte Sheedy Agency on behalf of the author. All rights reserved.

The Call of the Wild retold by Dina McClellan. Copyright © 2014 by Escletxa. Reprinted by permission of Escletxa.

Don Quixote retold by Candy Rodó. Copyright © 2014 by Escletxa. Reprinted by permission of Escletxa.

"End Slave Literacy" from *Etched in Clay: The Life of Dave, Enslaved Potter and Poet* by Andrea Cheng. Text copyright © 2013 by Andrea Cheng. Reprinted by permission of Lee & Low Books, Inc.

"Etched in Clay" from *Etched in Clay: The Life of Dave, Enslaved Potter and Poet* by Andrea Cheng. Text copyright © 2013 by Andrea Cheng. Reprinted by permission of Lee and Low Books, Inc.

Dave's inscriptions found in "Etched in Clay" by Andrea Cheng from *Carolina Clay: The Life and Legend of the Slave Potter Dave* by Leonard Todd. Copyright © 2008 by Leonard Todd. Reprinted by permission of W. W. Norton & Company, Inc.

Helen Keller by Jessica Cohn. Copyright © 2014 by Escletxa. Reprinted by permission of Escletxa.

"Into the Burning Night" from *Something to Hold* by Katherine Schlick Noe. Text copyright © 2011 by Katherine Schlick Noe. Reprinted by permission of Houghton Mifflin Harcourt Publishing Company.

The Last Days of Pompeii by Dina McClellan. Copyright © 2014 by Escletxa. Reprinted by permission of Escletxa.

"A Leap of Faith" excerpted and titled from *Divergent* by Veronica Roth. Text copyright © 2011 by Veronica Roth. Reprinted by permission of HarperCollins Publishers.

Excerpt from *Looking for Me* by Betsy R. Rosenthal. Text copyright © 2012 by Betsy R. Rosenthal. Reprinted by permission of Houghton Mifflin Harcourt Publishing Company.

"A Poem!" from *Etched in Clay: The Life of Dave, Enslaved Potter and Poet* by Andrea Cheng. Text copyright © 2013 by Andrea Cheng. Reprinted by permission of Lee and Low Books, Inc.

Dave's inscriptions found in "A Poem!" by Andrea Cheng from *Carolina Clay: The Life and Legend of the Slave Potter Dave* by Leonard Todd. Copyright © 2008 by Leonard Todd. Reprinted by permission of W. W. Norton & Company, Inc.

Excerpt from *The Ramayana* by Ramesh Menon. Text copyright © 2001 by Ramesh Menon. Reprinted by permission of Farrar, Straus and Giroux.

Excerpt from *Real Kids, Real Stories, Real Change* by Garth Sundem. Text copyright © 2010 by Garth Sundem. Reprinted by permission of Free Spirit Publishing. All rights reserved.

"Researcher Explains How Crows Solved a Challenge from Aesop's Fables" by Virginia Morell from National Geographic online, April 2014. Text copyright National Geographic © 2014. Reprinted by permission of National Geographic.

Excerpt from *Spider Boy* by Ralph Fletcher. Text copyright © 1997 by Ralph Fletcher. Reprinted by permission of Houghton Mifflin Harcourt Publishing Company and Marian Reiner, on behalf of Ralph Fletcher.

The Strange Case of Dr. Jekyll and Mr. Hyde retold by Dina McClellan. Copyright © 2014 by Escletxa. Reprinted by permission of Escletxa.

Theseus and the Minotaur retold by Candy Rodó. Copyright © 2014 by Escletxa. Reprinted by permission of Escletxa.

Podcast Acknowledgments

"Oh Captain, My Captain" by Pha Le. Used by permission of Pha Le and The Moth.

NPR *All Tech Considered* news report "Storm Shelter App Helps Pinpoint People Amid Tornado's Rubble," May 21, 2013. Used by permission of KOSU, Oklahoma City, Oklahoma.

Excerpt from Fresh Air story "After WWII A Letter of Appreciation that Still Rings True," by Maureen Corrigan, May 27, 2013. Used by permission of Maureen Corrigan and *Fresh Air with Terry Gross/* WHYY Philadelphia.

"A Kind of Wisdom" by Ellie Lee. Used by permission of Ellie Lee and The Moth.